Improving Sustainability Through Information Governance

Improving Sustainability Through Information Governance

Phyllis L. Elin, PhD and Max Rapaport

BEP

BUSINESS EXPERT PRESS

Leader in applied, concise business books

Improving Sustainability Through Information Governance

Cover design by Charlene Kronstedt

Interior design by Exeter Premedia Services Private Ltd., Chennai, India

First published in 2024 by
Business Expert Press, LLC
222 East 46th Street, New York, NY 10017
www.businessexpertpress.com

ISBN-13: 978-1-63742-712-5 (paperback)
ISBN-13: 978-1-63742-713-2 (e-book)

Business Expert Press Environmental and Social Sustainability for Business Advantage Collection

First edition: 2024

10 9 8 7 6 5 4 3 2 1

Description

Improving Sustainability Through Information Governance offers a comprehensive exploration of environmental, social, and governance (ESG) frameworks through the lenses of people, process, and technology.

Delving into the intricacies of strategic alignment, management principles, and risk management, the book emphasizes the vital connection between ESG and organizational sustainability.

This book begins by elucidating the significance of ESG, core frameworks, and regulatory mandates. Part 2 delves into information governance (IG) elements such as data management, privacy, and security, alongside relevant International Organization for Standardization (ISO) standards. The final section outlines strategies for applying IG standards to enhance ESG reporting and outcomes.

Advocating for integrating IG best practices to bolster organizational ESG compliance efforts, **this book is a must-read for leaders seeking to navigate the evolving landscape of climate risk reporting and sustainability.**

Keywords

information governance best practices for ESG reporting; implementing data governance for ESG compliance; how to integrate information governance into ESG investing strategies; sustainability reporting and information governance frameworks; ESG data governance solutions for risk management; compliance-driven information governance strategies for ESG initiatives; enhancing ESG reporting through effective data governance; leveraging information governance for sustainable ESG outcomes; data governance frameworks for ESG investing and sustainability; the role of information governance in ESG compliance and risk management

Contents

Introduction

By Phyllis L. Elin, PhD

With a wealth of experience as a global consultant in information governance (IG) and compliance spanning over four decades, my journey has evolved in tandem with the transformative shift from conventional records management to the expansive domain of IG. Rooted in the foundational teachings of records and information management (RIM) best practices received in Cincinnati, Ohio, during the 1970s, my educational foundation was shaped by formidable mentors with extensive experience gained during World War II in the U.S. Federal Government.

Despite my initial academic background in English and Political Science, seemingly distant from RIM basics, the training immediately resonated with my sense of reason and organization. As I immersed myself in RIM principles, a profound academic excitement paralleled my experiences at New York University. This transformative journey instilled in me essential traits of patience, meticulousness, and logic.

Over my career, which has traversed numerous countries and continents, I have been exposed to diverse approaches to RIM in various organizational contexts. Interacting with subject matter experts (SMEs) across functional areas provided insights into record-keeping requirements, workflow challenges, and organizational nuances.

Amidst technological advancements and evolving governance landscapes, the industry has undergone substantial transformations. However, enduring principles and best practices persist, forming the core focus of this volume, which is uniquely tailored to the context of environmental, social, and governance (ESG) reporting, specifically homing in on climate impact reporting and the positive impact of IG on companies' ability to develop robust and compliant governance structures and overall accountability.

Central to my observations is the ISO 15489 standard, established in 2001 as the inaugural globally recognized requirement for RIM.

The workflows outlined in this volume adhere to a structured protocol: Capture; Check; Record; Consolidate and Review; and Act, complemented by principles of Accountability, Transparency, Integrity, Protection, Compliance, Accessibility, Retention, and Disposition. The integration of these principles with ESG reporting is fundamental, particularly in the context of climate risk reporting.

Moreover, the book explores key subject areas from the vantage points of people, process, and technology, aligning these perspectives with climate risk reporting and ESG frameworks. Topics include strategic alignment, management principles, continuous improvement, organizational continuity, metrics, and risk and operations management—all intricately tied to the environmental aspects of ESG.

This book is organized into three parts. The Part 1 addresses why ESG is important, describes the core ESG frameworks, and discusses the various laws and standards mandating ESG reporting. Part 2 addresses the most important IG elements that are relevant to the world of ESG including data management, privacy, security, and defensible deletion and also includes a discussion of various relevant International Organization for Standardization (ISO) standards. Finally, Part 3 addresses different ways that these IG standards can be applied to improve ESG reporting and outcomes. The overall goal is to present a series of cogent arguments and strategies for incorporating IG best practices to improve and augment organizational ESG compliance efforts.

We look forward to having you join us on this journey!

PART 1

ESG Importance, Elements, Drivers, and Benefits

Why Is ESG Important?

In recent years, the business landscape has undergone significant transformation, with a growing emphasis on how companies conduct their operations. Stakeholders increasingly prefer associations with organizations demonstrating responsible business practices. Initially, ESG strategies were primarily driven by compliance requirements, but there is a gradual shift toward optimization and efficiency, exemplified by the growing focus on net-zero ambitions in various sectors.[1]

Changing expectations are evident among both employees and customers, who are increasingly conscious of sustainability issues. They expect organizations to fulfill ESG commitments and conduct business responsibly. The validation of these expectations relies on various reports that incorporate qualitative and quantitative data.[2] The imperative for innovation is underscored by government directives and regulatory body mandates, with many organizations committing to achieving net-zero targets by 2030. Meeting such targets requires innovative approaches in business processes, demanding a data-driven assessment of the current state and continuous progress monitoring.[3]

Investors now recognize ESG as a differentiator that ensures better returns and resilience against business disruptions. This recognition has led investors to urge companies to integrate ESG into their operations. However, the integration of ESG with existing processes necessitates careful consideration of data governance, as inaccurate and inconsistent data can undermine the communication of the intended message.[4]

Regulatory actions are aligning with global efforts to address climate change and sustainability, resulting in increased scrutiny from regulators and heightened ESG disclosure requirements. Organizations invest considerable time in analytics and reconciliations for reporting purposes, emphasizing the importance of having robust governance controls to enhance the overall value of data.[5]

In the absence of international consensus on ESG disclosures, various frameworks and indexes have emerged to guide company disclosures and inform investors. Leading international frameworks include the Global Reporting Initiative (GRI) Standards, Sustainability Accounting Standards Board (SASB) Standards, United Nations Principles for Responsible Investment, and United Nations Sustainable Development Goals. The proliferation of ratings, including those from entities such as Morgan Stanley Capital International (MSCI), Sustainalytics, Moody's, and S&P (Standard and Poor's) Global, reflects the growing influence of these frameworks and rating agencies. Estimates suggest that the global market for ESG ratings, currently valued at $200 million, could grow to $500 million within five years, indicating their potential to shape future regulations.[6]

ESG considerations are also shaped by public opinion, with these issues being inherently tied to reputational concerns, particularly in light of recent societal events. As more companies disclose their ESG commitments and actions, the rapid responses of social media and the news cycle can lead observations about a company's ESG stance to be widely disseminated and sometimes go viral. Companies that diverge from public opinion and market demands may face significant reputational consequences.

What Are the Elements of ESG?

The individual elements of ESG generally encompass the following ideas and criteria:

- The "E" in ESG, representing environmental criteria, encompasses factors such as an organization's energy consumption, waste discharge, resource utilization, and impact on living beings resulting from operations. This includes critical elements such as carbon emissions and contributions to climate change, as every company has an environmental footprint.

- "S" pertains to social criteria, addressing the relationships your company maintains and the reputation it builds within the communities where it operates. This includes considerations such as labor relations and diversity and inclusion, recognizing that every company operates within a diverse societal context.
- Finally, "G" signifies governance, encompassing the internal practices, controls, and procedures your company adopts to govern itself effectively, make informed decisions, comply with laws, and meet the needs of external stakeholders. Governance is inherent to every company as a legal entity.[7]

The interconnected nature of these ESG elements is evident, with social criteria overlapping with environmental criteria and governance, especially when striving to comply with environmental laws and broader sustainability concerns. While our primary focus is on environmental and social criteria, governance is inherently intertwined, emphasizing the need to excel not only in complying with laws but also in embodying their spirit.[8]

What Are the Drivers for ESG Compliance?

PwC offers three core reasons for why organizations have sought to emphasize and develop their ESG programs.

- The first is changing expectations. Both employees and customers are increasingly conscious of sustainability issues. They expect organizations to fulfill ESG commitments and conduct business responsibly. The validation of these expectations relies on various reports that incorporate qualitative and quantitative data.
- Additionally, investors now recognize ESG as a differentiator that ensures better returns and resilience against business disruptions. This recognition has led investors to urge companies to integrate ESG into their operations. However, the integration of ESG with existing processes necessitates careful consideration of data governance, as inaccurate and

inconsistent data can undermine the communication of the intended message.

- Finally, regulatory actions are aligning with global efforts to address climate change and sustainability, resulting in increased scrutiny from regulators and heightened ESG disclosure requirements. Organizations invest considerable time in analytics and reconciliations for reporting purposes, emphasizing the importance of having robust governance controls to enhance the overall value of data.[9]

The imperative for innovation is underscored by government directives and regulatory body mandates, with many organizations committing to achieving net-zero targets by 2030. Meeting such targets requires innovative approaches in business processes, demanding a data-driven assessment of the current state and continuous progress monitoring.[10]

What Are the Benefits of ESG for Companies?

Already by 2019, ESG-oriented investing had seen significant growth, surpassing $30 trillion globally, driven by increased attention on corporate impact and the realization that a robust ESG proposition safeguards long-term success. The substantial investment flow underscores that ESG is more than a trend; it is a meaningful exercise with tangible benefits. Moreover, at the start of 2021, ESG assets were valued at $35 trillion, and that figure is projected to grow to $50 trillion by 2025. In 2021, global mutual funds and exchange traded funds focused on ESG grew their net asset value by 53 percent, to a total of $2.7 trillion.[11]

Research further consistently demonstrates that companies prioritizing ESG concerns do not experience a drag on value creation; instead, they often see enhanced equity returns and reduced downside risks. This underscores that a strong ESG proposition is not merely a feel-good initiative, but a strategic approach linked to sustained business performance.[12]

In the realm of ESG, a significant study noted by McKinsey reveals that companies engaging in socially beneficial activities, as perceived by the public and social stakeholders, enjoy more straightforward access to resources with minimal planning or operational delays. These socially engaged companies demonstrate higher valuations than competitors with lower social capital. Furthermore, ESG factors can wield influence over consumer preferences. McKinsey's research highlights that customers express a willingness to pay a premium for environmentally friendly products. Approximately 70 percent of surveyed consumers across various industries indicated a readiness to pay an additional 5 percent for a green product that matches the performance standards of its nongreen counterpart.[13]

The impact of ESG on value creation is multifaceted and extends to five essential aspects, including cost reductions, top-line growth, regulatory and legal interventions, employee productivity uplift, and investment and asset optimization. For instance, effective ESG implementation can substantially reduce operating costs, combat rising expenses, and enhance resource efficiency, correlating with improved financial performance. Moreover, a strong ESG proposition provides companies with greater strategic freedom by mitigating regulatory pressures and reducing the risk of adverse government actions.[14]

In terms of employee productivity, a robust ESG proposition attracts and retains quality talent, fostering higher job satisfaction and motivation. Companies with positive social impact often experience higher productivity levels. Lastly, ESG can optimize investments by allocating capital to sustainable opportunities and avoiding stranded investments that may not pay off in the long term.[15]

The personal dynamic of ESG engagement involves recognizing individual causes that inspire executives and prioritizing initiatives that align with the company's mission. CEOs play a crucial role in rallying support for ESG initiatives that map to the company's circumstances and mission. Emphasizing the practical value creation of ESG is essential, linking priorities to hard metrics that impact the business model. An honest appraisal of ESG acknowledges the potential for value destruction if mishandled and underscores the importance of transparent risk assessment. Thoughtful and transparent engagement with ESG, even if uncomfortable in the short term, enhances long-term value and resilience. The journey toward ESG excellence requires strategic thinking, practical implementation, and a commitment to transparency.[16]

Summary of Critical ESG Standards

Global Reporting Initiative Standards

The GRI is an important international, independent nonprofit organization whose goal is to help businesses, governments, and other entities to transparently communicate their impact on the world. In the sphere of ESG reporting, GRI plays a crucial role in providing a standardized methodology, ensuring that sustainability reporting is not only accurate but also easily assessable. This information can then be used and digested both, internally, by the individual reporting organizations, who can leverage it to assess policies, strategies, and guide decision making and by outside stakeholders such as investors, analysts, policymakers, regulators, and academics, who can utilize it for benchmarking, policy formation, and research.[17]

GRI is used by a diverse spectrum of entities, including governments, corporations, and other organizations of varying sizes. With over 10,000 reporters spanning more than 100 countries, the GRI Standards have become the most widely used framework for sustainability reporting. These standards prove particularly instrumental for organizations aiming to navigate their low-carbon journey and achieve net-zero emissions targets.[18] This approach is particularly useful for multinational organizations operating in diverse regions with distinct sustainability requirements who seek to provide a standardized reporting "language," facilitating cross-border compliance.[19]

Sustainability reporting using GRI Standards signifies a forward-looking approach, with reports maintaining relevance and comparability over time. In an era where structured ESG reporting is gaining economic importance, GRI provides applicable and comparable standards that guide organizations worldwide, aligning with stakeholder and investor reporting requirements and ensuring transparency in decarbonization efforts. The growing trend, evidenced by the substantial number of S&P 500 companies publishing sustainability reports, underscores the economic imperative of structured ESG reporting, with GRI playing a central role in providing a robust framework for organizations globally.[20]

The GRI Standards operate through a modular, interconnected system, divided into three sections: universal, sectors, and topics. While all reporting organizations use the universal standards, they also have the flexibility to choose sector and topic standards that align with their specific circumstances.

This allows for a structured process that identifies "material topics," and creates the specificity needed for highly regulated organizations.[21]

The general standards, commonly known as Universal Standards (GRI 1, GRI 2, GRI 3) form the foundation applicable to all organizations. GRI 1 outlines key concepts, principles, and reporting requirements. GRI 2 encompasses disclosures related to organizational structure, practices, governance, and stakeholder engagement, providing insight into an organization's profile. GRI 3 guides the process of determining material topics, focusing on impacts, and managing each topic.[22]

Sector Standards, on the other hand, are designed to enhance reporting quality, completeness, and consistency, and are developed for specific sectors. These standards list likely material topics and relevant disclosures, ensuring a sector-specific approach to reporting. The Sector Standards serve as an aid in identifying and assessing impacts, aligning with the organization's specific circumstances.[23]

With respect to content, the following illustration provides an example of the types of requirements covered by GRI.

GRI 403 outlines various management approach disclosures and topic-specific disclosures, offering a comprehensive framework for organizations to report on this critical aspect. The GRI Standards are structured to help an organization and its stakeholders understand the context of the report so that they can better see the significance of its impacts.[24]

Within this standard are a number of disclosures.

Management approach disclosures

- Disclosure 403-1: Occupational health and safety management system;
- Disclosure 403-2: Hazard identification, risk assessment, and incident investigation;
- Disclosure 403-3: Occupational health services;
- Disclosure 403-4: Worker participation, consultation and communication on occupational health and safety;
- Disclosure 403-5: Worker training on occupational health and safety;
- Disclosure 403-6: Promotion of worker health;
- Disclosure 403-7: Prevention and mitigation of occupational health and safety impacts directly linked by business relationships.

Topic-specific disclosures

- Disclosure 403-8: Workers covered by an occupational health and safety management system;
- Disclosure 403-9: Work-related injuries;
- Disclosure 403-10: Work-related ill-health.[25]

Benefits of GRI include

- Improved reporting, which enables organizations to measure, disclose, and manage their impacts effectively, fostering better understanding and identification of strategic opportunities;
- Increased consistency, which improves trust, strengthening relationships with communities, industries, and internal stakeholders

GRI in the Context of ESG Sustainability Reports[26]

The sustainability report, also known as an ESG report, serves as a crucial communication tool for companies or organizations to transparently share information about their impacts on the environment, social aspects, and governance practices. This report plays a vital role in fostering transparency, enabling companies to articulate the risks and opportunities they encounter. It serves as a means of convincing skeptical observers about the sincerity of the company's actions.

The growing significance of sustainability reports is underscored by the increasing demands from investors and stakeholders for comprehensive disclosure of sustainability, ESG strategies. Legislative initiatives are underway to enforce such disclosures, exemplified by regulations such as the EU Taxonomy Regulation (REGULATION (EU) 2020/852) in force since July 2020 and others.

Ideally, these standards should be based on criteria such as those set forth in the GRI. These standards, although nonmandatory and nonbinding, are widely used globally, helping companies identify and report on their impacts related to climate change, environment, human rights, and corporate governance.

SASB Standards

Established in the United States, the SASB was created to streamline and standardize the language used in sustainability reporting. These standards pinpoint sustainability disclosure topics deemed relevant across 77 diverse industries, incorporating a concise set of primarily quantitative metrics to assess performance in each area. The development of SASB Standards resulted from extensive engagement with companies and investors, ensuring a comprehensive understanding of the information necessary for investors to make informed decisions about a company's value.[27] For example, the SASB Standards provide a framework to enable organizations to disclose industry-specific information on sustainability-related risks and opportunities. These disclosures are aimed at providing insights into factors that could impact an entity's cash flows, access to finance, or cost of capital across various timelines.[28]

The standards are the outcome of a rigorous standard-setting process, involving evidence-based research, active participation from companies, investors, and SMEs, and oversight and approval by the independent SASB Standards Board.[29]

Globally, SASB Standards are acknowledged by investors as essential requisites for companies aiming to deliver consistent and comparable sustainability disclosures. In August 2022, the International Sustainability Standards Board (ISSB) of the International Financial Reporting Standards (IFRS) Foundation took on the responsibility for SASB Standards. The ISSB has committed to maintaining, enhancing, and evolving these standards, urging preparers and investors to continue their use.[30]

The SASB Standards also hold a critical role within the IFRS Sustainability Disclosure Standards, generally. The ISSB's IFRS S1 General Requirements for Sustainability-related Disclosures and IFRS S2 Climate-related Disclosures, for example, incorporate and align with SASB Standards. This integration underscores the role of SASB Standards in supporting the application and implementation of the IFRS Sustainability Disclosure Standards, marking them as integral tools for comprehensive sustainability reporting.[31]

They do this by providing a clear starting point for determining financial material sustainability topics and providing industry-specific metrics relevant to investors. With the creation of the ISSB, SASB Standards serve as a foundational building block for global standards, particularly in the ISSB's first two standards that directly reference or incorporate SASB guidance. However, for companies aiming to address a broader stakeholder audience, additional standards such as those from the GRI or the EU's Corporate Sustainability Reporting Directive (CSRD) may be necessary.[32]

The SASB Standards also hold relevance for companies planning to adopt the ISSB's IFRS Sustainability Disclosure Standards. Notably, IFRS S1 requires companies to refer to and consider SASB Standards when identifying sustainability-related risks and opportunities. Additionally, IFRS S2, focusing on climate-related matters, aligns its content with SASB Standards, emphasizing the advantage for companies familiar with SASB when adopting IFRS Sustainability Disclosure Standards.[33]

Task Force on Climate-Related Disclosures (TCFD)

In 2015, the Swiss-based Financial Stability Board (FSB) established the TCFD with the aim of formulating recommendations for enhanced disclosures related to climate considerations.[34] This initiative sought to facilitate more informed decision making, providing financial stakeholders with a clearer understanding of the concentrations of carbon-related assets and the exposure to climate-related risks.

The Task Force officially released their recommendations in 2017, outlining:

- Four broadly applicable recommendations spanning Governance, Strategy, Risk Management, and Metrics and Targets. These can be summarized as follows:
  - Governance: The company is required to disclose the oversight role of its board and the involvement of management in evaluating and addressing climate-related risks and opportunities.
  - Strategy: The company must reveal its climate-related risks and opportunities across different timeframes (near, medium, and long terms), elucidating their potential

impacts on business, strategies, financial planning, and corporate governance. Additionally, the company should outline its resilience in various climate scenarios, such as a 2°C or lower climate scenario analysis.

o Risk Management: The company is obligated to disclose its procedures for identifying, assessing, and managing climate-related risks. This includes integrating these processes into overall risk management strategies.

o Metrics and Targets: The company must disclose the metrics and targets employed to gauge success in addressing climate-related risks and capitalizing on opportunities. Furthermore, the company should reveal its transition plan, outlining actions and initiatives aimed at achieving net-zero emissions by 2050. This encompasses the disclosure of metrics and targets related to three greenhouse gas (GHG) emissions categories or scopes:

■ Scope 1 Emissions: Direct emissions resulting from operations owned or controlled by the reporting organization.

■ Scope 2 Emissions: Indirect emissions linked to the generation of purchased energy, such as electricity, heat, or steam. While indirect, these emissions can be owned and directly controlled by the reporting organization.

■ Scope 3 Emissions: Emissions that the organization doesn't directly control but are a consequence of its operations or value chain. Estimates from the Carbon Disclosure Project (CDP) suggest that scope 3 emissions constitute, on average, 75 percent of companies' GHG emissions.

• Eleven suggested disclosures organized around these thematic areas, constituting fundamental aspects of an organization's operations. These disclosures are designed to interconnect and mutually inform each other.

• Provision of both general and sector-specific guidance to assist in implementing the framework.

• Seven key principles for effective disclosure, emphasizing the need for information to be relevant, specific, and complete, clear, balanced, and understandable, consistent over time, comparable within the sector, industry, or portfolio, reliable, verifiable, and objective, and provided in a timely manner.[35]

o These principles can be outlined as follows:

- Principle 1: Present information that is relevant.
- Principle 2: Ensure disclosures are specific and comprehensive.
- Principle 3: Strive for clarity, balance, and understandability in disclosures.
- Principle 4: Maintain consistency in disclosures over time.
- Principle 5: Foster comparability of disclosures among organizations within a sector, industry, or portfolio.
- Principle 6: Uphold reliability, verifiability, and objectivity in disclosures.
- Principle 7: Provide disclosures in a timely manner.[36]

The TCFD framework divides a company's climate-related risks into two main categories: physical risks and transitional risks. Physical risks are linked to the direct impacts of climate change, ranging from acute risks driven by extreme weather events to chronic risks associated with long-term shifts in climate patterns. On the other hand, transitional risks are inherent in the process of transitioning to a low-carbon economy. These risks involve evolving climate-related policies, regulations, and disclosure requirements, encompassing issues such as GHG emissions, net-zero carbon initiatives, carbon tax policies, energy costs, and national or global energy policies.[37]

The TCFD recommendations are applicable globally and span various industries, including banks, insurance firms, asset management firms, and other financial sector organizations. Companies in the financial sector are additionally responsible for disclosing not only their climate-related risks but also those faced by the companies in which they invest.[38]

The TCFD framework is integral to the broader context of ESG reporting. This is because the TCFD recommendations offer a consistent and comparable framework for organizations to disclose their climate-related risks, opportunities, and financial impacts, spanning the three pillars of ESG reporting: environment, social, and governance.[39]

While the TCFD recommendations were initially introduced as voluntary guidelines, they have gained significant regulatory traction and support. As of November 2022, for example, over 4,000 organizations across 101 jurisdictions, with a combined market capital value of USD 27 trillion, have expressed support for TCFD. And, the number of companies disclosing TCFD-aligned information has seen a notable 26 percent increase from 2017 to 2021.[40] In addition, nearly 60 percent of the world's 100 largest public companies claim to either support or align with TCFD recommendations, it has become a leading standard globally[41]-and, in fact, the ISSB, formed in 2021, has specifically stated its intent to deploy existing TCFD guidance for climate-related scenario analysis, providing specific guidance based on industry and jurisdiction.[42]

The TCFD framework is also becoming increasingly aligned with major financial reporting laws. Moreover, TCFD recommendations are progressively becoming a part of mandatory regulatory frameworks in various jurisdictions, including the European Union, Singapore, Canada, Japan, and South Africa. New Zealand and the United Kingdom have mandated climate risk disclosures aligned with the TCFD framework by 2023 and 2025, respectively. Regarding specific mandates, in March 2022, the U.S. Securities and Exchange Commission (SEC) proposed legislation on climate-related risk disclosures, aligning with key aspects of the TCFD framework.[43] And, in addition, the UK Financial Conduct Authority and UK Government have set the United Kingdom on a path to mandatory TCFD reporting, with premium-listed companies required to state their TCFD consistency in annual reports since January 2021, with the UK Government extending this mandate to over 1,300 of the largest UK-registered companies and financial institutions.

CDP Standards

CDP, founded in 2000, operates as a global disclosure system, assisting companies, cities, states, and regions in assessing and managing environmental risks and opportunities, spanning climate change, water security, forestry management, and more. Companies voluntarily disclose or respond to requests from investors and customers, impacting their CDP scores. CDP annually collects data, scoring entities from A to F based on the quality of disclosure, environmental risk awareness, and management practices. An A denotes environmental leadership, while an F signals inadequate information reporting.[44]

Currently, 746 investors with over US$136 trillion in assets and 330+ large purchasers with over US$6.4 trillion in procurement spend are requesting thousands of companies to disclose their environmental data through CDP.[45]

Investors, as CDP signatories, access the disclosure database for informed investment decisions, showcasing commitment to environmental engagement. CDP questionnaires cover climate change, forests/deforestation, and water security, with climate change aligned with TCFD recommendations. Industries with significant environmental impact face sector-specific questions. The climate change questionnaire explores indicators such as governance, risks/opportunities, business strategy, emissions data, and carbon pricing. Forests/deforestation and water security questionnaires assess relevant indicators specific to their domains.[46]

CDP provides three distinct questionnaires¡ covering (1) climate change, (2) forests/deforestation, and (3) water security. The climate change questionnaire aligns fully with TCFD recommendations, tailored to sectors with significant environmental impact such as agricultural commodities, capital goods, cement, chemicals, coal, construction, electric utilities, financial services, food/beverage/tobacco, metals and mining, oil and gas, paper and forestry, real estate, steel, transport original equipment manufacturers (OEMs), and transport services.

- The climate change questionnaire evaluates indicators including governance, climate-related risks and opportunities, business strategy (e.g., transition plans), targets and performance (e.g., emissions and low-carbon energy targets), emissions methodology, emissions data (scopes 1 to 3, emissions intensity), emissions breakdown, energy (e.g., energy spend), additional climate metrics, verification, carbon pricing (including carbon accounting and carbon credits), engagement on climate, and biodiversity.

- The forests questionnaire assesses indicators such as the type of commodities (e.g., timber, palm oil, soy), the current state (association of business model with forests-related resources and issues), procedures to manage issues and risks, forest-related risks and opportunities, governance regarding forest-related issues (including commitment to reduce deforestation or forest degradation), business strategy on forests-related issues, implementation of policies and commitments (e.g., targets, traceability of commodities, third-party certification, control system for noncompliance, compliance with the Brazilian Forest Code, legal compliance, engagement, ecosystem restoration), verification of reported data, and barriers and challenges in the process of removing deforestation from value chains.
- The water security questionnaire examines indicators such as the current state (dependency on freshwater sources, accounting on interactions with water resources, water intensity, and value chain engagement), business impacts (water-related detrimental impacts on the organization, compliance impact from fines and enforcement orders), procedures to manage risks and water pollutants, risks and opportunities related to water, facility-level water accounting, governance (e.g., approach to water-related issues at the board level and management level, employee incentives, policy that includes water-related issues, engagement that may influence water-related public policy, and inclusion of water-related risks in financial reporting), business strategy (e.g., water-related capital expenditure [CAPEX] and operating expenditure [OPEX], use of scenario analysis, setting of internal water price, impact of products and services on water), and water-related quantitative targets and qualitative goals.[47]

Specific modules exist under each questionnaire for companies responding to requests from customers who are part of CDP's supply chain program. CDP scores, ranging from D- to A, reflect a company's environmental disclosure and performance, aligning with a 1.5-degree, deforestation-free, and water-secure future. Companies aiming for A or B scores demonstrate environmental awareness and action consistent with the Paris Agreement. While CDP scores aren't exhaustive metrics of overall sustainability, they showcase reported environmental actions during the year.[48]

Benefits of disclosure include enhancing reputation, gaining a competitive edge in markets and tenders, tracking progress against industry peers, uncovering risks and opportunities, and staying ahead of evolving regulations. CDP, aligned with TCFD recommendations, serves as the gold standard for corporate environmental reporting. The scoring methodology follows a four-level progression: Disclosure (D-/D score), Awareness (C-/C score), Management (B-/B score), and Leadership (A-/A score). The failure to disclose results in an F score. The weighted scoring categories reflect relative importance to the overall score.[49]

UN Global Compact[50]

The United Nations Global Compact outlines 10 principles that are synthesized from key international declarations and agreements, namely, the Universal Declaration of Human Rights, the International Labor Organization's Declaration on Fundamental Principles and Rights at Work, the Rio Declaration on Environment and Development, and the United Nations Convention Against Corruption.

Human Rights

Principle 1: Businesses should support and respect the protection of internationally proclaimed human rights

The first principle requires businesses to support and respect internationally proclaimed human rights. This commitment involves employing due diligence to prevent human rights infringements, addressing adverse impacts, and voluntarily contributing to the protection and fulfillment of human rights. Vulnerable groups, including women, children, and indigenous peoples, merit special attention. Failure to respect human rights poses multifaceted risks such as reputational damage, legal liabilities, and erosion of social license.

To ensure compliance, companies must undertake and be able to document a comprehensive human rights due diligence process. This involves assessing potential impacts on all human rights, ensuring adherence to applicable laws, and internationally recognized human rights, and recognizing corporate responsibility irrespective of states' duties. Policies reflecting these commitments are crucial, requiring integration into broader corporate sustainability policies or codes of conduct, with communication and reporting of progress on an annual basis.

Businesses can also support their compliance with this principle through core activities, social investment, advocacy, and partnerships. Practical examples include providing safe workplaces, preventing displacement, contributing to local communities, and fostering education opportunities that promote understanding of human rights within the company, emphasizing their relevance and practical actions, and integrating human rights into existing business processes and procedures.

Principle 2: Make sure that they are not complicit in human rights abuses

The second principle obligates businesses to ensure that they are not complicit in human rights abuses. Practically, this includes being implicated in human rights abuses perpetrated by another entity or person.

Complicity consists of two key elements: an act or omission that assists another in committing a human rights abuse and the company's awareness that its actions could provide such assistance. To comply with this principle, companies need to maintain systematic management approaches and due diligence processes covering their business relationships. Allegations of complicity can arise in various forms, such as direct complicity, beneficial complicity, and silent complicity, each carrying distinct implications. Companies expanding into regions with poor human rights records face particular challenges, necessitating a robust approach to avoid complicity.

Practical compliance steps include integrating human rights policies, conducting thorough human rights assessments in their operational areas, and establishing monitoring systems to ensure policy implementation—especially in regions that are either less developed or that have poor human rights records. Engaging in open dialogue with stakeholders, utilizing leverage to influence actors committing abuses, and having explicit policies on security arrangements are also crucial compliance measures.

Labor

Principle 3: Businesses should uphold the freedom of association and the effective recognition of the right to collective bargaining

Businesses seeking to establish their compliance with this principle should maintain documentation showing that they uphold the freedom of association and the effective recognition of the right to collective bargaining. Freedom of association involves allowing both employers and workers to freely establish and join groups to promote and defend their occupational interests without interference from the State or other entities. This freedom encompasses activities such as rule formation, administration, and the election of representatives.

To support this principle, companies should respect workers' rights to join trade unions without intimidation, implement and document nondiscriminatory policies, provide facilities for effective collective agreements, and avoid interfering with workers' representatives' activities. Examples include using collective bargaining constructively to address working conditions, providing necessary information, and balancing their dealings with trade unions. And, from an ESG standpoint, this fosters the general sustainability and social goals of creating a positive work environment, promoting social dialogue, and supporting sustainable growth.

Principle 4: The elimination of all forms of forced and compulsory labor

Forced or compulsory labor, defined as work or service exacted from an individual under the threat of penalty without voluntary consent, demands attention from businesses, not only as a violation of fundamental human rights but also due to its broader societal and economic implications.

To effectively combat forced labor, companies should implement comprehensive measures within both the workplace and the broader community of operation. Within the workplace, the foundation lies in establishing a clear policy against forced labor, ensuring strict compliance with national laws and international standards. Educating company officials about the nuanced nature of forced labor is crucial, fostering a collective understanding of the issue.

In instances where companies engage prison labor, ensuring favorable terms and conditions, including occupational health and safety, coupled with the informed consent of the prisoners, reflects a commitment to ethical practices. By integrating these comprehensive measures, companies can actively contribute to eradicating forced labor and fostering a workplace and community that upholds the dignity and rights of every individual.

Principle 5: The effective abolition of child labor

Child labor, as distinguished from youth employment or student work, constitutes a violation of human rights, and is universally condemned by international instruments. The International Labor Organization (ILO) conventions, particularly Convention No. 138 and Convention No. 182, provide a framework for establishing minimum age standards for employment and eradicating the worst forms of child labor.

Child labor, defined by Convention 182, encompasses various forms, including slavery, trafficking, forced labor, involvement in armed conflict, prostitution, production of pornography, illicit activities, and work that harms a child's health, safety, or morals. Businesses should prioritize eliminating these worst forms of child labor.

Risks of breaching this principle not only go beyond the ethical reasons but also involve the potential damage to reputation, particularly for transnational companies with extensive supply chains. Economic exploitation of children, even by business partners, can tarnish a brand's image and have severe repercussions on profit and stock value. Beyond reputation, child labor hampers a child's physical, social, mental, and psychological development, depriving them of education and dignity.

To effectively combat the issue of child labor, companies should implement a multifaceted approach within both the workplace and the broader community of operation. Within the confines of the workplace, a crucial first step involves fostering regional awareness, enabling companies to identify regions, sectors, or economic activities where child labor is more prevalent. This heightened awareness should be met with the swift implementation and enforcement of appropriate policies and procedures tailored to each context.

Principle 6: The elimination of discrimination in respect of employment and occupation

Principle 6 focuses on the elimination of discrimination in employment and occupation. Discrimination encompasses differential treatment based on nonmerit or job-related characteristics, such as race, gender, religion, age, disability, and more. It occurs across various employment aspects, including recruitment, remuneration, job assignments, and training. Companies must ensure nondiscriminatory practices, considering additional grounds where discrimination may occur beyond those specified in national law.

To address discrimination, companies must adhere to local and national laws, respecting diversity in language, culture, and family circumstances. Managers should understand different forms of discrimination and their impacts. Practical actions include instituting policies based on qualifications, skills, and experience, evaluating job requirements to avoid systematic disadvantages, maintaining transparent records, conducting unconscious bias training, and establishing grievance procedures. Beyond the workplace, companies can contribute to the community by encouraging tolerance, supporting equal access to opportunities, and accommodating cultural traditions in foreign operations.

Environment

Principle 7: Businesses should support a precautionary approach to environmental challenges

Principle 15 of the 1992 Rio Declaration emphasizes the precautionary approach in environmental management, asserting that lack of full scientific certainty should not hinder timely, cost-effective measures to prevent irreversible damage. This involves systematic risk assessment, management, and communication, especially when suspicions of harm arise, necessitating a careful balance between scientific evaluation and public acceptability.

For companies, adopting a precautionary approach is economically prudent, as early prevention outweighs the substantial costs associated with environmental remediation. Investment in sustainable production methods proves more financially sound than practices depleting resources and degrading the environment, mitigating long-term financial risks.

Research and development focused on environmentally friendly products not only aligns with responsible business practices but also yields significant long-term benefits.

To actively support a precautionary approach, companies can take specific steps. Establishing a code of conduct affirming commitment to environmental stewardship and health sets the foundation. Developing comprehensive guidelines for consistent application of the approach across all operations reinforces corporate responsibility. Creating managerial committees or steering groups dedicated to overseeing risk management in sensitive areas ensures systematic implementation.

Principle 8: Undertake initiatives to promote greater environmental responsibility

Chapter 30 of Agenda 21, emerging from the 1992 Rio Earth Summit, directs businesses to enhance self-regulation through codes, charters, and integrated initiatives, fostering openness and dialogue with employees and the public. The Rio Declaration emphasizes businesses' responsibility to prevent environmental harm, aligning with societal expectations for responsible corporate citizenship. Cleaner processes and efficiency not only enhance resource productivity but also yield lower costs and potential tax incentives for environmentally responsible practices. Growing interest from employees and consumers in responsible business further underscores the need for sustainable practices.

Companies aiming to be environmental leaders face the challenge of innovating in environmental management. Key steps to promote environmental responsibility include defining a vision for sustainable development, establishing targets across economic, environmental, and social aspects, and implementing long-term sustainable production programs. Collaboration with stakeholders, adoption of voluntary codes, and transparent communication enhance companies' responsible environmental performance.

Appropriate management systems play a crucial role in addressing organizational challenges, utilizing assessment or audit tools (e.g., environmental impact assessment), management tools (e.g., environmental management systems and eco-design), and communication and reporting tools (e.g., corporate environmental footprinting and sustainability reporting). These mechanisms empower companies to meet their sustainability goals effectively.

Principle 9: Encourage the development and diffusion of environmentally friendly technologies

The call for businesses to encourage the development and diffusion of environmentally friendly technologies, as outlined in Agenda 21 of the Rio Declaration, underscores the importance of adopting technologies that protect the environment, minimize pollution, and utilize resources sustainably. These environmentally sound technologies encompass cleaner production processes, pollution prevention methods, end-of-pipe solutions, and monitoring technologies, along with know-how, goods, services, equipment, and organizational procedures. Embracing these technologies allows companies to address day-to-day inefficiencies, reduce emissions, protect workers from hazardous materials, and mitigate the risk of environmental disasters.

Companies seeking to comply with this principle should implement improvements in technology at both the basic factory level and the strategic corporate level. At the factory level, changes to processes, manufacturing techniques, input materials, and product design contribute to improved technology. Strategic-level approaches involve the establishment of corporate policies supporting the use of environmentally sound technologies, the dissemination of information showcasing environmental benefits, and a shift in research and development toward "design for sustainability." Such measures align with the principles outlined in the Rio Declaration, emphasizing the importance of adopting technologies that lead to sustainable practices and resource efficiency.

Anti-Corruption

Principle 10: Businesses should work against corruption in all its forms, including extortion and bribery

Companies seeking to comply with this principle should not only abstain from corrupt practices but also to proactively develop policies and programs addressing corruption internally and within their supply chains. The UN Convention Against Corruption (UNCAC), in force since 2005, serves as a global tool supporting this principle. Transparency International's definition emphasizes the abuse of entrusted power for private gain, spanning both financial and nonfinancial advantages.

The UN Global Compact recommends a three-pronged compliance approach for participants. Internally, companies should establish anti-corruption policies and programs. Externally, they should report on their anti-corruption efforts and share best practices through annual Communications on Progress. Embracing collective action, companies are encouraged to join forces with industry peers and stakeholders to scale up anti-corruption efforts, level the playing field, and foster fair competition. Additionally, signing the "Anti-corruption Call to Action" demonstrates a commitment to addressing corruption and promoting effective governance for a sustainable global economy.

The OECD Guidelines for Multinational Enterprises and ISO 26000, Guidance on Social Responsibility

The main focus of these standards is to guide multinational organizations on integrating social responsibility into an organization's operations.

The OECD Guidelines for Multinational Enterprises were first adopted in 1976 by the Organization for Economic Cooperation and Development (OECD). These guidelines provide voluntary principles and standards for responsible business conduct consistent with applicable laws and internationally recognized standards. Over the years, the guidelines have been updated to reflect changes in the global business environment and societal expectations. One significant update occurred in May 2011, marking an effort to ensure that the guidelines remain relevant and effective in addressing contemporary challenges related to multinational enterprises.

ISO 26000, Guidance on Social Responsibility, on the other hand, is a set of international standards developed by the ISO. The first edition of ISO 26000 was published in November 2010. This standard outlines principles and provides guidance on integrating social responsibility into the core activities of organizations. It emphasizes the importance of considering societal, environmental, legal, cultural, political, and organizational diversity while being consistent with international norms of behavior. ISO 26000 aims to assist organizations in contributing to sustainable development and acting in an ethical and transparent manner.

The following chart[51] summarizes the main priorities and responsibilities of these frameworks, as they apply to organizations seeking to establish evidence of their ESG compliance:

Concept	ISO 2600	OECD Guidelines
Accountability	Organizations are urged to uphold accountability for their impacts on society, the economy, and the environment, with a specific focus on addressing significant negative consequences. This entails a dual responsibility, involving management being answerable to both controlling interests within the organization and legal authorities. The emphasis is placed on transparently accounting for the effects of decisions and activities, underscoring the importance of acknowledging and preventing adverse outcomes while fostering a commitment to responsible and ethical behavior.	Emphasizes accountability through compliance with laws, periodic review of compliance, and providing information on all material matters regarding activities, structure, financial situation, and governance.
Transparency	Organizations should be transparent in decisions and activities affecting society and the environment and should ensure that they clearly, accurately, and completely disclose relevant information to stakeholders in a timely and factual manner.	Organizations should maintain high-quality standards for accounting and disclosure, encompassing both financial and nonfinancial dimensions and adhere to rigorous standards in their reporting, ensuring transparency in their financial and operational information. Ideally, enterprises are urged to go beyond mandatory requirements by actively communicating additional information when possible.
Ethical Behavior	Organizations should conduct themselves ethically, guided by principles of honesty, equity, and integrity. Specific actions include respecting animal welfare and avoiding involvement in activities contrary to international norms, emphasizing a commitment to responsible and ethical behavior.	Emphasizes the need for good ethical behavior based on values, emphasizing support for good corporate governance, self-regulatory practices, and refraining from discriminatory or disciplinary actions against workers reporting violations.

Stakeholder Engagement	Organizations should respect, consider, and respond to stakeholder interests, involving actions such as identifying stakeholders, evaluating their engagement capacity, and taking into account their views, even if they lack formal governance roles.	Enterprises should consider established policies in the countries where they operate, including engagement with relevant stakeholders. The encouragement extends to supporting cooperative efforts promoting responsible business conduct.
International Behavior Norms	Organizations should respect international norms of behavior, particularly in situations where local laws do not provide adequate safeguards.	Organizations should follow internationally recognized human rights norms and observe the guidelines worldwide but considering the circumstances of each host country.
Human Rights	Organizations should respect human rights, particularly in situations lacking protection, and are encouraged to adhere to international norms of behavior when local laws are inadequate. Organizations must not only respect human rights but also engage in due diligence to identify, prevent, and address actual or potential human rights impacts arising from their activities or relationships. Due diligence allows organizations to recognize and address the responsibility to influence the behavior of others, especially when they might be the cause of human rights violations that implicate the organization.	Organizations should contribute to economic, environmental, and social progress while respecting internationally recognized human rights. They should also conduct risk-based due diligence to identify, prevent, and mitigate adverse impacts on human rights. Moreover, where possible, the organization, acting alone or in cooperation with other entities, should use its leverage to influence the entity causing the adverse human rights impact to prevent or mitigate that impact.
Governance	Organizations should deploy effective governance standards that incorporate the principles of social responsibility into decision making and implementation. Additionally, when establishing and reviewing governance systems, organizations should account for social responsibility practices, core subjects, and related issues. It is essential for organizations to establish processes, systems, structures, or mechanisms that facilitate the application of social responsibility principles and practices.	Enterprises should ensure sound corporate governance principles, implementing robust practices consistently across enterprise groups. In terms of disclosure policies, enterprises should provide comprehensive information, including details on governance structures and policies. This encompasses the content and implementation processes of corporate governance codes or policies, ensuring transparency and accountability in their organizational practices.

(Continued)

Concept	ISO 2600	OECD Guidelines
Employment and Labor Practices	Labor practices form a crucial aspect of an organization's social responsibility, encompassing all policies and practices related to work performed within or on behalf of the organization, extending to sub-contracted work. Recognizing their impact on the rule of law, societal fairness, and overall social justice, socially responsible labor practices are deemed essential for fostering stability and peace in society. Specific issues within labor practices include employment relationships, conditions of work, and social protection, as well as promoting social dialogue. It is imperative for organizations to integrate these principles into their broader framework of social responsibility.	Organizations should uphold fundamental principles such as respecting the freedom of association, supporting workers' right to collective bargaining, actively contributing to the eradication of child labor, and taking immediate measures against any forms of forced or compulsory labor. They should also promote nondiscrimination, provide facilities for effective collective agreements, furnish workers with essential negotiation information, and ensure transparency on company performance, observe labor standards meeting basic needs, prioritize occupational health and safety, employ local workers, and facilitate training. Finally, enterprises should provide notice of major changes, collaborate with worker representatives to mitigate adverse effects, and ensure the involvement of workers' representatives in negotiations and decision-making processes related to collective bargaining and labor issues.
Environment	Organizations should follow key principles such as environmental responsibility, the precautionary approach, environmental risk management, and the polluter pays principle. They should also assess the relevance and employ approaches such as the life-cycle approach, environmental impact assessment, cleaner production, eco-efficiency, product-service system approach, environmentally sound technologies, sustainable procurement, and learning and awareness raising. Addressing pollution, sustainable resource use, climate change mitigation and adaptation, and the protection of the environment, biodiversity, and restoration of natural habitats are paramount. This involves preventing pollution, improving resource efficiency, and	Enterprises should establish and maintain an environmental management system that encompasses monitoring, evaluating, and verifying the environmental, health, and safety impacts of activities and objectives. Transparency is emphasized through providing measurable and verifiable information to the public and workers, engaging in timely communication and consultation with affected communities, and continually seeking improvement in corporate environmental performance. This involves assessing and addressing foreseeable environmental, health, and safety-related impacts over the entire life cycle, avoiding or mitigating them, and maintaining contingency plans for serious environmental and health damage.

	contributing to climate change actions and biodiversity protection, including valuing, and protecting biodiversity, using land and natural resources sustainably, and promoting environmentally sound urban and rural development. Additional guidance is provided for related actions and expectations in these areas.	Enterprises should also adopt technologies reflecting environmental standards, develop environmentally friendly products and services, promote customer awareness of environmental implications, and explore long-term strategies for emission reduction, efficient resource utilization, recycling, and biodiversity. Additionally, they are encouraged to provide education and training on environmental health and safety matters and contribute to the development of environmentally meaningful and economically efficient public policies. Further guidance can be found in the "Commentary on the Environment" section.
Fair Operating Practices	Organizations should ensure ethical conduct in their interactions with other entities, encompassing relationships with government agencies, partners, suppliers, contractors, customers, competitors, and relevant associations. Anti-corruption measures address the abuse of entrusted power for private gain, including bribery, conflicts of interest, fraud, money laundering, embezzlement, and trading in influence are particularly critical. Organizations should also support public political processes while avoiding undue influence and coercive behavior. The commitment to fair competition opposes anticompetitive practices such as price fixing, bid rigging, and predatory pricing. Finally, organizations are urged to promote social responsibility along the value chain, influencing other entities through procurement and purchasing decisions. Respect for property rights extends to both physical and intellectual properties, including interests in land, copyrights, patents, geographical indicators, and various other rights.	Enterprises must refrain from offering bribes for obtaining or retaining business advantages and resist the solicitation of bribes or extortion. This involves not providing undue monetary or other advantages to public officials or employees of business partners directly or through intermediaries. Measures to combat bribery include adopting internal controls, ethics, and compliance programs based on risk assessments, monitoring, and reassessing risks regularly, and prohibiting facilitation payments. Due diligence is crucial when hiring and overseeing agents to ensure legitimate services and promoting transparency by disclosing antibribery control systems. Employee awareness and compliance with policies are emphasized, along with ensuring political contributions comply with disclosure requirements. In the realm of competition, enterprises should adhere to competition laws, avoid anticompetitive agreements, cooperate with investigating authorities, and foster employee awareness of applicable competition laws and regulations.

(Continued)

Concept	ISO 2600	OECD Guidelines
Consumer Rights	Organizations should follow the principles outlined in the UN Guidelines for Consumer Protection and the International Covenant on Economic, Social, and Cultural Rights, encompassing safety, information, choice, voice, redress, education, and a healthy environment. Additional principles involve respecting the right to privacy, the precautionary approach, the promotion of gender equality, the empowerment of women, and universal design. In addressing consumer issues, enterprises should uphold fair marketing, provide factual and unbiased information, and ensure fair contractual practices. Attention to protecting consumers' health and safety, promoting sustainable consumption, and providing consumer service, support, and effective dispute resolution is essential. Issues such as consumer data protection and privacy, access to essential services, and education and awareness are integral to socially responsible practices in consumer-related matters.	Enterprises must ensure that their goods and services comply with agreed or legally required consumer health and safety standards, including relevant health warnings and safety information. They should provide accurate, verifiable, and clear information to enable consumers to make informed decisions, facilitating product comparisons. Ensuring access to fair, easy-to-use, timely, and effective nonjudicial dispute resolution and redress mechanisms without unnecessary cost or burden is crucial. Enterprises may not engage in deceptive, misleading, fraudulent, or unfair practices, with a commitment to supporting consumer education for informed decision making and sustainable consumption. Respecting consumer privacy, implementing measures for data security, cooperating with authorities to combat deceptive marketing, and addressing the needs of vulnerable and disadvantaged consumers, including challenges posed by e-commerce, are integral aspects of socially responsible consumer-related practices.
Science and Technology	Organizations should consider supporting small- and medium-sized organizations. This support includes raising awareness about social responsibility issues, sharing best practices, and providing additional assistance such as technical support, capacity building, or other resources to help these organizations meet socially responsible objectives.	Enterprises should strive to align their activities with the science and technology policies and plans of host countries, actively contributing to the development of local and national innovative capacity. They should adopt practices that facilitate the transfer and rapid diffusion of science, technology, and know-how and intellectual property rights. Enterprises should also engage in science and technology development in host countries to address local market needs, employing and training local personnel. Finally, they should contribute to the long-term sustainable development of the host country when granting the use of intellectual property rights or transferring technology.

		Establishing connections with local universities and public research institutions and participating in cooperative research projects is also encouraged, especially if relevant to commercial objectives.
Taxation	Organizations should fulfil their tax responsibilities and provide authorities with the necessary information to correctly determine taxes due.	Enterprises are expected to contribute to the public finances of host countries through punctual tax payments, ensuring full compliance with both the explicit provisions and the underlying principles of the tax laws in host countries. This includes providing relevant and timely information to authorities as required by law, especially for tax determination purposes, and adhering to transfer pricing practices guided by the arm's length principle. Tax governance and compliance should be integral components of oversight and broader risk management systems within enterprises. Adopting tax risk management strategies is crucial to identifying and evaluating financial, regulatory, and reputational risks associated with taxation comprehensively.

Sustainalytics

Sustainalytics' ESG Risk Ratings are designed to help investors identify and understand financially material ESG risks at the security and portfolio levels. The ratings focus on capturing an issuer's exposure to material, industry specific ESG risks and evaluating the management of these risks. The resulting ESG Risk Rating score reflects the extent to which a company's exposure to ESG risk is unmanaged.[52]

Unmanageable risk represents the portion that remains a threat regardless of management practices, such as health risks associated with certain products. Manageable risk is the portion that can be controlled through policies and programs, and the proportion of manageable versus unmanageable risk is defined at the subindustry level for each material ESG issue (MEI).[53] The ESG Risk Rating score is the sum of unmanaged risk for each MEI. Exposure, management, and resulting risk scores are assigned to one of five ESG risk categories: negligible, low, medium, high, and severe, providing investors with insights into the material financial impacts driven by ESG factors.[54]

Sustainability also analyzes controversies, assessed at the MEI level, which are considered to be breakdowns in management, with more severe controversies leading to higher decreases in the management score. Idiosyncratic risks resulting from severe controversies may further reduce the overall management score.[55]

To this end, Sustainalytics staff review ESG-related controversies involving over 10,000 companies. Using a daily news screen, incidents are collected and analyzed by analysts within 48 hours. If an incident is deemed to have significant ESG relevance, it is categorized as a controversy and rated on a scale of 1 to 5, with higher ratings indicating more severe issues. Serious controversies pose substantial risks to stakeholders and are closely tracked. Sustainalytics provides an analyst outlook on the likelihood of the rating being upgraded or downgraded over the next 12 to 24 months, ensuring ongoing assessment and responsiveness to evolving circumstances.[56]

The assessment of exposure involves an analysis across 138 subindustry classifications, considering 20 MEIs for each. Sustainalytics staff then reviews the potential impact of these issues on subindustries and selects up to 10 MEIs per subindustry through an intensive consultation process. Corporate governance is universally applicable. The exposure score includes company-specific adjustments, and idiosyncratic risks from severe ESG controversies may be added. Sustainalytics measures sustainability performance by identifying relevant ESG issues within industries.[57]

Companies are assessed on three dimensions (preparedness, disclosure, and performance) within each E, S, and G pillar. More than 70 indicators are developed, weighted by importance within 42 industry groups. The resulting ESG score is on a 1 to 100 scale with a percentile ranking relative to industry peers. Controversies are also evaluated, with serious ones impacting stakeholders and rated from 1 to 5, monitored for potential rating changes over 12 to 24 months. Analysts oversee the process, providing a qualitative assessment, and scores are updated annually.[58]

Social Value International (SVI)[59]

SVI outlines eight principles of social value that collectively form a comprehensive framework that is intended to guide organizations seeking to adopt a principled and accountable approach to social value measurement and decision making. The goal of these principles is to create a framework for measuring and managing social, environmental, and economic value in decision making.

By involving stakeholders, valuing relevant impacts, and ensuring transparency and verification, SVI aims to drive a global movement toward decision making that prioritizes equality, well-being, and reduced environmental degradation.

The SVI principles can be summarized as follows:

Principle	Description
Involve Stakeholders in the Process of Measuring Social Impact	Stakeholders, those directly affected by activities, should actively contribute to decisions about what to measure and how to measure it. This ensures that the social value measurement accurately represents the perspectives and priorities of those experiencing the impacts.
Articulate and Evaluate Changes	Comprehensively assess both the intended and unintended consequences of each social activity. By understanding the dynamics of change, decision makers can better gauge the overall impact on stakeholders' well-being and make informed choices to optimize positive outcomes.

(Continued)

Principle	Description
Prioritize Stakeholders' Values	Decision making should recognize the values of stakeholders. Value, in this context, refers to the relative importance of different outcomes from the perspective of stakeholders. The principle encourages decision makers to consider stakeholders' preferences and prioritize actions that contribute significantly to their well-being.
Ensure Relevance	Information included in the accounts should provide a true and fair picture, enabling stakeholders to draw reasonable conclusions about the impact. This ensures that the focus is on relevant and significant aspects of the activity.
Do Not Overclaim	Organizations should ensure that they are honest and accurate in representing the impact of an activity. It ensures that the social value claimed is proportionate to the actual positive change attributable to the organization's actions.
Transparency	Organizations should demonstrate the basis on which their analysis may be considered accurate and honest. By openly sharing the methodologies, assumptions, and processes used in social value measurement, organizations foster credibility and accountability.
Verify Results	Independently validate the accuracy and reliability of social value accounts to promote trust, credibility, and accountability.
Be Responsive	Ensure that all information that is used and presented supports decision making that optimizes impacts on well-being across all materially affected groups. Being responsive means using the information to inform timely decisions that align with the organization's goals for optimizing well-being.

IIRC Framework (International Integrated Reporting Council)[60]

The International Integrated Reporting Council (IIRC) was established as a global coalition in 2010, to become a collaborative force comprising regulators, investors, companies, standard setters, the accounting profession, and nongovernmental organizations (NGOs).

This primary theme of the IIRC framework is that the communication of value creation should be the logical progression in the evolution of corporate reporting. The IIRC's vision anticipates a world where integrated thinking is deeply embedded within mainstream business practices across public and private sectors, facilitated by the widespread adoption of integrated reporting (IR) as the standard in corporate reporting.

IR, as championed by the IIRC, is designed to contribute to more efficient and productive capital allocation by elevating the quality of information available to providers of financial capital. The International IR framework, introduced by the IIRC, adopts a principles-based approach that attempts to strike a balance between flexibility and prescription, acknowledging the diverse circumstances of different organizations while promoting a sufficient degree of comparability for relevant information needs.

Notably, the framework not only applies to private sector and for-profit companies but is also adaptable for use by public sector and not-for-profit organizations, emphasizing its versatility in promoting transparency, accountability, and the efficient allocation of capital.

The framework categorizes resources and relationships as "capitals," spanning financial, manufactured, intellectual, human, social and relationship, and natural capital. An integrated report, therefore, aims to articulate how an organization interacts with these capitals and the external environment to generate value over varying time horizons.

The guiding principles and content elements of the framework provide a structured approach to the preparation of an integrated report and can be summarized as follows:

Principle	Description
Strategic Focus and Future Orientation	All integrated ESG reports should provide insight into the organization's strategy and how it aligns with the ability to create value over the short, medium, and long terms. Organizations should maintain a forward-looking perspective, ensuring stakeholders understand their strategic direction and its implications on value creation.
Connectivity of Information	Organizations should ensure that their reports present a holistic picture that captures the combination, interrelatedness, and dependencies between factors affecting an organization's ability to create value over time. The goal of this principle is to create a mechanism to break down silos in reporting and showcase the interconnected nature of various aspects influencing value creation.
Stakeholder Relationships	Organizations should strive to achieve a high-quality understanding, consideration, and response to legitimate stakeholder needs and interests. Effective stakeholder engagement is critical for sustainable value creation.

(Continued)

Principle	Description
Materiality	Organizations should ensure that they adequately disclose information about matters that significantly impact their ability to create value in the short, medium, and long terms. This principle ensures that the report prioritizes information that is relevant and significant, helping stakeholders make informed decisions.
Conciseness	Integrated reports should be succinct and focused. Organizations should strive to omit unnecessary details, and ensure that these reports remain clear, accessible, and neither overwhelming nor confusing. This promotes efficient communication and enhances the report's accessibility.
Reliability and Completeness	Organizations should strive to present all material matters, both positive and negative, in a balanced manner without material error. They should aim to build trust in the information presented and ensure that stakeholders can rely on the report for a comprehensive understanding of their performance and prospects.
Consistency and Comparability	Organizations should aim to present information consistently over time and in a way that enables meaningful comparisons with other organizations, using a standardized yet flexible approach.

FTSE4 Good Index Series[61]

The FTSE4Good Index Series, which was developed and maintained by the Financial Times Stock Exchange-Russell Group (FTSE) and initiated in 2001, is a collection of socially responsible or ESG stock indexes. Their goal is to highlight companies that are determined, based on specific ESG-oriented criteria excel in corporate social responsibility (CSR).

Representative indexes focus on a specific geographic region, such as the United States, Australia, Japan, and Latin America. Investors can use these indexes for individual stock selection or as benchmarks for investment products. Notably, the U.S.-based index's top holdings as of April 2023 featured well-known technology companies such as Apple, Microsoft, NVIDIA, and Alphabet.

The Index Series employs a score-based methodology to assess a company's management of ESG issues. It breaks down a total score and rates companies on three pillars and 14 themes, utilizing over 300 indicators. The three pillars encompass ESG issues, while the themes delve into specifics such as biodiversity, climate change, customer responsibility, human rights, anti-corruption, and more, including strong policies in human rights, labor relations, anti-corruption measures, and environmental sustainability within their supply chains.

Transparent management and defined ESG criteria render the FTSE-4Good indexes valuable tools for creating financial products, conducting research, establishing benchmarks, and tracking the performance of sustainable investment portfolios. Investors can also opt for products such as the Vanguard FTSE Social Index Fund, which measures its performance against the FTSE4Good U.S. Select Index.

The Dow Jones Sustainability Indices (DJSI)[62]

Initiated in 1999, DJSI stands out as the first global sustainability benchmark and is intended to monitor the stock performance of preeminent companies worldwide. Developed through the collaborative efforts of S&P Dow Jones indexes and SAM,* the indexes aggregate the proficiency of an established index provider with the specialization of a sustainable investing expert. This collaboration aims to identify and select the most sustainable companies across 61 industries.

The DJSI endeavors to provide a transparent, rules-based process for component selection, relying on the companies' Total Sustainability Scores derived from the annual S&P Global Corporate Sustainability Assessment (CSA). The assessment encompasses economic, environmental, and social criteria, ensuring a comprehensive evaluation. Only the top-ranking companies within each industry, constituting the Global Indices' top 10 percent, Regional Indices' top 20 percent, and Country Indices' top 30 percent, earn inclusion in the DJSI family. Notably, no industries are exempted from this rigorous selection process, contributing to the index's credibility and thoroughness.

The stated goal of the DJSI is to function as a platform for investors who actively integrate sustainability considerations into their portfolios and to serve as an engagement tool for investors committed to encouraging companies to enhance their corporate sustainability practices. The

---

* SAM is a global investment company focused exclusively on sustainability investing. The indexes are created to track financial success of leading sustainability companies.

composition of the DJSI undergoes an annual review every September, utilizing the S&P Global ESG Scores generated from SAM. To maintain relevance, the indexes are rebalanced quarterly, adapting to evolving sustainability trends and corporate performance.

The DJSI family encompasses a range of benchmarks, including the DJSI World, DJSI North America, DJSI Europe, DJSI Asia Pacific, DJSI Emerging Markets, and more. Additionally, S&P Dow Jones indexes offers DJSI indexes with exclusion criteria for investors looking to minimize exposure to controversial activities such as Armaments and Firearms, Alcohol, Tobacco, Gambling, and Adult Entertainment. All DJSI indexes are calculated in both price and total return versions, providing investors with comprehensive and real-time insights into sustainable investment opportunities.

ESG Reporting Laws and Initiatives

Europe

EU Nonfinancial Reporting Directive (NFRD): Requires certain large companies to disclose information on environmental and social matters, as well as aspects of corporate governance.[63]

The goal of the NFRD, Directive 2014/95/EU, was to enhance transparency in the disclosure of nonfinancial information among certain large undertakings. Adopted in 2014 as an amendment to the Accounting Directive (Directive 2013/34/EU), its primary objective is to raise the transparency of social and environmental information provided by public interest entities, including large, listed companies, banks, and insurance companies, each with more than 500 employees.

Under the NFRD, these entities must publish reports on policies related to social responsibility, treatment of employees, human rights, anti-corruption, bribery, and diversity on company boards. The disclosure encompasses business models, policies, outcomes, risks, risk management, and key performance indicators (KPIs) relevant to the business. Approximately 6,000 of the largest EU companies are obligated to disclose nonfinancial information under the NFRD.

Importantly, the NFRD offers flexibility in implementation, allowing companies to choose the format of disclosure. It does not mandate the use of specific reporting standards or frameworks, providing companies significant latitude in presenting relevant information. They can utilize international, European, or national guidelines for their statements. The "comply-or-explain" principle is incorporated, requiring companies to provide a clear and reasoned explanation if they do not pursue policies in specific areas.

The concept of "double materiality" is emphasized, necessitating companies to disclose information necessary for understanding both how sustainability issues may affect the company ("outside-in risks") and how the company affects society and the environment ("inside-out risks").

Regarding assurance of nonfinancial reports, the NFRD includes a minimum requirement for statutory auditors to check whether nonfinancial information has been provided. Member States have the option to exceed this minimum requirement, requiring additional checks or verification by an independent assurance services provider.

The transposition deadline for Member States was December 6, 2016, with covered undertakings reporting for the first time in 2018 for the 2017 financial year. The European Commission issued nonbinding guidelines in 2017, and additional guidelines on reporting climate-related information were published in 2019.

Sustainable Finance Disclosure Regulation (SFDR): Aims to improve transparency on how financial market participants integrate ESG factors into their investment decisions.[64]

Regulation (EU) 2019/2088 on sustainability-related disclosures in the financial services sector, commonly known as the SFDR, was enacted by the European Commission to introduce harmonized ESG transparency rules for financial market participants and financial advisers. The SFDR's primary objectives are to foster sustainability and provide advice to these entities on how to integrate ESG factors into their investment decisions and financial advice. A fundamental concern addressed by SFDR is the prevention of greenwashing, where financial products are marketed as sustainable but fail to meet established ESG standards in practice.

The SFDR requires strategic business and investment decisions by financial market participants and advisers to be transparently communicated through disclosures, leading to greater accountability, discipline, and efficiency in financial markets, and fostering healthy competition within sustainable finance markets.

Key aspects of the regulation include entity-level transparency requirements, mandating financial market participants and advisers to publish information on negative externalities associated with their business models. Additionally, subject entities must explain how sustainability risks are integrated into their investment decision-making processes and give financial advice. The regulation extends its reach to remuneration policies, emphasizing consistency with the integration of sustainability risks.

Regarding financial products, the SFDR distinguishes between those that promote environmental or social characteristics and those that aim to have a positive impact on the environment and society. Each category is subject to specific transparency requirements, ensuring that precontractual and periodic documents elucidate how ESG sustainability goals are achieved and how sustainability risks are considered in investment decisions. Furthermore, the disclosure must identify the potential impact of investments on profitability.

The SFDR also establishes the roles of European supervisory authorities, tasked with developing regulatory technical standards on information content, methodology, and presentation. It sets reporting obligations on best practices, recommendations on voluntary reporting standards, and annual reporting to the European Commission. EU Member States are responsible for ensuring compliance with the legislation and may extend its application to certain pension product manufacturers and microinsurance intermediaries.

The SFDR has been in effect since March 10, 2021, with additional specific provisions on adverse sustainability impacts becoming applicable to larger financial market participants from June 30, 2021. However, its ongoing evaluation by the European Commission reflects a commitment to assessing its effectiveness and considering potential amendments.

The United States

Currently, in the United States, a majority of ESG information is disclosed voluntarily. While some specific areas have formal rules issued or proposed by U.S. regulators, the voluntary disclosure of information related to ESG factors, following globally recognized frameworks, remains a significant aspect of ESG reporting. Despite the frameworks discussed earlier and other similar frameworks, companies often conduct materiality assessments independently or with the assistance of legal counsel to identify ESG factors relevant to long-term profitability. Following the assessment and evaluation of associated disclosure risks, the development of an ESG strategy requires collaboration among internal stakeholders such as compliance, general counsel, human resources, technology, and information security. This collaborative effort is essential to establish realistic goals, benchmarks, internal processes, and controls with the necessary accountability.[65]

SEC: The SEC has been exploring the implementation of mandatory climate-related disclosures for public companies.

On March 22, 2022, the SEC announced proposed amendments to rules and reporting forms aimed at enhancing the consistency, comparability, and reliability of information available to investors regarding the incorporation of ESG factors by funds and advisers. The scope of these proposed changes would extend to certain registered investment advisers, exempt advisers, registered investment companies, and business development companies.[66]

SEC Chair Gary Gensler expressed support for the proposal, highlighting its potential to establish disclosure requirements specifically tailored for funds and advisers with an ESG focus. Emphasizing the diverse nature of ESG investments and strategies, Gensler underscored the importance of transparency, allowing investors to gain a comprehensive understanding of the underlying components of these strategies. According to the related press release, the proposal aligns with the SEC's core mission of protecting investors, enabling them to allocate their capital efficiently in line with their needs.[67]

The proposed amendments outline a framework to categorize various ESG strategies broadly, requiring funds and advisers to provide more specific disclosures in fund prospectuses, annual reports, and adviser brochures based on the specific ESG strategies they pursue. For instance, funds emphasizing environmental considerations would need to disclose the greenhouse gas emissions associated with their portfolio investments.

Those claiming to achieve specific ESG impacts would be required to articulate the intended impact(s) and summarize their progress in achieving these objectives. Funds utilizing proxy voting or engagement with issuers as a primary means of implementing their ESG strategy would need to disclose details about their voting on ESG-related matters and information regarding their engagement meetings.[68]

The disclosure encompasses scope 1 and scope 2 emissions, and if significant to the company or relevant to its GHG reduction targets, scope 3 emissions. Furthermore, companies must provide an independent third-party attestation report from a GHG emissions expert regarding their scope 1 and scope 2 emissions disclosure. Reporting companies would also need to provide an independent third-party attestation report from an expert in GHG emissions on the company's scope 1 and scope 2 emission disclosure.[69]

Under the proposed amendments, registrants would be required to disclose information on various aspects related to climate-related risks, governance, and risk management processes. This includes details on the oversight and governance of climate-related risks by the registrant's board and management. The disclosure framework encompasses climate-related risks and their potential material impacts on the registrant's business, strategy, and outlook. Additionally, registrants would need to provide information on their GHG emissions, with certain filers subject to assurance for specified emissions.[70]

The proposed rules cover a range of climate-related disclosures, including financial statement metrics, information about climate-related targets and goals, and transition plans. Aligning with established disclosure frameworks such as the TCFD and the GHG protocol, these proposed disclosures seek to enhance the transparency and comparability of climate-related information provided by registrants.[71]

Registrants are expected to outline processes for identifying, assessing, and managing these risks and describe any integrated risk management systems over various time horizons. Additionally, the proposed rules address scenario analysis, internal carbon pricing, and the impact of climate-related events on financial statements.[72]

To ensure consistent presentation, the SEC proposes specific ways that registrants should provide these disclosures, including separate sections in registration statements and annual reports, and the use of Inline XBRL for electronic tagging. Accelerated and large accelerated filers may also be required to obtain an attestation report from an independent service provider covering scopes 1 and 2 emissions disclosure.[73]

Finally, the proposed rules include phase-in periods based on registrant status, with additional accommodations for scope 3 emissions disclosure, assurance requirements, and exemptions for smaller reporting companies as well as safe harbors for liability and forward-looking statements, acknowledging the challenges associated with forecasting climate-related impacts.[74]

More recently, in late 2023, unveiled a series of proposed rule amendments designed to mandate the disclosure of specific climate-related information by registrants. These proposed rules would apply to both domestic and foreign registrants, impacting their registration statements and periodic reports, such as Form 10-K. The objective is to provide investors with comprehensive insights into how registrants address and manage ESG impacts, particularly those related to climate risks and impacts.[75]

Failure with the SEC reporting rules can result in fines—in 2022, for example, the SEC collected $4.2 billion in penalties. Fines can also erode brand reputation, investor confidence, and loss of stakeholder trust.[76]

In addition to the these, in August 2021, Nasdaq approved Board Diversity Disclosure requirements for companies listed on its U.S. exchange. These regulations mandate that such companies must have a minimum of two diverse board members. This includes the stipulation that at least one director must self-identify as female, and at least one director must self-identify as an underrepresented minority or LGBTQ+. Alternatively, companies must provide an explanation if they do not have directors meeting these diversity criteria.[77]

U.S. Department of Labor Guidance

The U.S. Department of Labor (DOL) has provided guidance to fiduciaries of company-sponsored pension plans, outlining considerations for incorporating climate change and other ESG factors into investment decisions. Additionally, the DOL issued a climate request for information (RFI) to explore whether Form 5500 Annual Return/Reports could be used to gather data on climate-related financial risk to pension plans. The inquiry also questions whether plan administrators should be mandated to report on how they manage climate-related financial risk for pension plans. It's worth noting that this regulatory action by the DOL may have implications for auditors and record-keepers.[78]

California

Not surprisingly, California leads the way with respect to state law reporting requirements. Recently, on October 7, 2023, Governor Newsom of California enacted two pivotal climate-related disclosure laws on October 7, 2023, marking a significant shift for large U.S. companies. These legislations, set to take effect as early as 2026, mandate expansive climate-related disclosures that surpass the SEC's proposed rule and prevailing practices of most public companies. The impact will be profound for businesses operating in California, as the disclosure requirements delve into scopes beyond the SEC's proposed climate-related disclosure rule.[79]

The first law, S.B. 253, known as the Climate Corporate Data Accountability Act, necessitates certain companies to reveal their direct (scope 1), indirect (scope 2), and value chain (scope 3) GHG emissions. The second law, S.B. 261, named the Climate-Related Financial Risk Act, compels specific companies to disclose climate-related financial risks in alignment with the TCFD recommendations.[80]

While these bills lack crucial details and clarity on key aspects, companies anticipate further amendments or implementing regulations to decipher their true implications. Compliance will demand substantial resources and expenses as companies prepare to establish the infrastructure necessary for these new disclosure requirements. Notably, some companies subject to the California laws may also navigate the EU's CSRD, adding complexity to the landscape with overlapping yet distinct climate-related disclosure requirements across multiple jurisdictions.[81]

Fines for failure to disclose in California can reach up to $500,000 per year.[82]

The United Kingdom

Streamlined Energy and Carbon Reporting (SECR): Requires certain companies to report on their energy use and GHG emissions, enhancing disclosure on environmental matters.

SECR is a mandatory sustainability reporting framework in the United Kingdom for large organizations. Introduced on April 1, 2019, SECR aims to enhance transparency around an organization's energy and carbon use while encouraging cost savings and emission reductions. Quoted companies, large unquoted companies, and large Limited Liability Partnerships (LLPs) incorporated in the United Kingdom are required to comply with SECR reporting.[83]

SECR reporting goes beyond simply disclosing GHG emissions; it contextualizes emissions by requiring organizations to provide a narrative, methodology, and intensity ratio. The narrative explains efforts undertaken, the methodology uses independent standards such as GHG Reporting Standards, and the intensity ratio compares emissions data with a business metric.[84]

SECR became effective alongside the end of the Carbon Reduction Commitment (CRC) Energy Efficiency Scheme, replacing a complex framework with a broader, more standardized reporting approach. The SECR framework aligns with global ESG reporting frameworks and follows recommendations from the G20 FSBs TCFD.[85]

Mandatory reporting applies to over 11,900 organizations, including quoted companies and large unquoted companies or LLPs meeting specific criteria related to turnover, balance sheet, or employee count. Exemptions exist for organizations using a low level of energy (40MWh or less) or those in the public sector. While not mandatory, public-sector organizations are encouraged to report similarly on their energy and carbon use.[86]

SECR reporting involves disclosing energy use, GHG emissions, methodology, efforts to improve energy efficiency, and intensity ratios. The framework offers flexibility in methodology and intensity ratio calculation, allowing organizations to choose the most relevant indicators for disclosure. Prior-year figures are required for comparison.[87]

Though scope 3 emissions reporting (upstream and downstream supply chain) is currently voluntary, it may become integral to SECR in the future. SECR disclosures should be easily accessible and understandable, typically included in a company's Directors' Report or equivalent annually.[88]

Following is a summary of several specific SECR reporting requirement highlights:

- SECR disclosures, included in the annual report, require reporting on total UK energy use, GHG emissions, intensity ratio, comparative figures, and energy efficiency actions. Methodologies used in calculations must be disclosed, encouraging the use of recognized independent standards such as GHG Reporting Protocol, ISO, CDSB, or GRI.
- Data collection for energy usage should use verifiable data, including meter data, supplier invoices, or statements. If unavailable, reasonable estimates based on direct comparison, pro-rata extrapolation, or benchmarking are acceptable.
- Intensity ratios normalize emissions against factors such as total production, staff numbers, turnover, or office floor space. While an explanation of the chosen ratio(s) is recommended, it's not mandatory.
- The accuracy of disclosures lacks a de minimis or materiality level in the regulations, but the guidance suggests a materiality of 2 to 5 percent of overall emissions. While external assurance is not mandatory, statutory auditors must consider consistency with financial statements and legal requirements. Voluntary independent assurance is encouraged.[89]

Asia

Hong Kong Stock Exchange (HKEX) ESG Reporting Guide: Encourages listed companies to report on their ESG performance.[90]

Core recommendations of the HKEX include advising issuers to:

- **Board Governance and Oversight**
    - o Disclose information about their board of directors' role in overseeing ESG risks and opportunities to address stakeholder demands for transparency;

- o Provide details to investors on the processes, controls, and procedures used to monitor and manage ESG matters;
- o Provide information on the relevant expertise, interaction between the board and its committees, the frequency of discussions on ESG issues, and its available resources; and
- o Align ESG governance with their business strategy.

- **Monitor ESG Goals**
  - o Include information on the measurement system used for assessing ESG goals, their mode of data collection and verification process, and comparisons with historical data; and
  - o Provide details on the results of the review, reasons for unmet targets, and actions or adjustments planned for the future.

- **Climate Change**
  - o Acknowledge the substantial impact of climate change on issuers' sustainability and profit;
  - o Consider the requirements established by Switzerland-based FSB, which established the TCFD in 2015;
  - o Encourage issuers to adopt quantitative targets for climate-related issues and disclose scope 1 and scope 2 GHG emissions separately;
  - o Consider reporting on scope 3 GHG emissions and climate-related scenario analysis;
  - o Improve climate disclosure standards, aligning them with TCFD recommendations and ISSB standards;
  - o Prepare for reporting on climate-related matters and scenario analysis; and
  - o Disclose the results of climate-related reviews and reasons for unmet targets.

- **Social Issues:**
  - o Emphasize the importance of social issues in governance structures
  - o Comply or explain initiatives related to social KPIs, including new KPIs related to supply chain management and anti-corruption training; and

o Address the lower reporting level of new social KPIs and ensure comprehensive reporting on these aspects.

Japan's Stewardship Code and Corporate Governance Code: Encourages institutional investors and companies to consider and disclose ESG-related factors.[91]

Japan's Stewardship Code establishes a comprehensive set of principles and corresponding guidance for institutional investors seeking to effectively fulfill their stewardship responsibilities. Its primary objective is to foster sustainable growth in companies in which these institutional investors invest, ultimately enhancing medium- to long-term investment returns for clients and beneficiaries. The code is made up of eight core principles:

1. **Principle 1: Clear Stewardship Policy**
   Institutional investors should proactively engage with companies in which they invest through purposeful dialogue, concentrating on improving corporate value and sustainable growth. Transparent policies, publicly disclosed, should articulate how stewardship responsibilities are executed, with a specific emphasis on considering sustainability in alignment with investment strategies.

   On a practical level, this means that institutional investors should constructively and meaningfully interact with their investee companies to develop a deep understanding of those companies and their business needs. Moreover, on an internal level, they should encourage their asset managers to align with their stewardship perspectives. And, in particular, they should explicitly outline the necessary stewardship principles required for asset managers, ensuring the effectiveness of stewardship endeavors. Finally, institutional investors should have robust audit and review policies that emphasize their commitment to good stewardship policies and place a distinct emphasis on the qualitative aspects of those activities.

2. **Principle 2: Managing Conflicts of Interest**
   Investment companies should enforce clear policies on conflict management, including the disclosure of key measures for ensuring that the interests of clients and beneficiaries are safeguarded. These policies should include clear, established governance structures, such as independent boards, which have the power to prevent conflicts.

3. **Principle 3: Monitoring Investee Companies**

   Investment companies should continually monitor their investee companies focusing on enhancing medium- to long-term corporate value and supporting sustainable growth including their governance, strategy, performance, and risks, and the social and environmental aspects of their operations.

4. **Principle 4: Constructive Engagement**

   Institutional investors should actively engage in constructive dialogue with investee companies to seek common understanding and address risks, contributing to medium- to long-term value enhancement and sustainable growth. This dialogue should be active and consistent with their investment strategies and geared toward sustainable growth.

5. **Principle 5: Voting Policy for Sustainable Growth**

   An institutional investor's voting policy should align with the results of its monitoring efforts and dialogue related to sustainable growth. Institutional investors should particularly avoid using a mechanical checklist. They should also keep detailed voting records that include the specific reasons for their board of directors' votes. And, when using a proxy, institutional investors should disclose the proxy's name and how they use the proxy's services.

6. **Principle 6: Periodic Reporting**

   Asset managers and owners should periodically report to clients and beneficiaries on stewardship responsibilities. The report format and content should be tailored to recipient needs, agreements, and cost considerations, maintaining transparency without disclosing confidential information. In addition, the report should be adapted to the specific recipients' needs, agreements, and cost considerations and should omit confidential information.

   Reports should be adapted to recipient needs, agreements, and cost considerations.

   Confidential information should not be disclosed in asset management reports.

7. **Principle 7: Developing Skills and Resources**

   To contribute positively to sustainable growth, institutional investors should develop skills and resources for effective engagement, ensuring unbiased and capable management.

8. **Principle 8: Continuous Improvement**

Institutional investors should continuously review and improve policies and activities to promote consistency with the stewardship code. This includes conducting regular self-evaluations and transparent disclosure of results to enhance governance structures and overall stewardship activities.

PART 2

Information Governance Principles[1]

Introduction

As its name implies, information governance, or IG, is a comprehensive strategy for managing an enterprise's people, processes, and technology, with an emphasis on risk, legal compliance, information management, and business intelligence. IG also subsumes a number of disciplines such as e-Discovery, data privacy, big data, architecture, operations, organizational continuity, and audit.

Broadly defined, IG includes the management of information within an organization or enterprise. It includes a broad range of policies, procedures, and technology used to manage the life cycle of information from creation to disposal. Its central purpose is to ensure that information is managed in a way that supports an entity's goals and objectives, while also complying with legal and regulatory requirements. These goals include promoting regulatory compliance, helping employees find the "right information at the right time," ensuring the disposal of unneeded or duplicate data, and helping entities to ensure that the right versions of documents are preserved.

One widely accepted definition of IG comes from The Sedona Conference, which is a nonprofit organization dedicated to the advanced study of law and policy in areas of antitrust law, complex litigation, and intellectual property rights. Unfortunately, like many definitions for IG, the Sedona Conference couches the term in somewhat academic language. Specifically, the Sedona Conference defines IG as "an organization's coordinated, interdisciplinary approach to satisfying information compliance requirements and managing information risks while optimizing information value."

This definition highlights the need for IG to be a cross-functional effort that involves various stakeholders across an organization.

More importantly, perhaps, the Sedona Conference established a set of principles for IG, known as the Sedona Principles. These principles guide organizations on how to develop and implement effective IG programs. The principles are as follows:

- Organizations should have a sound and reasonable basis for their IG policies.
- IG policies should be consistent with the organization's legal obligations, industry standards, and business objectives.
- IG policies should be designed to minimize the risks and costs associated with the preservation and disclosure of electronically stored information.
- Organizations should identify and manage information in a timely and efficient manner, taking into account the nature of the information and the needs of the organization.
- Organizations should have an ongoing process for monitoring and improving their IG policies and procedures.
- Organizations should implement policies and procedures to ensure that the information they collect, use, and disclose is accurate, complete, and up to date.
- Organizations should implement appropriate security measures to protect information from unauthorized access, use, disclosure, alteration, or destruction.
- Organizations should implement policies and procedures to ensure that information is disposed of in a timely and secure manner when it is no longer needed.

Another definition of IG comes from Gartner, a leading research and advisory company. Gartner defines IG as "the specification of decision rights and an accountability framework to ensure appropriate behavior in the valuation, creation, storage, use, archiving, and deletion of information." This definition highlights the importance of assigning responsibility and accountability for managing information throughout its life cycle.

But, that is not all…

- The ISO defines IG as "the system of controls, policies, procedures, and technologies used to manage information throughout its life cycle, from creation to disposal, in order to minimize risk, ensure compliance with legal and regulatory requirements, and maximize value."
- The Healthcare Information and Management Systems Society (HIMSS) defines IG in the health care context as "a strategic approach to managing enterprise information assets that enables an organization to support its business objectives, maximize its value, minimize its risks, and ensure its compliance."
- The Association for Information and Image Management (AIIM) defines IG as "the activities and technologies that organizations employ to maximize the value of their information while minimizing associated risks and costs."
- The Electronic Discovery Reference Model (EDRM) defines IG as "the process of creating, implementing, and enforcing policies and procedures to manage information assets in order to meet legal, regulatory, and business requirements."

Finally, when communicating the need for IG, however, we have often found it to be more effective to rely on simpler, nonacademic language, and on the net organizational impact of adopting defensible and understandable IG best practices.

What Questions Does Information Governance Help to Answer?

IG best practices help organizations to identify, manage, and protect their important data throughout all phases of their life cycle. Based on our experience, this understanding can be broken down into three general categories:

- Knowing what information they need: IG helps organizations to identify the types of information they need to operate effectively. One of the critical elements of this process is the inventory data assets, which includes both the automated and manual review of structured and unstructured data. This review can help organizations to make informed decisions about where to focus their data management efforts and prioritize their information management initiatives. In a typical use case, the organization would conduct a data inventory of its collections, including its physical and digital assets, to determine which resources are most important to its mission and which should be deprioritized or deselected based on either an absence of need or based on the requirements of a retention schedule (or privacy laws). When conducted properly, the overall result is generally an optimization of the use of resources and a measurable record showing that the organization is investing its time and budget wisely.

- Understanding how to use information: Once an entity has identified which data assets are the most critical, IG best practices can be harnessed to help it to further define how that information should be used. This definition includes creating policies around data access, usage, and sharing, as well as establishing rules around retention, archiving, and disposal, and guidelines around data use. The end result is that the enterprise can ensure that its information is being used in a way that aligns with its strategic objectives and complies with applicable laws, regulations, and industry standards. An example of this process is a case where the organization cooperates with other staff to establish policies and procedures governing data retention and disposal. This process generally includes identifying which types of data should be archived or preserved and which can be deleted or destroyed (and how the data should be destroyed). The end result is that the organization will play a key role in helping to optimize the use of storage resources and to ensure that it is only retaining data that is truly valuable and necessary for its operations.

- Allocating responsibility for information management:
  IG can also help organizations to define clear roles and
  responsibilities around their data ownership, management,
  and protection. This type of enterprisewide accountability
  helps to ensure that all relevant personnel understands its
  role in managing and protecting the organization's critical
  information assets. In addition, it helps organizations to
  identify the right data stewards and custodians who should
  be responsible for managing specific data assets, establish
  clear policies governing data access and usage, and enforce
  and promote sound data management standards through
  regular training and education. An example of this role is
  A could work with the organization's legal team to ensure that
  it is compliance monitoring, to promote compliance with
  applicable laws and regulations governing data management
  and privacy that is bolstered by ongoing training and
  education for staff around best practices for data handling.

Good Information Governance Versus Bad Information Governance

In the context of organizational management, inadequate IG in an organization that manages various types of data from multiple sources manifests in various ways. These include:

- Inconsistent Metadata: Metadata is crucial for the effective
  management and discovery of organizational resources. Poor
  IG practices involve the use of inconsistent, inaccurate, or
  incomplete metadata, making it challenging to find relevant
  materials, leading to increased data search times, and
  introducing errors related to version control.
- Duplication of Effort: Ineffective information management
  necessitates organizational staff to duplicate routine tasks such
  as cataloging, indexing, and storing information. This results
  in unnecessary costs and, similar to metadata issues, increases
  the likelihood of mistakes.

- Lack of Standardization: Good IG practices emphasize standardization across an organization's departments or divisions. Poor IG practices often lead to a lack of standardization across collections, making it difficult to compare and analyze information from multiple sources and compromising quality control.
- Limited Access: Improper information management can hinder granting appropriate access to employees, stakeholders, and the public, causing delays, frustration, and negative impacts on organizational operations.
- Inadequate Security: Organizations often manage sensitive or confidential information, and staff are typically responsible for ensuring appropriate security measures. Poor IG protocols can result in inadequate security controls, leaving data vulnerable to unauthorized access, theft, or other threats.
- Poor Preservation: Organizations often manage sensitive and easily degradable data. Poor IG may lead to a lack of proper preservation measures (e.g., temperature controls), resulting in the deterioration or obsolescence of materials.
- Inefficient Workflows: Inadequate IG can lead to inefficient workflows that impact productivity and cause delays in organizational operations.
- Excess Storage: An essential element of good IG is reduced storage space. Organizations failing to dispose of redundant, obsolete, and trivial (ROT) data and materials with low business value face high online storage costs and wasted physical space.

Conversely, organizations with robust IG protocols tend to exhibit traits that contribute to cost reduction, improved regulatory response, enhanced security, and improved employee engagement.

Governance and Steering Committees

A governance or steering committee is a group of executives or senior managers who provide guidance, authority, and approval on strategic initiatives in organizations. This oversight mechanism is intended to ensure that the goals and objectives of key initiatives are aligned with organizational goals in general. As such, the steering committee will have final authority on budgets, scope, and resources and meet periodically to ensure that initiatives are headed in the proper direction. They will also help identify risks, prioritize key deliverables, and establish appropriate and measurable success criteria. A steering committee is generally led by a chairperson who is formally or informally elected and serves as a sort of mediator to keep the committee on track and help resolve disputes or disagreements. This is particularly important in complex organizations where different groups, teams, or entities are not just cross-impacted but have the potential to operate at cross purposes.

Considering the level of complexity in technology operations in many medium and large organizations, a governance committee must also be able to rely on a team of senior SMEs who have the hands-on, day-to-day experience to advise on and support their strategic decisions. In most cases, they should have an intimate working knowledge of the subject areas at hand, including testing, validation, and KPIs. A common scenario, therefore, is a sort of triumvirate of executives, senior SMEs, and project management staff.

In most cases, a project manager (PM) will sit at the helm of each enterprise initiative to manage day-to-day activities, ensure deliverables are met on time, and serve as a focal point among various stakeholders. A PM's job comes down to providing timely and accurate reporting or, in certain regards, serving as a single source of truth for the real-time status of the initiative. This will be true from the early stages of research and planning through execution and closure.

A PM needs to have not just strong communication skills but a strong will, particularly in moments where they must inform a room full of executives something they might not necessarily want to hear. That being the case, a skilled PM frames the challenges, risks, and workarounds in a succinct and informed manner that will allow the governance committee to make the most effective and educated decisions or course corrections. With good communication comes trust and confidence, and that usually starts with the truth.

Experienced leaders generally understand that projects rarely run according to plan. So, the expectation is not perfection, but that material issues will be escalated in a timely fashion. This will put them in the best position to do their jobs and provide guidance and leadership that will help get a project back on track and completed on budget and on time. Waiting too long to get information from the governance committee for fear of a bad reaction can become a self-fulfilling prophecy. Not only does delayed information weaken their ability to make good decisions, but it also tends to reflect poorly on their leadership. In cases where critical information may be pending, unavailable, or incomplete, it is all the more vital to advise the governance committee what is known, any limitations of the current information, and that updates will be provided immediately as they become available. It is also recommended to formalize these escalation protocols to eliminate any gray areas.

There is no standard size of a governance committee in organizations. It depends on the size of the initiative and the number of groups or organizations that may be directly or indirectly cross-impacted. Too few members tend to err on the side of underrepresentation. Too many members, alternatively, present the challenge of mob rule. In most cases, the governance committee may be comprised of roughly five to eight members. There is a balance to be struck between representation and effectiveness, not to mention how difficult it is to get their attention to schedule regular meetings. There is a balance to be struck between representation and effectiveness, not to mention how difficult it is to get their attention to schedule regular meetings. In the best of all worlds, a PM will effectively manage deliverables and keep the team properly informed so that the time, however limited, is time well spent.

Following are two use cases indicating good versus bad practices:

Good Practice

The governance committee of a credit union meets periodically to review and approve strategic initiatives, such as the implementation of a new technology system. The committee is composed of experienced leaders from various departments within the organization, as well as SMEs in technology and project management. A PM is designated to manage day-to-day activities and provide regular updates to the committee. The committee trusts the PM to escalate any issues in a timely manner and provide updates on a regular basis. The PM communicates effectively with the committee, presenting challenges and risks in a clear and concise manner, allowing the committee to make informed decisions. The committee is not overly large, consisting of about five to eight members, ensuring effective representation without succumbing to the challenges of mob rule.

Bad Practice

The governance committee of a public sector organization is composed of only a few members who are not experienced leaders in the organization or SMEs in the initiatives being discussed. The committee does not meet regularly, and when they do meet, they do not have a clear understanding of the initiatives being discussed. The PM is not designated, leading to confusion and inefficiency in managing day-to-day activities. The PM does not communicate effectively with the committee, withholding critical information for fear of a bad reaction. When issues do arise, they are not escalated in a timely manner, leading to delays and cost overruns. The committee is too small to provide effective representation, leading to underrepresentation and lack of diversity in decision making.

Strategic Alignment and Strategic Vision

Strategic alignment in organizational management aims to connect an entity's organizational needs with its internal structure, teams, and resources for optimal efficiency. Any shortcomings in the organization's structure or its parent entity can jeopardize its success. Organizations neglecting the importance of strategic alignment face significant risks.

Four principal areas involve strategic alignment in organizations: budget, technology, operations, and legal. Management drives strategic goals, plans initiatives, estimates return on investment (ROI), and collaborates with internal teams and external parties. Leadership and governance committees, formed by the organization, support development.

When a project or initiative is identified, relevant stakeholders collaborate. The technical operations team determines effective plans, working with budget and operations to establish scale and infrastructure. Operations collaborates with technology for project management and technical oversight, ensuring security and organizational continuity. Legal assesses risk, compliance, and legal exposure.

Use cases include developing a new digital service, implementing a management system, and reducing the organization's carbon footprint. Each case requires collaboration with stakeholders to align the project with strategic goals, considering technology, budget, and legal aspects.

Strategic vision is deemed crucial for organizational management, as it offers direction and purpose. A strong vision statement guides decision making and can be the difference between success and failure. Developing a vision demands understanding the organization's unique context and inspiring the team toward common goals.

A leader sets challenging yet achievable targets, leading to concrete goals and meticulous planning. IG goals stem from the organization's vision, confronting obstacles in execution. A strong vision unifies the organization, providing common purpose and direction for implementing IG best practices.

An illustrative use case involves an organization implementing an IG program. The organization's vision is to provide easy access to information while ensuring compliance. A committee from various departments develops policies and procedures, implements a metadata management system, and establishes regular reviews and audits. The program enhances resource management, discoverability, and accessibility, reducing legal and compliance risks.

Organizational Drivers

Organizational drivers are the collective resources and activities that contribute to operational or financial outcomes. An organization must be able to establish and rely on goals and objectives, which in turn require an intimate understanding of the resources that combine to achieve those measurable and achievable objectives. They include but are not limited to, the quality and quantity of human resources, organization locations, costs, production, social media presence, and so on. It is therefore critical to understand organizational drivers along with their strengths, limitations, and codependencies.

Of course, each organizational challenge is unique and requires a process of assessment and analysis to accurately identify key variables, which is recursive in nature. Meaning, that to solve a problem, one must have a thorough understanding of its underlying root causes, as well as the chain of causes and effects that lead to it.

Organizational drivers are critical for the success of an organization, which relies on goals and objectives to achieve operational and financial outcomes. Understanding the resources and activities that contribute to these outcomes is essential for organizations to thrive. These drivers include but are not limited to, the quality and quantity of staff, organization locations, production, marketing, and community engagement.

Organizational drivers and metrics operate hand in hand. Specifically, variables must be quantified to make accurate representations up and down the organizational structure, especially for the purpose of building accurate financial assumptions and projections. And, the amount of time and resources given to a problem is generally proportional to its overall impact.

One use case for organizational drivers is the development of a new branch of a retail organization. Understanding the community demographics, including population size, age, and socioeconomics is a critical driver in determining the success of a new branch. This information helps the leadership team to make informed decisions about the location, size, and services offered at the new location. Additionally, understanding the budget and funding sources, as well as the availability of staff and resources, will impact the feasibility of opening a new branch.

Another use case is the implementation of a new technology or service at a bank. Understanding the current technology infrastructure, including hardware, software, and staff expertise, is critical in determining the feasibility and success of a new technology or service. Additionally, understanding the user base and their technology needs and preferences is essential in developing a service that meets their needs. This information can help leadership to make informed decisions about the resources needed to implement the new technology or service.

Strategic Planning

Strategic planning is an essential part of organizational management, enabling organizations to align their activities with their vision and goals. Strategic planning involves the development of a comprehensive plan that outlines specific and measurable actions, objectives, and resources necessary for execution. It is a process that requires a clear understanding of the organization's key drivers, including its strengths, limitations, and codependencies.

Strategic planning should be driven and supported by the executive leadership of the organization, with the support of PMs. The strategic vision of the organization should then be translated into a series of finite goals, which are then reverse engineered into a methodical structure in the form of constituent and dependent tasks. A comprehensive project plan is then developed with as much detailed information as possible, including objectives, resources, budgets, deliverables, and risk controls. PMs play a critical role in the success of strategic planning, working closely with leadership and staff to ensure that the project plan is achievable and comprehensive.

Strategic planning should involve stretching limitations and being just a little uncomfortable, balancing options and budgets to facilitate a degree of certainty. An innovative organization should encourage strategic thinking and, if so, is more likely to endure conditions when they do not go precisely according to plan, or when circumstances on the ground require a pivot in direction or tactics. A risk response strategy provides protection, and a PM with risk management experience can help to reduce risks, although no guarantee can be made that risks will be eliminated. Leadership provides guidance and strategic thinking to the project management team.

Obstacles to IG Improvement

Organizations of all types can face significant challenges when seeking to improve or maintain their IG practices. These challenges include:

- Resistance—Improving IG practices often requires organizations to make significant changes in the way that they operate, which can be challenging for staff. Combating this resistance requires a concerted effort to achieve buy-in by training staff and emphasizing the positive impact that IG best practices can have on their work.

- Lack of Awareness—Challenges can arise when employees do not see why they need to improve their practices. This is especially true for organizations that employ a mix of transient employees such as students and long-term workers.

- Keep Everything Mentality—Organizations must comply with legal and regulatory requirements related to data management, privacy, and security. Also, many employees tend to see keeping everything as the surest way to comply with retention laws. This is not only dangerous in a legal sense (especially regarding privacy laws) but also costly and potentially risky, particularly in the case of litigation. Combating this mentality requires organizations to continually communicate the needs and importance of IG best practices to their staff and to gauge staff buy-in on a regular basis.

- Costs—One of the main challenges that organizations face is a lack of resources, including funding, staffing, and technology. Without adequate resources, it can be difficult to implement and maintain effective IG practices. Therefore, it is critical for organizations to secure the funding that they need for an IG improvement project before the project begins and to maintain executive-level support within the organization throughout the engagement.

- Data Volumes—Organizations manage a huge volume of data in multiple formats, ranging from legacy formats such as microfilm to cloud storage and physical storage. Staff may not be "up to date" on the most current data management standards. This requires training, clear policies and procedures, and a concerted and unified approach to data management.

- Obsolete Systems/Legacy Technology—Many organizations use legacy systems that may not be compatible with modern IG practices. Updating these systems can be costly and time-consuming, which can impede IG progress. This issue is closely related to both "cost" and "awareness." Organizations seeking to implement IG practices must factor in the cost of upgrading systems and choosing the right repositories and storage formats.

Why Is Big Data Such a Big Problem?

Managing extensive data is critical for organizations because it enables them to make informed decisions and provide better services to their patrons and other stakeholders. Oracle defines Big Data as datasets that contain greater variety, arrive in increased volumes, and with additional velocity. According to Statista sources, approximately 64.2 zettabytes of data are created, captured, copied, and consumed in the entire digital universe, a number likely to triple by 2025.

Despite its significance, Big Data is a term yet to be operationally defined. An analysis of 1,437 articles discussing Big Data identified four centralized themes: information, technology, methods, and impact. Authors defined Big Data as "the information asset characterized by such high volume, velocity, and variety to require specific technology and analytical methods for its transformation into value." Essentially, Big Data involves accumulating past and present information on individuals in various areas of life to predict future behaviors or needs. Volume represents the large amount of data to be managed, velocity refers to the speed of data collection and storage, variety describes different file types and sources, veracity examines data quality, and value refers to data usefulness.

Despite numerous innovative analytics tools in the market, many struggle to scale, and our ability to make sense of the volume, variety, and velocity of collected data cannot keep pace with our ability to collect it. Sampling, the methodical selection of a smaller data set for analysis, is an effective way to address this challenge. Poor sampling methods can lead to inaccurate conclusions, emphasizing the importance of focusing on the accuracy and utility of the sample size.

The unprecedented growth of data can be attributed to business adaptation in response to COVID-19. In a survey published in the World Economic Forum (WEF)'s 2020 Future of Jobs report, employers, especially those with significant numbers of home workers, are accelerating the digitalization of work processes and automation of tasks, generating more data in return. Companies in various sectors surveyed in the report also indicated that Big Data analytics, AI, Internet of Things (IoT), and connected devices are some of the technologies likely to be adopted by 2025.

The Role of Records and Information Management

Information and records management are crucial for organizations as they ensure that needed information is secure and available to meet organizational obligations, delivering services consistently and equitably while providing continuity in the event of a disaster. A good records management program must protect records from unauthorized access, meet statutory and regulatory requirements for archiving and audit oversight activities. This program should also provide protection and support during litigation, enable quick storage and retrieval of documents and information, and improve efficiency and productivity from an operational perspective.

Organizations may be subject to various legal and regulatory requirements related to records and information management, including data privacy laws, copyright regulations, and freedom of information requests. A records management program can help ensure that the organization is in compliance with these requirements and is able to respond to legal or regulatory requests promptly.

The technology used to store and access information is critical for organizations. Failure to maintain a proper records and document management platform can result in a direct threat to the security, integrity, and availability of data, leading to potential problems such as questions of veracity or authenticity due to a degradation of data quality. Compliance with legal and regulatory requirements for records management is essential for organizations to safeguard data and information assets.

There are three phases to responsible records retention compliance: identification and retention, preservation and safekeeping, and destruction and disposal of records that have fulfilled their life cycle and outlived their usefulness. An up-to-date, comprehensive records and information management program documents the organization's intent and commitment to compliance, reducing potential punitive and compensatory damages that can result from litigation or regulatory fines.

Maintaining updated policies and procedures for the systematic control of records is exceptionally important for organizations. Without proper records management, organizations may be storing records too long, not long enough, or not at all. Failing to maintain records and data necessary for regulatory auditing, compliance reporting, and other valid organizational requirements presents great risk, which can be mostly unreasonable if not negligent in this day and age.

Any risks related to noncompliance with records retention regulations could lead to penalties, blemished public reputation, and any number and variety of legal liabilities. RIM controls are needed to demonstrate proactive and transparent efforts to satisfy compliance requirements. Consistent records management processes, policies, and practices can also dramatically reduce litigation costs, both in terms of improved efficiency and in terms of mitigating or eliminating risk.

Ultimately, a proper records management function ensures that records of vital historical, fiscal, and legal value are identified and preserved, while nonessential records are discarded in a timely manner according to established rules or guidelines. With the increasing digitization of organizational collections, organizations need to have robust records and information management practices in place to ensure that digital materials are properly preserved and accessible over time. This includes adherence to metadata standards, appropriate version control, and regular backups to guard against data loss.

The Records Life Cycle

The records management life cycle refers to the process of managing the creation, use, retention, and disposal of records. The life cycle includes seven phases: creation and capture, collaboration and use, taxonomy and classification, version control and management, retention and archiving, preservation and hold, and disposition and destruction.

To effectively manage records, it is essential to identify, organize, and classify them using a taxonomy and retention schedule. This enables organizations to comply with laws and regulations governing the retention and disposal of records. Secure storage is also necessary to protect the records and ensure that they remain accessible and reliable until they are no longer needed.

Before we return to the life-cycle phases, first, a brief introduction to metadata, which is basically data about data and essential to the entire aforementioned data life cycle. It is the reason a document can be indexed and searched and enhanced and grouped with or separated from other similar documents. It describes the document, who created or modified it, and when they created or modified it. An e-mail includes server information and senders and recipients and whether it has attachments. It describes where it came from and where it resides and includes unique technical information, ensuring its uniqueness. It is used to determine access rights and whether it is related to other documents or clusters of documents. It can be hashed to create a unique fingerprint to identify it or eliminate duplicative copies. And over time, it will be enhanced to include everything that can be known about its journey during that life cycle, most importantly, when it was created, to which retention rules or legal holds it may be subject, and whether or when it can be destroyed.

Creation and capture represent the date, time, and file type the moment a document comes into existence. Once it exists, it can be used by one or many individuals who have the right to access it. If a number of individuals collaborate on a document, it will be subject to version control, which will track and preserve changes among multiple users. Depending on the status of our users, whether they are on a legal hold or subject to regulatory retention, the document will be retained and archived with a set of rules to prevent it from being destroyed or spoliated. And finally, if the document should outlive its retention requirements, legal holds, and usefulness, it will be subject to destruction.

So, records need to be identified, organized, and classified using a taxonomy and retention schedule so that they can be managed, retained, retrieved, and disposed of in accordance with the laws and regulations that govern them. They must be securely stored to ensure that they are protected, accessible, and reliable until they are no longer of value to the organization or required due to regulations or legal holds. They should be inventoried in tandem with asset management and data mapping to ensure their accessibility and efficient access. Some modern tools enable and empower this process with automation. Their data quality and metadata should be preserved and enhanced over time to increase their value to the organization. They should be migrated and consolidated when it makes sense to improve security, availability, and searchability, or to reduce duplicative costs. And again, a proactive destruction or disposition program reduces the risk of overretention, unnecessary storage costs, and improved bandwidth.

Data quality and records inventories are essential to quality records management and should be revisited by operations and compliance on a periodic basis. A completed record inventory can also provide each organizational unit with information to enable better management and organizational intelligence. There are six important concepts to keep in mind when creating the records inventory: Identifying required records to add to the inventory is likely to highlight duplicates and unnecessary retention of information. Adding records to the inventory will instigate discussions about whether efficiencies can be made in the volumes of information held and replicated. A data map will also be useful. Classification of records sets out clearly why records are held, what value they provide, and how they fit into the wider context of the organization.

Over time, the retrieval of records is improved when there is an accurate inventory of where they are stored. Use of records over time may change, including ownership and storage location. The inventory will help track those changes, making long-term management of records easier. Understanding whether there is an ongoing requirement to retain records will in part be supported by the record inventory and the record classes that have been identified, which will help hedge against resignation in the form of the "keep everything" approach.

Finally, confidence in disposing of records starts with a clear link between records and retention schedules. The record inventory will make that link with structured and consistent governance. It will make for more effective management of data. It will help reduce and eliminate redundancies. It will reduce costs for storage and duplicative systems. It will reduce legal liability and monetary risk by avoiding spoliation. It can even hedge against cybersecurity breaches since you cannot hack what does not exist.

Data Governance

Data governance is a critical process for organizations as they manage large volumes of information. It involves managing, archiving, accessing, and controlling the exponential growth of data and data types that are now extending to thousands of platforms and applications. Organizations need to meticulously plan their data management from scope and architecture to policies, asset management, and operational frameworks, which serve organizational needs while meeting regulatory and compliance standards.

One significant challenge faced by organizations in managing data is the proliferation of ROT data. The existence of this type of data is often the result of backups, multiple users, and inefficient data management, leading to dozens of copies of the same documents. The problem of ROT data can be mitigated by using deduplication, classification methods, and single-instance storage, which preserve a single version of a record with a reference pointer to the e-mails, documents, or file systems from where the file(s) originated.

An essential component of good data governance in organizations is asset management and data mapping. This involves protecting and backing up physical assets, including legacy systems, storage devices, and applications that present substantial risk and should be replaced and migrated from as a part of the process of data life-cycle management. Migrations provide an opportunity to port only those records that are still subject to retention requirements while leaving behind and destroying those that have outlived their retention schedules or usefulness.

Data consolidation into a single or federated archive is an effective way for organizations to reduce risks associated with compliance and security, reduce the potential for spoliation or unintended destruction, allow for more efficient retention and disposition, eliminate duplicative resources and risks, and reduce the inefficiency in maintaining an array of systems and SMEs. Consolidation also reduces the likelihood of data remediations and facilitates a more defensible, efficient, and reliable process overall.

A well-managed data governance program in organizations allows custodians and responsive data to be searched and extracted in hours and days. In organizations with poorly designed, integrated, and managed systems, the same process can often drag on for weeks and months, frustrating stakeholders, particularly in legal or compliance. Failure to identify, search, or extract data can be a major frustration to stakeholders who must review data or evidence and pass it on to regulators, investigators, or opposing counsel. Therefore, organizations must consider these risks and challenges when building a reliable and defensible enterprise data governance program.

Following are a few use cases illustrating good versus bad data governance practices for organizations:

Good Data Governance Practices

An organization invests in a modern data management system to manage their collection, users, and operational processes. They also conduct regular reviews of their data to ensure that they are not storing ROT data. They establish retention schedules and dispose of data that is no longer needed. They make sure their system is backed up and have a plan in place for data recovery in the event of system failure.

An organization consolidates their data into a single archive, which reduces the risk of data loss or duplication, and makes it easier to maintain and manage their data. They have a clear plan for integrating different types of data and ensure that their archive is accessible, secure, and searchable.

An organization implements security protocols to safeguard sensitive data, limit access to authorized staff, and requires secure authentication for access. They also have a process in place for detecting and responding to security incidents and have a disaster recovery plan in case of a security breach or other disaster.

Bad Data Governance Practices

An organization fails to establish a retention policy for their data, which leads to data overload and increases the risk of data loss, duplication, and other issues. They continue to store data that is no longer needed and fail to dispose of it in a timely manner.

An organization fails to maintain their data management system, which leads to outdated, unstable systems that are prone to failure. They also fail to back up their data, increasing the risk of data loss in case of system failure or other disaster.

An organization fails to implement appropriate security protocols for their data, such as limiting access to sensitive data or using weak authentication methods. They also fail to have a plan in place for detecting and responding to security incidents, increasing the risk of data breaches and other security incidents.

Data Minimization[2]

The increasing volume of data, doubling each year, is primarily driven by the widespread use of mobile applications and collaboration platforms, particularly in the context of remote work trends. Organizations, for various reasons such as corporate inertia, budget constraints, and a belief in the potential sales benefits of retaining large datasets, tend to keep more information than is deemed necessary.

Information management professionals assert that only 15 percent of the data created holds value for an extended period, highlighting the importance of discerning valuable information. Legal considerations play a crucial role in data retention, with laws and regulations specifying the need for retention based on business and geographic factors. Privacy laws, particularly those concerning personal privacy, emphasize data minimization, imposing fines for noncompliance, and allowing private rights of action.

The consequences of overretention extend beyond mere storage costs. Keeping unnecessary data requires additional servers and databases, presenting attractive targets for hackers and increasing the likelihood and costs associated with cybersecurity incidents. Fear of legal consequences, such as being found in the wrong during litigation, used to drive companies to retain data unnecessarily. However, recent legal updates, such as the 2015 amendments to federal civil procedural rules, have narrowed the scope of discoverable information, reducing the need for speculative data retention.

Another major issue is cost. Despite decreasing unit costs of data storage, the total costs for companies may rise due to the explosive growth in unstructured data. The International Data Corporation predicts a substantial increase in worldwide unstructured data from 33 zettabytes in 2018 to 175 zettabytes by 2025. A global survey identifies data storage among the top drivers for IG projects.

Overretention also leads to litigation and investigation costs. The obligation to preserve relevant data during legal proceedings becomes cumbersome when dealing with large volumes of unnecessary information. Compliance costs are on the rise, with the evolution of privacy regulations, exemplified by General Data Protection Regulation (GDPR) and various state-specific laws. Violations of data-handling regulations can result in significant fines, as evidenced by cases in 2022 against companies such as EyeMed and online custom merchandising platforms.

Data breaches, a significant risk associated with overretention, incur substantial costs. The global average cost of a data breach, according to IBM's 2022 Cost of Data Breach Report, has reached $4.35 million. These costs include penalties, class-action lawsuits, and intangible damages such as reputational harm. The article provides examples, such as the Facebook Cambridge Analytica scandal and the Equifax data breach, highlighting the long-lasting impact on trust and reputation.

To mitigate these risks, organizations should implement a defensible disposition plan. This plan involves systematically deleting data in a reasonable and good-faith manner, considering the company's business, legal, and regulatory obligations. A defensible disposition plan is part of an overall IG program and requires support from high-level executives. It includes protocols for defining information objectives, identifying data subject to disposition, assessing retention obligations, deciding whether to retain or dispose of data, and periodically reassessing the plan.

It is further important to leverage the right suite of tools and technologies to assist in the disposition process, including legal hold management tools, e-mail platforms, collaboration platforms, advanced search applications, and artificial intelligence (AI) tools. Additionally, extending the defensible disposition plan to third parties, such as vendors and service providers, is crucial to avoid the costs associated with breaches involving third-party data.

Records Management Surveys

The record survey is the primary source of information necessary to develop classification schemes, to associate retention schedules, and to understand one's organization. These surveys will also capture the information needed for our gap analysis, risk assessment, and vital records documents. These surveys consist of interviewing appropriate staff.

Essential elements of our approach are as follows:

- Data Collection: Includes record types, activity patterns, and other related information.
- Surveys and File Evaluations: The scope of the survey process will include interviews with users from departments that are significant generators of the above-captioned records (in a scheduled series of meetings). During these meetings, any of our questions relevant to our projects should be answered.
- Validation: Review of survey data by one's staff will ensure validation by the data source.

For organizations, the record survey process can be adapted to gather information about the organization's data and how it is managed.

Legal Research

The objective of this process is to identify the specific legal retention requirements, legal citations, and governing authorities for each record class.

The legal research project involves these subtasks:

- Legal Group Classification: Linking record classes to legal groups of records that are viewed similarly by the law or regulatory bodies.
- Legal Research: A database of legal and compliance research is reviewed and updated to relate the law to the legal group and hence the record classes.
- Auditing: Interpreting and auditing the legal research.

Application of Management Principles

The sophistication and complexity of management theory are slowly catching up to the sophistication of technological advancement in an increasingly complex global marketplace—and this is true, even for traditional institutions. In some regard, it might seem the reverse would be true; that to design effective systems, we must ourselves become more systematic and robotic. That is only half true. Indeed, we can and should increasingly rely on formal and semiformal systems to improve and maximize process efficiency while minimizing human error. But most of us are not robots and do not wish to be treated as such. Which largely explains why the vast majority of turnover can be attributed to a sense that management often undervalues and underappreciates its employees. While we often talk about people, process, and technology, managers can often confuse people with process or technology and reduce them to components. A good manager is sensitive to human complexity while recognizing the systematic nature of process and organization to maximize human potential. Fortunately, as it turns out, what is best for employees is often what is best for management and the organization at large. The current market for knowledge workers is also having a restorative effect. With greater mobility and opportunity than ever, skilled employees, particularly in technology, need not be reduced to automatons.

At the same time, and somewhat paradoxically, organizations are becoming more process- and data-oriented, which provides the objectivity necessary to remove or at least minimize emotion and personality from the task at hand. But any good and effective manager has to understand, first and foremost, that they are working with human beings, who have friends and families; hopes and dreams; and personal and professional aspirations. Which is why a manager should spend time looking inward and considering how he or she is perceived by employees and whether the fealty they command is through respect or fear. Are their employees excited to go to work? Do they like, or at least, respect their boss or the people with whom they share the majority of their waking hours? And how, if at all, are those perceptions impacting productivity?

It seems obvious that a manager should want to earn the respect of his employees. But too often they are more interested and invested in their own success, even at the expense of their team. Satisfied employees and doing good hard work are not mutually exclusive; a type of obsolescent thinking that goes back to the early industrial revolution. But let us be clear: while soft skills are crucially important to good leadership and good management, they are by no means a replacement for experience or expertise. A poor leader or manager can make a successful career for themselves being a creep who happens to be very skilled at their job. Whether they have any meaningful or trusting relationships is another story.

A manager should also make an effort to establish trust with employees. It is especially effective to reinforce the notion that their privacy and confidentiality will be respected. This, in turn, encourages greater trust and honesty between boss and subordinate, which is better for the team and the individual. Employees often become discouraged when their superiors appear not to value their ideas or recommendations, or at least, give them the light of day. For selfish and unselfish purposes, it can be useful to let them know that, even if their ideas or suggestions fail to make it past the concept stage, they will nevertheless get a hearing. Similarly, a manager should give credit where credit is due. One who takes credit for others' efforts will never be respected or establish trust. Alternatively, there are times when mistakes must be revealed or papered over. A manager who turns mountains into mole hills merely to exert power will similarly fail to earn the esteem of his employees. People make mistakes. Unless it is the end of the world, a good manager should use leadership jujitsu to convert a mistake or error of judgment into a constructive learning experience, which will also increase the probability of greater respect and trust with one's employees in the future.

Another underrepresented skill among managers is the ability to recognize aptitude and, to the extent possible, orient employees in a direction that will have the most productive impact on the team, the organization, and on their careers. Different people have different personalities, interests, and aptitudes. A manager should take the time to learn where an employee's sweet spots are to increase the probability of their success, as well as the overall capacity of the team. It may be wise, for example, not to force one's introverted database manager into the role of client success manager. Or select an employee who is uncomfortable speaking in public to conduct critical presentations. There is always an opportunity to discuss such matters with employees, if only we would find the time. Even if the exercise in no way changes the substance of their job or the direction of their career, they will recognize and appreciate the effort, and both will learn something in the process.

Indeed, there are times when a manager has little choice but to do the best with the team he or she has. So, if certain exigencies require that creative or talented employees pull staples on a particular day, then so be it. A wise manager will acknowledge when a job is unpleasant or distasteful and make light of it rather than displaying a lack of sympathy. Or worse, gaslight employees by pretending it is not that bad. It also would not kill a manager to use it as an opportunity for team building or find painless ways to make it up to them.

To be clear, none of this is to suggest that employees be coddled; or are not obliged to maintain ownership and accountability; or are not responsible for their mistakes and missteps; or can in any way take their time management or their deliverables for granted; or do not have a professional obligation to their manager and their team; or that they need not follow rules or process requirements. Nothing about being a good manager suggests a diminution of employee responsibilities. In fact, it is the opposite one should expect in a give-and-take relationship.

Though it does not always come naturally, a manager must learn to be flexible and adaptive to change, especially in an increasingly dynamic and complex global environment. A manager who can pivot with the technology and the times will stand out to executive management. Excessive rigidity on the other hand often leads to poor adaptation, poor communication, and poor outcomes. It is at times necessary to teach and more often, to learn, and the best managers tend to be the best students, whether they acquire skills formally or informally. But good and poor habits are all a matter of practice. Invest in good skills and good communication and you will generally receive dividends over time.

A struggle that often arises and can pit a manager between his employees and executive leadership is training. Most employees see the value for themselves and for the organization in improving their skills, especially when those efforts are acknowledged and reciprocated. Regrettably, many enterprises undervalue the virtue of training and developing their employees. Thus, when putting budgets together, education and employee training often get short shrift. By contrast, more innovative organizations tend to invest more time and effort training their employees, realizing not just the benefits of improved efficiency and performance but employee satisfaction. Conversely, enterprises who do not invest in their employees tend to receive negative returns on their investment in the form of low employee satisfaction.

Considering the type of effective, low-cost training available today, there are not a lot of good reasons for more focus on training. Surveys repeatedly indicate that, while salary is of course especially important, employees tend to be more motivated by job fulfillment. If an employee believes that his boss and his firm are loyal and have his or her best interests at heart, they are much less likely to jump ship. But even if it were the case that better trained employees were leaving in modest numbers—and it is not obvious—it would nevertheless be to the firm's advantage to have better skilled employees during their employment. Whether one is a manager or employee, improvement requires time, investment, and commitment.

It is critically important for a manager to have a strong relationship with his or her PMs. Where the ultimate accountability rolls up to a manager, having weak PMs is a ticking time bomb. A manager also needs to be effective and maximize human potential. So, delegation is also important, as is becoming solutions oriented and improvement minded; that is, proactive in terms of always looking for a better solution or greater efficiencies and encouraging the team, as a team, to do the same.

At the end of the day, managers and employees must be accountable. So, like much in life, there needs to be a balance. For example, expressing empathy and trust on the one hand, and strength on the other. Sure, employees want a sympathetic leader but not at the expense of one who is competent and worthy of respect.

Understanding one's strengths and weaknesses is crucial to good leadership, as well as surrounding oneself with a talented team of individuals. Some managers of a lower order of primate can become jealous or politically concerned if they have employees who they believe might outshine them. This betrays a transparently flawed character. The best managers will look smart by surrounding themselves with talent so that the whole of their collective efforts is always greater than the sum of its parts.

Last of all, managers and employees alike should have a realistic understanding of their limitations or opportunities. Many of us focus on our strengths rather than our weaknesses and then wonder why our careers are in limbo. Or receive a less than stellar review and, instead of taking personal responsibility, let our egos blame our managers or co-workers. It is similarly ironic how often individuals fail to apply best organizational practices to their own lives or profession. One should conduct a periodic needs assessment and a review of the objective data available to visualize a better, more fulfilling future state. We should all want to be the best version of ourselves in whatever we do. But organizational or personal change requires more than motivational speeches and self-help books, it requires a plan and executing on that plan. Having a mentor in or out of the workplace is also advisable.

Project Management

In the context of organizations undertaking IG projects, project management is a crucial methodology that enables planning, executing, and monitoring projects to completion within a specific time frame. IG projects, such as those related to data management or compliance, require careful planning and execution to achieve their goals successfully.

In this context, ongoing work related to customer, or technical services can be managed, as well as errors or issues that require resolution can become distinct projects. The project life cycle for IG projects consists of initiation, planning, execution, and closure.

During project initiation, the high-level goals, scope, risks, and dependencies of the IG project should be established, and roles and responsibilities should be assigned. In the planning phase, details of resources, costs, deliverables, and timelines should be refined, and a single-page project charter should be created to communicate the project's core elements. Communication and reporting are crucial for the success of the project, and the PM should be responsible for collecting, recording, centralizing, and sharing information and metrics with stakeholders.

The project charter should summarize the key information about the project, including senior management, key players, goals, scope, success criteria, risks, dependencies, and what is out of scope. Time in project management for IG projects refers to the aggregate number of hours required for a task, and duration is the overall time frame in which the task will be completed.

In the context of organizations undertaking IG implementation projects, time management is crucial for the successful completion of the project. The implementation of IG requires careful planning, execution, and monitoring of the project to ensure that it is completed within a specific timeframe.

The PM must estimate the aggregate number of hours required for each task and the overall timeframe in days, weeks, months, and so on, in which the task will be completed. This will involve communicating with team members to assess how long it will take for them to complete their activities and whether it will impact the overall project timeline. The PM must also go beyond the surface to get a thorough understanding of the work requirements, resource availability, and reliability, especially for resources attached to critical path tasks.

A good project plan will have alternative or tactical solutions ready as necessary, connected to a PM's risk response assessment. For example, what is the backup plan if a key resource quits, or if there is a competing exigency that commands their time or attention.

Communication with resources on a regular, and often daily, basis, is crucial, as is estimating time, which has a direct impact on budgets and completion dates. Making decisions about work and time based on guesswork can be calamitous. It is not unusual to make educated guesses during the process, but they are not so much guesses as well-researched and well-considered due diligence.

The nature or complexity of the project will dictate how long it will take to complete. For example, a data migration or disposition project could take months or even years, depending on the amount of data to be analyzed, searched, copied, or classified.

In addition, a wise PM should not rely solely on their team's representations. Precise estimation of work takes effort, time, and understanding all variables and unknowns that can impact it. Therefore, it is advisable for PMs to take a relatively conservative approach to estimating deliverables to avoid a negative cascade that reflects poorly on the PM and the team in general. PMs must also understand that a lack of dependability from a resource may not be due to subpar performance but because they are higher performing and overtasked. In such cases, a PM should communicate with program management to ascertain whether competing work or projects might impact the resource's availability.

Having a program or portfolio management office can help ensure consistent standards for documentation, tools, processes, and reporting.

A good project management system should simplify complex tasks and assume as little time, energy, and communication as possible. Kanban boards or similar project management tools, for example, are becoming increasingly popular due to their simplicity, efficiency, and malleability.

During the project execution phase, the more time and consideration dedicated to planning and risk mitigation, the smoother and more efficient the execution stage will be. Human beings are flawed, including managers, and can make mistakes that can be costly. However, having a culture that values honesty, communication, trustworthiness, and teamwork can help mitigate these mistakes. PMs must also avoid thinking too high level and must have hands-on knowledge and understanding of the project to ensure its success.

Similarly, one of the more common blunders is thinking too high level when more hands-on knowledge or understanding is necessary or critical. Or making assumptions about a challenge, process, or deliverable, which may appear minor, but which could theoretically sabotage or at least threaten the success of the entire project. If for no other reason than protecting one's caboose, it is wise to perform the proper due diligence and not leave anything to chance.

The term RACI is a project management acronym for "Responsible, Accountable, Consulted, and Informed." Typically represented by a matrix, it defines who is Responsible for completing tasks, who is Accountable for ensuring tasks are done correctly, who should be Consulted for input and expertise, and who needs to be Informed about progress. This structure helps prevent confusion, ensures accountability, and improves communication and efficiency within the project team. There are several variations on this theme, but they all essentially address the same challenge of clarifying roles and responsibilities. It may seem obvious to the uninitiated, but it is an area too often ignored or underestimated, particularly in less formal project management settings. It might be less critical on smaller projects with fewer personalities, responsibilities, and moving parts, but it is still highly recommended. A project with merely two or three stakeholders can go sideways, so there is frankly no good reason for trying to avoid confusion. Documenting roles and responsibilities is useful not just for communicating duties or obligations to various stakeholders but as part of the project documentation overall. It is often the case that a historical project may inform a similar implementation in the future.

Similarly, after our planning and hard work, when we finally arrive at the end of the project, we must secure our planning materials and documentation to soberly reflect on our successes and failures. Did we meet or fail to meet our success criteria and to what extent? What did we miss during planning or execution? What could we have done better? Once a project is completed, everyone tends to move on very quickly and set their sights on the next priority. Where a project has not run particularly smoothly, that is the time people are less likely to want to revisit errors or misjudgments. But, of course, there is no better time or opportunity, which is the point of a lessons-learned exercise. Little surprise, then, when many of the mistakes or inefficiencies in an organization are repeated from project to project. A fresh review of a project at its conclusion, however brief, much less uncomfortable, will increase the probability of a more efficient project in the future. Needless to say, if that exercise is not conducted constructively and with a certain degree of sensitivity, it could devolve into throwing one another under the bus, which defeats the purpose of the exercise in the first place. So, it is even more important for senior managers to take the lead while also assuming the role of a crisis negotiator.

That said, it bears repeating that accountability is no less crucial to improvement, and a lack of accountability will not only encourage a repeat of poor performance but also have a destructive effect on morale and cohesion for those who did perform well. Still, if a team member did not pull their weight, it is often better to have that conversation in private. Embarrassing one's employees helps no one and undermines morale and trust, as employees might have good reason to believe that they could suffer the same embarrassment at a point in the future. Alternatively, there may be less obvious reasons to explain their inadequate performance such as overburdening them with work when they had limited bandwidth.

IG Needs Assessment and Gap Analysis

The goal of an IG needs assessment and gap analysis is to identify disparities between their current approach and industry best practices and to then map IG-based solutions to improve organizational priorities.

The analysis typically involves collecting and analyzing information on the customer's current IG practices through surveys, interviews, and policy reviews. The related deliverables include creating and distributing IG survey materials, along with conducting postsurvey interviews. Through this process, the consulting team will then measure and score the customer's IG practices, benchmarking them against industry standards. The related deliverables encompass analyzing survey data and benchmarking data.

The consulting team then typically prioritizes recommendations based on the severity of gaps, internal priorities, and available resources. The deliverables in this phase include analyzing survey data, benchmarking data, and drafting a comprehensive report with recommendations.

Once the analysis is finalized, the project team will then, typically, compile a final project report that includes an action plan and roadmap with timelines, resource estimates, responsibility allocation, and measurable progress goals. The related deliverables will also generally include drafting a comprehensive report with recommendations and reviewing and amending it for final approval.

Elements of the project process often involve creating and distributing IG survey materials, conducting postsurvey interviews, analyzing survey data, benchmark data, and drafting a comprehensive report with recommendations for final approval by senior decision makers.

Clients participating the needs assessment and gap analysis project are expected to collaborate with the vendor to ensure an understanding of project requirements and execute project deliverables. Another important element is to provide a single point of contact for the project, ensure staff participation in surveys, interviews, meetings, and respond to vendor queries. And, to ensure success, the client must proactively assist with reviewing, budgeting, and approving the refined estimate and scope.

Vendor Management

In the context of IG implementation projects, the need to manage and control relationships with vendors and suppliers is becoming increasingly demanding. The most obvious risks involve security breaches or organizational continuity failures. A good vendor management program should ensure that the relationships with vendors and suppliers provide maximum benefits while minimizing risks and help with cost containment measures.

A vendor manager should be responsible for supply chain management, contract negotiations, reporting, procurement, audit, and documentation. They must find a balance between holding the vendor's feet to the fire and working as partners and equals. It is critical to anticipate challenges, legal or otherwise, by scrupulously documenting all material interactions as if every line of a contract, every issues log, and every quarterly and annual organizational review could be used in future litigation. The greater the discipline applied to the relationship, the greater the service in return.

A successful request for proposal (RFP) requires that all stakeholders participate throughout the entire process, with involvement proportional to need and expertise. There is often so much at stake in terms of time and opportunity cost; the vendor manager must insist on full cooperation. A good prospective vendor will ask and understand most or all the pertinent questions about one's organizational needs. It is equally important to develop specifications and requirements that can be clearly and concisely communicated to vendors so both parties are on the same page in terms of expectations.

In the world of IG vendor management for organizations, experienced information technology (IT) or IG professionals have learned from past mistakes. They have encountered vendors who have excelled in demos and RFPs but have failed to deliver in real-world conditions. Therefore, it is crucial to assess a platform or service's performance at scale and gather references and recommendations. A well-prepared list of questions and topics should be used to evaluate the vendor and service to determine how they are likely to perform. Inconsistencies between references should raise red flags or require maximum protection in the contract.

The process for vendor management usually begins with a perception of a need, which leads to brainstorming and information gathering. Demos with vendors follow, and the scope begins to narrow, leading to an RFP. All stakeholders should participate throughout the process, with involvement proportional to need and expertise. The development of specifications and requirements should be clear and concise to communicate expectations. Depending on scope, the process could be informal or take years.

A good vendor will ask pertinent questions to understand the organizational needs and translate the problem into detailed specifications. They will also assess whether their product or service is a suitable solution and determine whether the organization is seeking a new product or process or replacing an older one. If the latter, they will identify why the previous vendor failed and what the expectations are for the replacement. Sales and marketing will initiate these conversations, but technical SMEs will eventually take over to facilitate decisions and be responsible for implementation, maintenance, future performance, and vendor interaction.

Two significant red flags during the vendor selection process come down to politics and expertise. Every day, an objective effort to assess, grade, and select a vendor is undermined by political maneuvering. Years of effort can be undermined over a single cup of coffee between two executives. The combination of authority and a lack of applied knowledge and expertise are often destructive and demoralizing to a team who may have spent years carefully and diligently trying to make the right strategic decision for the organization only to have it upended by hubris and abuse of authority. While this is not something for which there is a surefire cure, a vendor manager and a team should document all their risks and concerns to the executive management team responsible for the final decision.

Development of Vital Records Programs

Only a very small portion of a typical office's records—usually no more than 2 to 4 percent—are vital.[3] To consider which records are vital, a critical question is whether, in the absence of these records a company could effectively resume and maintain operations for up to 30 days, or ensure the security of personnel, operations, or facilities, without access to some of those records.[4]

Given the importance of these records, a vital records program is a crucial component of an organization's RIM and IG initiative. Integrated into operational policies and procedures, it plays a key role in effective vital records protection throughout the entire records life cycle. By utilizing risk management techniques, the program assesses the potential impact of losing vital records on the organization, ultimately aiming to enable the resumption or continuation of business operations at the highest quality level.[5]

Typically overseen by RIM/IG professionals in collaboration with business continuity, disaster recovery, or emergency management teams, the program development may vary based on the organization's size and resources. In some cases, especially in smaller organizations, RIM or IG professionals may lead the vital records program development independently. Despite the organization's size, ongoing evaluation and updates are essential to reflect technological advancements and evolving business requirements.[6]

The process of developing a vital records program involves multiple steps, including assigning responsibilities, identifying vital records, verifying their inclusion in retention schedules, implementing a risk management process, developing protection strategies and policies, selecting offsite storage methods, and establishing procedures for the effective use of vital records in case of a disaster. The program also addresses issues such as remote access to electronic vital records, backup methods, identifying individuals authorized for decision making during restoration, developing training materials, and periodically evaluating program effectiveness.[7]

Identification and classification of vital records are integral parts of the program, aligning with operational, legal, and regulatory record-keeping requirements. Records are deemed vital if they are absolutely necessary to resume operations, preserve rights and obligations, protect assets, and safeguard the organization's legal and financial status. The development of a vital records schedule includes activities such as assigning attributes to each vital record, assessing the cost of protection, vulnerability, and necessary information for reconstruction or access. Records are classified as vital, important, or useful, each contributing to business resumption in the event of a disaster. The vital records schedule details essential attributes, including name, location, protection method, and recovery actions, providing a comprehensive guide for recovery in case of a disaster.[8]

Distinguishing between vital, important, and useful records is crucial due to the fact that only a small fraction of your overall records holds critical significance during emergencies. It is imperative to clearly identify those records essential for maintaining uninterrupted operations under abnormal or extraordinary conditions. The distinctions are outlined as follows:[9]

Vital Records

- Contain information crucial for the continuation of office functions during emergencies.
- Required to sustain operations under extraordinary circumstances.
- Contain information essential for confirming the office's legal and financial status.
- Essential for protecting rights and confirming obligations for the organization, its personnel, and stakeholders.
- Crucial for recovering or safeguarding critical systems, equipment, facilities, or workspaces.
- Unique and irreplaceable or would incur extremely high costs for reproduction.
- Their unavailability would lead to severe negative consequences.

Important Records

- Hold value for the office, aiding in the restoration of operations during or after an emergency.
- Losing or damaging them would inconvenience the office, but it would not halt operations.
- Can be replaced at a moderate cost.

Useful Records

- Contribute to keeping the office's business going but are not critical during emergencies.
- Their loss or damage would cause minimal or temporary inconvenience to the office.
- Can be replaced at a moderate cost.

Ensuring the safety of vital records involves not only general record-keeping practices but also additional measures tailored specifically for their protection during emergencies. Master copies of vital records within the office can be safeguarded by adopting daily record-keeping procedures.

This includes securing paper vital records in fire-proof or bomb-proof safes, lockable storage cupboards, or drawers. Formal procedures for regular updates and maintenance of vital records, both in physical and digital forms, should be established. Efficiently managing all records systems is crucial to enable easy location and handling of vital records in emergency situations, preventing confusion with less critical records. It is imperative to collaborate with RIM/IG specialists to establish best practices for safeguarding vital records in various formats or mediums, emphasizing the comprehensive backup of electronic records, including operating systems and application software.[10]

An effective strategy for protecting vital records involves offsite storage in a secure remote location. Authentic copies or originals, if applicable, should be stored far enough from the office to avoid potential damage during emergencies but close enough for quick retrieval or access as needed postdisaster. The offsite location must adhere to stringent standards, including secure access only for authorized personnel, robust security measures, disaster prevention measures equivalent to those in the office, capability to store, protect, and use vital records in all formats, and ensuring protection against adverse environmental conditions for the entire life of the records. Additionally, the offsite location should provide necessary connectivity, such as telephone and Internet access, to facilitate easy retrieval and utilization of vital records in emergency situations.[11]

Continuous Improvement

Continuous improvement is a formal methodology that can benefit organizations seeking to undertake IG projects by identifying and executing on opportunities for improvement incrementally, minimizing disruption to operations and the organization. The approach emphasizes the reciprocal relationship between improving products, services, or processes, and engaging employees to encourage constructive feedback and engagement.

Implementing major organizational transformations can often prove to be challenging for organizations and their staff. Change is an inevitable aspect of human nature, and employees can become habituated and comfortable with systems and processes, preferring the "devil they know," even if changes have the potential to make their jobs easier or processes more efficient. Additionally, cynicism can arise within the organization if senior management makes top-down changes without input from the teams who perform the work or develop the very processes and systems. Changes sold as improvements can fail to live up to the benefits advertised, often because they were not properly vetted or assessed in the first place.

Continuous improvement methodology is critical in engaging employees as a value within the organizational culture, as they know best where the shoe pinches. Strong managers and organizations understand that treating employees with trust and loyalty breeds trust and loyalty in return, as well as greater ownership and accountability. Encouraging constructive feedback on issues or inefficient processes generally comes at little or no cost, and it is hard to conceive of how less feedback and input from a team is better than more feedback.

Continuous improvement programs have made a resurgence in recent years, with different systems and verticals sharing the same basic objectives: to commit the organization to a culture of improvement, demonstrate employee value, extract intelligence from staff, improve trust and communication, never settle for the status quo, and maintain a structure that can evolve to changing circumstances.

Intentionally or not, managers sometimes get lost in the stress and urgency of their job and forget that the word "patrons" means "human beings who depend on the organization for their information needs." They have families and friends and hopes and dreams. They want to trust the organization as a reliable source of information; to be treated respectfully and taken seriously and believe that they are valued members of the community. Strong organizations understand that treating patrons with trust and loyalty breeds trust and loyalty in return, as well as greater ownership and accountability. Not to mention the fact that encouraging constructive feedback on issues or inefficient processes generally comes at little or no cost. Assuming that it takes up very little of their time, it is hard to conceive of how less feedback and input from a team is better than more feedback.

According to the theory of "the wisdom of the crowd," the collective opinion of the group is statistically more effective or accurate than single or fewer individuals. Imagine a visualization where each point of a scatterplot represents an idea to be considered before making important strategic decisions. It is a scientific fact that the more—diverse and informed—opinions one considers, the higher probability of success that decision will tend to produce. This is not to suggest that managers will or should make decisions based solely on statistical probability. It is simply to convey the idea that we should value our patrons, both because they are human beings and because they possess intrinsic value to an organization merely by virtue of their potential to contribute good ideas.

In terms of risk and reward, our instincts to fear dramatic change are not entirely without merit. The greater the change, the greater the risk. Incremental change allows us to make significant improvements in real time while measuring the impact and minimizing risk. So, it provides us an opportunity to analyze whether our proposed changes have led to actual improvements or whether a pivot may be necessary to seek out a better solution. And a pivot from incremental change is naturally easier than a pivot from a more dramatic commitment.

Formal or semiformal continuous improvement programs have made a resurgence in recent years, manifesting in different systems and verticals, but all sharing the same basic objectives: to commit the organization to a culture of improvement; demonstrate that patrons have value; extract intelligence from staff; improve trust and communication; never settle for the status quo; and maintain a structure that can evolve to changing circumstances.

Six Sigma offers a simple blueprint for continuous improvement represented by the acronym DMAIC, which stands for define, measure, analyze, improve, and control. First, define, detail, and document an opportunity for change and improvement; second, establish the way in which data can be used to quantify and measure performance; third, analyze the variables from a data perspective to isolate and determine root causes; fourth, develop a solution that will remediate or improve those root causes; and fifth, execute, monitor, and maintain those solutions by establishing proper controls.

The following scenario highlights how Six Sigma processes can be successfully deployed in the context of implementing an IG project:

- First, define and document the opportunity for change and improvement, such as improving the organization and accessibility of digital assets.
- Next, establish a way to measure and quantify performance, such as the average time it takes to locate and retrieve a digital asset, or the number of errors encountered in the process.
- Then, using data from measurements, analyze the variables to identify the root causes of inefficiencies or errors in the digital asset management process. For example, discover that the search functionality in the digital asset management system is not working effectively, resulting in longer search times and lower efficiency.
- With this information, develop and implement a solution that will remediate or improve the root cause. This might involve upgrading the digital asset management system or training staff in more effective search techniques.
- Execute, monitor, and maintain the solution by establishing proper controls, such as tracking search times and error rates to ensure that the new system is working effectively.
- Finally, establish metrics to measure the success or failure of improvement initiatives, such as a reduction in the average time it takes to locate and retrieve a digital asset or a decrease in the number of errors encountered.

By continuously monitoring and improving their digital asset management process, the organization can ensure that their IG project is successful and provides value to the organization.

It is critical to be able to establish metrics to measure the success or failure of improvement initiatives. Four key qualitative and quantitative metrics for improvement include risk, efficiency, quality, and patron satisfaction. Risk tends to be more qualitative in nature but might be measured and extrapolated—compared to previous years—as a reduction in legal actions, regulatory fines, data remediations, or data breaches. Efficiency is generally a measure of time.

The quality of a service can often be measured as a reduction in errors, complaints, calls, or returns. Patron satisfaction can be evaluated with internal or external surveys, as well as positive or negative reviews on social media.

Several use cases for organizational continuous improvement include:

- Process Improvement: Identification of inefficiencies in a process and implementation of changes to make the process more efficient. This can include eliminating nonvalue-added steps or automating manual processes.
- Quality Improvement: Diagnosis of defects in a product or service and implementation of changes to reduce or eliminate those defects, ultimately improving the quality of the product or service.
- Employee Engagement: Improvement of employee engagement by providing opportunities for employees to contribute ideas and feedback, and by recognizing and rewarding employees who make significant contributions to the organization.
- Customer Experience: Improvement of patron experience by identifying pain points in the patron's usage of organizational systems and implementing changes to address those pain points, ultimately improving customer satisfaction and loyalty.

KPIs and Metrics

Using effective IG project metrics is critical to obtaining the type of meaningful quantitative evidence required to address vital questions or hypotheses concerning enhanced or diminished performance. This can be effectively summarized by the concept of GIGO, or garbage in/garbage out, which epitomizes the repercussions of inadequate inputs leading to flawed outputs and consequential decision making within organizations.

However, having metrics alone is insufficient; they must be both meaningful and accurate, catering to specific questions or hypotheses. Without the integration of metrics in organizational IG projects, decision making becomes speculative, leaving too much to chance and elevating the stakes significantly.

Senior managers, when requesting reports, should always prioritize data over feelings or opinions, seeking specific conclusions that can shed light on the efficacy of new processes or technologies, ensuring advancements in organizational efficiency and responsiveness to industry standards. Metrics, although universally applicable, also possess unique characteristics, with each organization posing distinct questions based on its structure and interactions.

Identifying quality metrics that are reliable, repeatable, and conducive to decision making becomes paramount, especially in cases where the qualitative aspect outweighs the quantitative, such as reducing risk. Negative correlations between metrics, such as error and efficiency, become instrumental in pinpointing and eliminating waste or bottlenecks systematically. Metrics should further not only reveal what is working or not but also align with strategic goals and objectives, allowing leadership to track progress accurately.

However, poorly framed questions can render metrics useless or create more confusion than clarity. Therefore, a strategic approach to framing questions, such as in the example of AI, is essential to ascertain whether technological advancements lead not only to increased productivity but also efficiency.

In the implementation of IG projects, metrics play a vital role in guiding organizational resource commitments and providing insights for informed decision making.

Finally, carefully considering opportunity costs and regularly monitoring KPIs in alignment with key organizational goals are crucial for optimal outcomes. Good data is fundamental, and the metrics must be fit for purpose, reflecting the truthful status of performance over time. Continuous improvement in metrics, starting with limited data and expanding over time, is a common and effective approach.

Knowledge Management

In the realm of IG project management for organizations, knowledge management emerges as a pivotal discipline facilitating the capture, organization, and leverage of collective knowledge and information within organizations. The knowledge base of an organization stands as its paramount asset, necessitating formal capture, organization, and seamless accessibility for organizational staff.

The advent of technology has revolutionized knowledge management, simplifying the organization and extraction of information that might otherwise be lost or underutilized. However, the triumph of knowledge management in an organization hinges on the dedication invested in creating and maintaining a practical, user-friendly knowledge base. Establishing an effective knowledge management system demands a framework aligned with the organization's culture, starting from leadership.

Challenges in this endeavor include capturing information in a useful and educational format, ensuring its ongoing relevance, and finding the time and incentives to commit to knowledge management. Overcoming these challenges and establishing an effective knowledge management system yields numerous benefits. The sharing of information fosters a culture that supports employees, aligning with the organization's goals. Invested and supported employees are more likely to be motivated, engage in collaborative efforts, and contribute significantly to the organization's success.

Knowledge sharing extends to cross-training, a practice that builds redundancy and enhances understanding between organizational teams. With a well-established framework and appropriate tools, an organization can harness its collective knowledge and information, optimizing redundancy, securing long-term prospects, and actively contributing to the growth and success of the organization.

Defensible Deletion

Many companies store excessive amounts of unnecessary data, which can lead to legal and compliance risks as well as financial burdens. The reduction of ROT data is essential for minimizing these risks. However, achieving defensible deletion, the strategic elimination of such data, can be perceived as a challenging task. This article outlines a framework to make defensible deletion an achievable objective, emphasizing the importance of planning.[12]

Defensible deletion involves the ongoing removal of unnecessary data, either in real time or according to a predetermined schedule, to prevent the accumulation of ROT. This process also includes the identification and deletion of previously accumulated ROT. The term "defensible" in this context pertains to the reduction of legal risk, particularly regarding the spoliation of evidence.[13]

Contrary to common concerns, companies are entitled to dispose of information they no longer require, as long as it aligns with regulatory and litigation preservation obligations. The U.S. Supreme Court, for example, in *Arthur Andersen v United States* (2005), affirmed the legitimacy of document retention policies, stating that it is not wrongful for managers to instruct employees to comply with valid retention policies. Best practices advocate for the destruction of records that are no longer necessary, citing various risks associated with overpreservation.[14]

To ensure defensibility, organizations should make disposal decisions based on legal and business judgment—and clearly defined rules. This involves implementing robust processes and procedures, including:

- Records Retention Policy and Schedule: Documenting retention requirements in a policy and schedule provides clarity on data eligibility for deletion.
- Inventory of Legal Preservation Obligations: Understanding data categories under legal hold enables efficient execution of defensible deletion.
- Buy-in and Support: Executive support is crucial to overcome opposition; identifying specific benefits for each stakeholder is key.[15]

Organizations also need to define the scope of the defensible deletion initiative, considering factors such as:

- Key Driving Forces: Events such a system upgrades, legal hold releases, or organizational transformations can create opportunities for defensible deletion.
- Departmental Focus: Targeting specific departments undergoing changes can facilitate a focused "house-cleaning" exercise.

- Enterprisewide IG: Prioritizing company wide IG efforts can serve as an ideal opportunity for defensible deletion, with the initiative divided into manageable projects.[16]

Another critical success factor in ensuring that ROT destruction efforts are both successful and defensible is to ensure collaboration among different organizational roles, including legal and compliance, business representatives, IT, records management professionals, and potentially external resources. C-suite sponsorship is particularly crucial for garnering support. Also, effective planning requires understanding that data deletion takes time, especially in large volumes. A "quiet" period should be anticipated for managing preservation obligations that may arise unpredictably.[17]

From a project management standpoint, to promote success, organizations should focus on feasibility by categorizing data into "easy," "medium," and "hard" buckets based on objective criteria. This approach allows for iterative culling and early wins with low-hanging fruit.[18]

In addition, defensibility hinges on thorough documentation, covering the overall approach, scope, data classification process, and final execution. Finally, the process of ROT deletion involves various iterative technical steps, including data deletion, validation, and further culling using advanced methods if necessary.[19]

Compliance and Risk Management

Compliance frameworks play a crucial role in establishing safeguards and controls to meet legal, regulatory, and industry certification requirements, while governance provides strategic direction and oversight. A comprehensive understanding of technology and its alignment with organizational strategic goals is imperative for compliance staff. Regular risk assessments and audits are integral to compliance with industry-specific standards and requirements, encompassing infrastructure, processes, rules, and retention criteria. For most organizations compliance and risk management functions encompass privacy and confidentiality, accessibility, copyright, and licensing requirements.

These assessments should adhere to ISO standards. Failing to meet compliance standards can result in significant consequences, including reputational damage and a loss of trust among patrons, stakeholders, and the research community. Compliance initiatives must be instilled from the top down, sensitizing employees to these consequences to become ingrained in the organizational culture. Providing relevant training is critical to keep employees updated on changing regulations and best practices. Stringent practices are necessary for maintaining documentation, ensuring general defensibility, and preparing for prospective audits and investigations.

Collaboration between compliance staff, IT auditors, and risk managers is also essential. Successful collaborative efforts require organizations to identify and eliminate material hazards that might impede operational goals tied to strategic organizational objectives. IT audits and assessments serve as an initial step in scrutinizing controls and measuring and quantifying risks.

Discovering risks and vulnerabilities in IG practices postimplementation is unfortunately common for organizations of all types. Therefore, comprehensive onboarding processes should extend beyond software vulnerability scanning to identify potential issues. Managing communications stored in organizational applications, especially data falling under regulatory retention requirements, poses a common challenge. Protocols should be established for retaining or destroying such data appropriately, ensuring compliance.

To maintain effective governance practices, guidelines must be codified across IT while remaining adaptable for use by other crucial staff stakeholders. Tailoring programs to specific groups or regions is important, but alignment with consistent strategic goals across the organization is crucial. A successful IG program must enforce fundamentals across all relevant IT stakeholders, addressing technical and operational challenges related to interoperability. Third-party audits during onboarding, RFP, and proof of concept phases ensure program effectiveness and alignment with best practices.

Additionally, senior managers should employ compliance principles to prevent unnecessary complications in IT audits. Recognizing human tendencies such as error, inconsistency, ego, and territoriality, effective auditors should conduct interviews, not interrogations, and heavily rely on SMEs familiar with day-to-day processes and operations.

The Importance of Information Management Policies

An organization's information management policy plays a pivotal role, serving dual objectives. First, it furnishes explicit guidelines for the creation, capture, and management of information assets, such as records, information, and data, aligning seamlessly with the organization's business, legal, and stakeholder requisites. Then, it methodically allocates responsibilities across the organizational landscape, fostering a unified and cohesive approach to information management. Importantly, this policy should harmonize with the principles, environment, and strategic directions articulated in the organization's overarching IG framework, adapting, and evolving as necessitated by dynamic operational landscapes.

From an IG best practices standpoint, a defensible information management policy encapsulates five core elements.

- **Outline Expectations.** The policy should outline expectations for information management practices, processes, and systems to be "fit for purpose," ensuring the creation, maintenance, and protection of reliable information. This involves articulating commitments to aligning practices with policy, defining which information assets staff can routinely destroy, and extending coverage to all business applications encompassing dedicated information management systems, databases, e-mails, and other mediums.
- **Describe Benefits.** Outline the organizational benefits of following sound information management practices. The policy should emphasize guidance for staff, clarify responsibilities, and underscore the advantageous outcomes of trustworthy, well-described, and readily accessible information.
- **Define Roles and Responsibilities.** The policy should clearly define the roles and responsibilities of all core stakeholders and users, presenting a comprehensive delineation of

the responsibilities of positions such as unit managers, supervisors, and the entity's chief technology officer (CTO). This extends to encompassing both permanent and contract workers, with managers and supervisors responsible for ensuring staff, including contract staff, are aware of and compliant with the outlined information management practices.

- **Strategic Alignment.** The policy should clearly align with the entity's commitment to meeting its business, legislative, and regulatory requirements, positioning it within the context of the organization's broader IG framework. It emphasizes the promotion of integrity and accessibility of information assets to support business outcomes.

- **Goal Orientation.** The policy should embody a strategic perspective, acknowledging the dynamic nature of the organization's operations and the necessity of keeping the policy aligned with the entity's strategic objectives. This involves careful consideration of how the policy supports the organization's overarching goals, intersecting with other strategic documents.

From a design standpoint, the policy formulator should tailor the policy to the entity's size, nature, and complexity. While smaller entities might consider consolidating information management policy with other governance documents, larger and more complex organizations may find this practice impractical. Additionally, attention must be given to addressing different policy statements to diverse audiences, ensuring that individual needs and sophistication levels are accounted for.

IG best practices underscore the importance of ensuring that the target audience comprehends various facets of information management, such as processes, approved systems, record destruction practices, roles, responsibilities, and the interrelation of the policy with other organizational documents. The complexity inherent in information management for large organizations necessitates a multifaceted approach, potentially requiring multiple policy documents integrated across organizational policies and procedures for accessibility and comprehension.

To enhance readability and usability, policy statements should further avoid the use of unnecessary references, to ensure clarity and relevance. Practical examples of appropriate guidance within the policy include listings of endorsed systems for information capture, details on information storage protocols, access controls, guidelines for third-party data transfers, training provision, and resources for additional information. Furthermore, it is essential to articulate the policy's commitment to regular review, compliance monitoring, and its adaptability to changes in the business or regulatory environment.

Finally, from a corporate governance perspective, policy formulators should furnish evidence of the policy's endorsement by the relevant officers or managers responsible for information management. Including a brief, signed paragraph from the internal supervisory authority not only acknowledges the critical role of information management but also directs staff to comply with and monitor the policy requirements.

Data Mapping and Classification

Capturing, as defined in information management, involves placing organization-generated records or data into a system and recording their existence in that system. ISO 15489 identifies three critical purposes for capturing records: establishing a relationship between the record, its creator, and the business context; ensuring the trustworthiness and authenticity of records; and creating links between the captured record and related ones. A significant portion of contextual information is captured through metadata, emphasizing the importance of recording a record's context as close to the event it documents as possible.

AIIM adds to these purposes by highlighting additional core reasons for capturing documents to support business goals and objectives. This includes enabling innovation by centralizing access to information, enriching customer, and system-user experiences, and minimizing risk and protecting data assets. Centralization of access often results from most capture approaches, allowing personnel to know that the version they have is correct, current, and approved. The capture process also supports efficient customer service, enabling quick responses to queries through self-service websites, portals, or mobile apps.

In practical IG best practices, making the capture process easy for all staff is crucial to reduce the risk of information and records not being captured. Automation and integration of the capturing process into normal business workflows are encouraged, along with providing clear instructions and support. It is essential for staff to know where information must be captured and to avoid keeping business records on personal drives. Digitizing physical records is recommended, considering factors such as the deterioration of physical records over time and the benefits of scanning incoming correspondence.

Data mapping plays a pivotal role in informing how data is stored, moved, searched, and accessed within an enterprise, carrying significant implications for operations, governance, data privacy, and organizational intelligence. A comprehensive data map should provide insights into the status of systems, their functions, strategic or tactical relevance, location, and interoperability levels. The governance and information security management principle of confidentiality, integrity, and availability (CIA) is closely tied to data mapping, emphasizing the need to designate data by sensitivity, prevent unauthorized modifications, and ensure appropriate data availability.

In the context of privacy compliance, effective data mapping proves crucial for identifying and tracking personal data, especially for cross-border transfers and responding to data subject access requests. Challenges in building and maintaining accurate data maps are prevalent, particularly for organizations such as libraries managing large volumes of diverse data. Constant changes in data systems and sources make manual approaches laborious and prone to inaccuracies, impacting data life-cycle management. A poor data map hampers an organization's ability to optimize search and analysis, essential for extracting organizational intelligence.

Data mapping begins with collaboration among key stakeholders and SMEs to inventory and identify key data assets. Technological advancements facilitate automated aspects of the mapping process, but the complexity of off-grid or third-party systems requires thorough validation and testing. A quality data map aids in identifying areas of improvement during the data life cycle, streamlining processes for greater efficiency. Furthermore, a well-established data map positions the enterprise for advancements in data classification, enabling categorization based on sensitivity, file type, or taxonomies for various use cases. Implementing a proactive data classification program offers benefits such as consolidation, improved analytics, and efficient data destruction. Depending on factors such as data architecture and scale, classification can be implemented manually, automatically, or through hybrid approaches, each with its own set of advantages and challenges. Establishing consistent rules, understanding platform limitations, and regular auditing contribute to the success and scalability of a strategic data classification program.

Incident Management

Incident management focuses on identifying and minimizing the impact of unanticipated events that may significantly disrupt operations and aims to restore functionality promptly. The incident management life cycle comprises five stages: planning, detection, containment, postmortem, and closure. Planning involves building an incident response team (IRT) alongside policies, training, checklists, and a communication plan. The detection phase defines incident priorities and types, utilizing monitoring tools for prevention, detection, and notifications. The containment phase tactically executes the planning and detection phases, documenting the incident's nature and initiating recovery procedures. The postmortem phase is a well-documented lessons-learned exercise, covering incident details, IRT execution, and prevention measures submitted to senior management for closure.

An impact or root cause analysis precisely outlines the incident's why, where, and when, advising on a solution and preventing recurrence. Collaboration among technical stakeholders is essential for a comprehensive understanding, considering cross-impacts on organizations, systems, or individuals. Given legal exposure potential, meticulous analysis, documentation, and guidance from legal, compliance, and senior management are crucial.

The response requires a proper communication plan to inform affected parties, particularly crucial in large organizations. Senior management may need to report material issues to executive management or the parent institution's General Counsel's office, possibly facing regulators if temporarily out of compliance. The remediation plan, reviewed and approved by management, prioritizes responses amid competing priorities. Incidents encompass various events, from physical system failures to security breaches and data spoliation.

Incident management naturally transitions to change management, involving a documented change request detailing reasons, solutions, testing, validation, and senior/executive management authorization. Specific and well-documented changes are crucial. Management may deny or propose modifications, subject to the same testing and validation life cycle before approval and implementation. A proper backout plan should accompany changes, preparing operations to restore systems to operational points. Postimplementation, changes require careful monitoring, with periodic status reporting to management based on criticality.

Digitization Practices

Before embarking on any digitization process, organizations should conduct a meticulous assessment of relevant considerations and priorities. Practically, this means a comprehensive internal policy framework becomes paramount, governed by fundamental principles that ensure the usability, integrity, authenticity, and legal defensibility of digitized records. This policy should address various aspects, including the appropriate criteria for document selection, allocation of roles and responsibilities across different departments, and strategies for managing risks associated with digitization.

In addition to this assessment, organizations must assess the risks associated with the destruction of source records, the cost implications of digitization versus maintenance, and the risks involved in not digitizing. These evaluations inform strategic planning, ensuring that digitization projects are not only successful but also that the resulting records are preserved appropriately.

The digitization policy framework should also encompass considerations related to format and indexing, emphasizing adherence to business needs and legal requirements. Specific attention is given to archival records, with guidelines recommending consultation with parent institutions or government entities for official guidelines. The framework must also detail the types of digitization, such as page images, full text, or encoded text, depending on the specific needs and access requirements. Metadata, both bibliographic and biographic, plays a crucial role in ensuring the accessibility, reliability, and proper management of digitized records.

Finally, organizations must ensure that they generate and maintain high-quality digitized images. Depending on the condition and format of source records, varying levels of preparation may be required. Quality assurance processes are integral to the digitization workflow, involving rigorous checks at different stages, such as image capture, indexing, and transfer of images. The documentation of quality assurance activities, including certifications for batches of digitized images, ensures defensibility and authenticity.

Once this process is finished, the next stage typically involves ensuring that digitized documents are properly classified and integrated into the organization's Electronic Document and Records Management System (EDRMS). This process involves activities such as assigning file numbers and applying retention and disposition information for all record formats. The fundamental principle guiding this integration is that the content of a record, not its format, determines essential attributes such as retention and disposition periods, sensitivity levels, and access permissions. Consequently, digitized versions must faithfully mirror the characteristics of their source records.

In cases where derivative copies are generated alongside the official version of the record, it becomes imperative to clearly identify them as such in the file title using standardized naming conventions. This practice ensures clarity and transparency regarding the authenticity and status of each record, preventing any ambiguity in the file management process.

Security considerations play a paramount role throughout the digitization journey. Institutions are advised to plan meticulously for both the physical security of records and the protection of information during the digitization process. Special attention should be given to records containing protected or classified information, with metadata of digitized records appropriately reflecting their sensitivity. Access restrictions applied to the source record should be seamlessly transferred to the digitized image. If source records undergo destruction, the process should align with their security level, ensuring a consistent approach to safeguarding sensitive information.

Efficient data transfer procedures are critical, particularly when departments or business units engage in the transfer of source documents and digitized files. Maintaining the security and authenticity of records during transfer is paramount. Establishing well-defined procedures, including the use of fixity information such as checksums, helps prevent any unauthorized alterations to digitized files during the transfer process.

Storage and preservation are vital components of the overall digitization strategy. Active records must find a home in a designated corporate repository that meets comprehensive requirements for records management across their entire life cycle. For digitized records placed in dormant storage, the chosen storage solution should possess robust search and access capabilities, ensure long-term management of records, preserve their authenticity, and remain responsive to regulatory and litigation requests. Departments or business units should plan for ongoing storage needs and develop a schedule for the migration and/or conversion of digital records, adapting to evolving technological landscapes.

Perhaps, the most critical ISO standard related to digitization is ISO/TR 21946:2018, which offers a series of comprehensive guidelines tailored for organizations engaged in appraisal processes, particularly in the realm of records management and digitization. Its primary focus is to provide a structured framework for the identification of records based on diverse criteria such as business value, legal requirements, and other relevant factors. In addition, the standard offers methodologies for evaluating the significance of these identified records, allowing organizations to measure their administrative, legal, financial, historical, or research value. Finally, helps organizations to reach thoughtful decisions for determining the most suitable retention and disposal schedules for digitized records, and aligning these decisions with applicable laws, including privacy regulations.

This standard emphasizes the importance of stakeholder engagement, ensuring that voices from records creators, researchers, users, and managers are considered during the decision-making process of which records to digitize. Consistency with records management policies is another focal point, preventing unnecessary confusion and ensuring that the appraisal process aligns seamlessly with established organizational procedures.

The guidelines of the National Data Stewardship Alliance (NDSA) complement ISO/TR 21946:2018 by presenting a structured framework consisting of four distinct levels to assess an organization's digital preservation practices. These levels progress from establishing fundamental policies and procedures to advanced strategies for actively managing and mitigating risks to digital content. This structured approach guides institutions to evaluate their current practices, identify areas for improvement, and communicate their commitment to best practices in digital preservation effectively.

Organizational Continuity

Successful organizational continuity planning, and preparedness is measured by an organization's ability to maintain or restore business-as-usual operations during a major disruption. That includes resiliency for virtually any type of natural or unnatural disaster that could impact operations, including branch offices, data centers, systems, third-party systems, or infrastructure on which the organization relies for critical functions.

The adoption of remote technology during the COVID pandemic is an example of a process and technology adjustment, which more or less maintained most business-as-usual operations in an efficient, cost-effective manner. A more critical and challenging example would be a document management or archiving system crashing, or actually being destroyed, which would suddenly make data unavailable to the organization, regulators, and various stakeholders.

An enterprise's organizational continuity model must first establish its strategic objectives. That starts with alignment across the organization as well as identifying and interviewing key stakeholders such as managers, employees, teams, and third parties. Roles must be understood and established along with any required training or individual action plans.

For example, where members of the team would physically locate if their regular location became inaccessible. Owing to the potential complications, many organizations maintain a formal organizational continuity management function, which includes a manager to coordinate activities and manage communications, and a team of organizational continuity specialists to support those efforts.

The first priority in applying organizational continuity standards is to conduct and document a thorough risk assessment. This will include identifying, classifying, and quantifying the level of risk to locations, technology, data, utilities, inventory, or third parties. Each will then require an understanding as to whether or to what degree they are mission-critical and what constitutes acceptable levels of reduced output or production. Next, the organizational continuity team should collaborate with key organizational units to design, document, and implement a resiliency plan, which accounts for those acceptable levels of reduced service during the recovery, as well as the underlying systems and applications that support them. The plan must outline specific and appropriate recovery time objectives (RTO) or the length of time it takes to restore organizational processes, and recovery point objectives (RPO), or the amount of data that can be lost during the recovery phase.

The resiliency plan must also include a detailed communication plan, which identifies and enumerates all of the entity's system's key stakeholders and who must be reported to and updated on a regular basis during a disruption, internally and externally. The details of the reporting will naturally vary depending on the roles of the recipients. A regulator or researcher is highly unlikely to see the same unexpurgated information as senior management. The communication plan will often include legal, compliance, public relations, and other important internal stakeholder departments.

In addition to identifying areas of vulnerability, a resiliency plan must consider the specific data and information that may be compromised, not just temporarily but permanently. Thus, it is critical to establish a data map, which includes critical or sensitive information, along with appropriate backup and recovery so that data can be secured and recovered. That data might include sensitive financial records, intellectual property, or customer information, and hard copy data as well as digital. Finally, testing and validation must be coordinated with audit departments or groups and conducted on a regular periodic basis to ensure that planning and readiness work under disaster conditions. For example, if a data site were actually destroyed, and all systems were shut down, a failover should kick in so that all key data is recoverable and available to the organization remotely from an alternative, mirrored data center.

Information Governance by Design

IG by Design is a proactive approach that integrates IG principles into the design, development, and implementation of information systems and processes. This approach emphasizes considering IG requirements from the early stages of system design, ensuring the embedding of data privacy, security, compliance, and records management considerations into the functionality of information systems.

The following graphic provides a summary of the core concepts of IG by Design:

What are the Principles of IG by Design?

This concept is closely related to Privacy by Design, a framework introduced by Dr. Ann Cavoukian in the 1990s. Privacy by Design encourages organizations to embed privacy-conscious practices into the design and operation of their systems, ensuring privacy considerations throughout the entire information life cycle.

As illustrated by the following graphic, IG by Design should include a robust and multifaceted approach to problem solving:

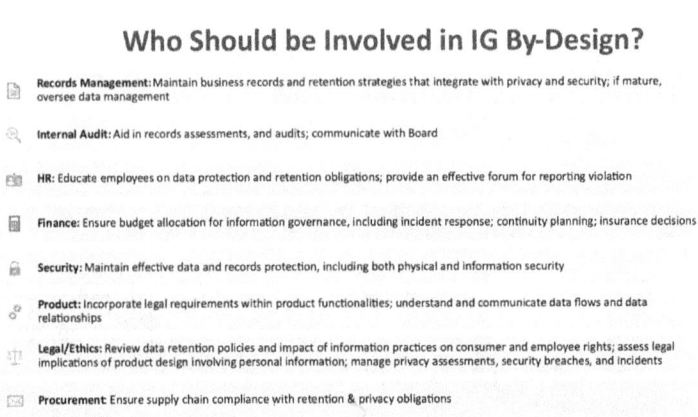

Who Should be Involved in IG By-Design?

Records Management: Maintain business records and retention strategies that integrate with privacy and security; if mature, oversee data management

Internal Audit: Aid in records assessments, and audits; communicate with Board

HR: Educate employees on data protection and retention obligations; provide an effective forum for reporting violation

Finance: Ensure budget allocation for information governance, including incident response; continuity planning; insurance decisions

Security: Maintain effective data and records protection, including both physical and information security

Product: Incorporate legal requirements within product functionalities; understand and communicate data flows and data relationships

Legal/Ethics: Review data retention policies and impact of information practices on consumer and employee rights; assess legal implications of product design involving personal information; manage privacy assessments, security breaches, and incidents

Procurement: Ensure supply chain compliance with retention & privacy obligations

Finally, organizations exhibiting good IG by Design practices tend to exhibit many of the same characteristics including:

What does good Information Governance by Design Look Like?

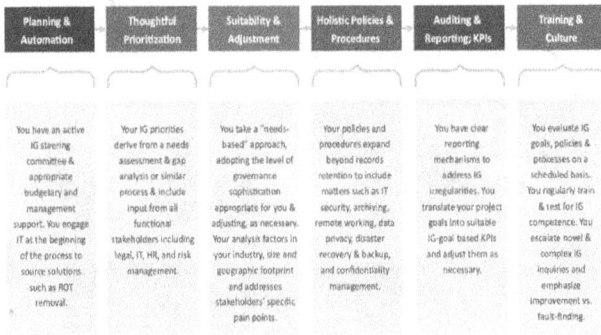

Planning & Automation	Thoughtful Prioritization	Suitability & Adjustment	Holistic Policies & Procedures	Auditing & Reporting; KPIs	Training & Culture
You have an active IG steering committee & appropriate budgetary and management support. You engage IT at the beginning of the process to source solutions such as ROT removal.	Your IG priorities derive from a needs assessment & gap analysis or similar process & include input from all functional stakeholders including legal, IT, HR, and risk management.	You take a "needs-based" approach, adopting the level of governance sophistication appropriate for you & adjusting, as necessary. Your analysis factors in your industry, size and geographic footprint and addresses stakeholders' specific pain points.	Your policies and procedures expand beyond records retention to include matters such as IT security, archiving, remote working, data privacy, disaster recovery & backup, and confidentiality management.	You have clear reporting mechanisms to address IG irregularities. You translate your project goals into suitable IG-goal based KPIs and adjust them as necessary.	You evaluate IG goals, policies & policies on a scheduled basis. You regularly train & test for IG competence. You escalate novel & complex IG inquiries and emphasize improvement vs. fault-finding.

IG by Design concepts are further enshrined in various ISO standards. For example, ISO/TR 26122:2008 offers nonbinding guidelines to promote the integration of record-keeping requirements into an organization's business processes. Emphasizing early consideration of record-keeping elements such as metadata, retention schedules, and other relevant requirements ensures effective incorporation into workflows and systems. Integration of this standard closely aligns with IG by design. This proactive approach involves incorporating IG principles, including recordkeeping, into the design and implementation of information systems. And, by integrating these requirements early on, organizations can ensure greater consistency, accuracy, and transparency in their record-keeping practices, aligning with industry standards and minimizing risks associated with inadequate recordkeeping.

Another related standard ISO 30301:201, focuses on important project planning elements such as policy development, accountability, records classification, retention, access controls, and system performance monitoring. Adherence to this standard enables organizations to plan and establish a robust and compliant records management system based on IG best practices.

ISO 30302 provides further guidelines for organizations seeking to address records management requirements before implementing a system. Recommendations include developing a project plan, involving key stakeholders, conducting a risk assessment, allocating sufficient resources, providing training, and ensuring continual improvement through regular audits and evaluations.

Critical ISO Standards and Practices[20]

Recordkeeping

ISO 15489, established in 2001 and revised in 2016, stands as the initial global standard for records management. Adopted in over 50 countries and translated into 15 languages, its fundamental premise lies in considering records not just as documents but as evidence of business activities and valuable information assets. The standard plays a pivotal role in guiding organizations toward creating effective records management policies.

The standard is built upon several core principles that contribute to its comprehensive approach. First, it emphasizes broad applicability, extending its reach beyond records to include records systems and metadata. This ensures a holistic view of records management, covering principles such as stated policies, assigned responsibilities, recurring analysis of business context, records controls, and processes for creating, capturing, and managing records.

The following chart describes how IG best practices can help organizations to comply with ISO15489 requirements:

How IG Best Practices Promote ISO 15489* Compliance

Principle	Standard	IG Solution
Provenance	Produce & maintain records in the course of business and ensure trustworthiness & reliability	Institute records quality controls, policies & procedures and use of uniform taxonomies
Integrity	Protect records from unauthorized alteration, destruction, or loss	Institute & maintain a comprehensive disaster recovery plan, ensure backup, & data labelling & access controls
Authenticity	Ensure that records are authentic, meaning that they are what they purport to be, and have been created and maintained in accordance with established procedures	Create uniform taxonomies, access & change controls & document tracking mechanisms; eliminate redundant, obsolete & trivial (ROT) data
Confidentiality	Protect records from unauthorized access & disclosure	Ensure compliance with NDAs (both internal employee agreements & external), institute access controls & review work-from-home policy compliance
Availability	Ensure that records are available for use when needed	Eliminate ROT data, institute defensible email policies that correlate with legal retention requirements, use uniform taxonomies and central records location control
Compliance	Make sure that records management practices accord with applicable laws including both comprehensive & sector-specific privacy laws and retention requirements as set forth in defensible retention schedule	Create and periodically review defensible retention schedule, ensure privacy compliance including defensible systems, engage in IG maintenance, training & policy review on continual basis

Critical elements of ISO 15489 include obligations to establish a records management policy, assign responsibilities, ensure necessary resources, and communicate the importance of records management. Planning involves developing a records management plan, identifying records for management, and creating ISO-compliant procedures. Support requires providing necessary resources, delivering training programs, and integrating records management into organizational processes.

In the operational phase, organizations must systematically create and capture records, classify and index them for easy retrieval, ensure integrity and authenticity, manage access, and oversee storage, retrieval, and timely disposal. Performance evaluation becomes crucial, with monitoring, internal audits, identification of areas for improvement, and reporting on program performance to management. Recognizing the challenges, the standard acknowledges that merely having standards is insufficient for achieving IG goals. It stresses the need for effective integration into broader information and records management policies, requiring collaboration across diverse disciplines, including IT, risk management, HR, legal, and information management.

Finally, the concept of improvement is embedded throughout the standard, urging organizations to identify opportunities for enhancement, implement corrective actions, and continuously refine the records management program.

ISO 15489 is complemented by related standards such as ISO/TR 21965:2019, ISO 22428, ISO 16175, ISO 23081, ISO 14721 (OAIS), and ISO 16363, each addressing specific aspects of records management, preservation, and digital repositories.

Digital Conversion and Migration

ISO 13008:2022 offers a comprehensive guide for the conversion of records between different formats and the migration of records from one hardware or software configuration to another. This standard is crucial for understanding records management requirements, organizational frameworks, technology planning, and the implementation of controls in the conversion and migration processes. It outlines specific steps, components, and methodologies, covering vital aspects such as workflow, testing, version control, and validation.

In the realm of digital preservation, the standard underscores the significance of conversion and migration in shaping an organization's preservation strategy. To ensure the authenticity, reliability, integrity, and usability of digital records, effective management of these processes is imperative. ISO 13008:2022 provides clarity on program components, planning considerations, and records management requirements essential for successful digital record conversion and migration. The standard emphasizes the preservation of record integrity and compliance with relevant legal and regulatory requirements.

Key elements of this standard include guidelines for the conversion and migration of digital records, encompassing metadata and contextual information, ensuring their long-term preservation and accessibility. It stresses principles such as maintaining authenticity, integrity, reliability, and usability, along with the need for comprehensive planning and scoping of projects. The standard recommends careful selection and evaluation of conversion and migration tools, emphasizing the importance of preserving and migrating metadata. Additionally, it highlights quality control measures, thorough documentation, and reporting as essential components for successfully managing digital records.

The principles of record integrity, authenticity, reliability, and usability apply to both ad hoc and ongoing conversion or migration programs. The standard advocates for future planning, integrating additional conversion and migration endeavors into the requirements for EDRMS to ensure sustained, long-term preservation.

ISO/TR 13028:2012—Information and documentation—Implementation guidelines for digitization of records begins by outlining potential benefits and risks associated with digitization, applicable across various business scenarios. It emphasizes advantages such as increased accessibility, networked access, integration with business systems, structured workflows, resource reusability, consistent classification, disaster recovery integration, reduced storage space, and heightened organizational productivity through streamlined workflows.

However, the standard also highlights risks, including long-term costs, technology and standards influence, legislative constraints, appropriateness of destroying nondigital records, and legal requirements for record retention. To mitigate these risks, organizations are advised to carefully devise digitization strategies aligned with legislative, regulatory, and IG requirements. This involves implementing processes for long-term digital record preservation, formulating policies for the authenticity and reliability of digital images, and providing staff training to manage associated benefits and risks effectively.

In the context of organizations undergoing digital transformation, the standard introduces the concept of master copies and derivative versions for managing digitized records. Master copies, the original digital files, are stored securely and used to produce derivative copies for organizational use. Organizations need to consider the legislative framework when deciding on creating master and derivative copies, especially for records serving as evidence of business actions.

The standard emphasizes the importance of planning, scoping, and documenting all digitization processes in organizations undergoing digital transformation. Documentation should include identification of business drivers, objectives, constraints, purpose, and expected uses of digitized records, along with technical standards, equipment, resources, quality control processes, and strategies for ongoing management.

Clause 6 of the standard establishes best practices for digitizing records, covering planning, material selection, preparation, digitization, quality control, preservation, and access and dissemination. Planning involves setting objectives, identifying project scope, resources, risks, and timelines. Material selection requires determining materials for digitization based on value, condition, and copyright status. Preparation involves physical preparation, metadata creation, and material description. Digitization demands adherence to industry best practices using high-quality scanners or cameras. Quality control is essential to verify that images meet standards and are error-free. Preservation involves selecting appropriate file formats, backup procedures, and creating multiple copies. Access and dissemination necessitate making digital materials accessible through various channels while respecting copyright laws.

Additionally, the standard sets essential criteria for selecting technical standards, urging the incorporation of the highest quality specifications, open-source or open standards, widespread support, readability, and the creation of master copies meeting the highest technical standards.

Archiving

ISO TC46/SC11, established in 1998, plays a pivotal role in the international standardization of archives management. This initiative was driven by the necessity to foster a common understanding of record-keeping globally, synthesizing developments from various initiatives worldwide. The core elements of this standard encompass rules for maintaining metadata, standards for digital repositories, preservation of digital records, records on the web, management, and business perspectives, e-Government, e-Business, and the intersection of data as records or records as data.

Recognizing the growing need for globalization, the establishment of common standards becomes imperative for effective communication and mutual understanding among people and organizations. Common standards facilitate trust, management, and maintenance of messages and vital information, with good recordkeeping being an essential component of this process. The standardization efforts of ISO/TC 46/SC11 are crucial for ensuring that common standards are in place to support the management and understanding of records on a global scale.

Within ISO/TC 46/SC11, the ISO 23081 series comprises three significant pieces of work related to metadata for records. Notably, ISO 23081-1 establishes a principles-based standard linking metadata requirements to the foundational ISO 15489-1. ISO 23081-2:2009 provides a practical approach to implementation, offering insights into implementation options, metadata management, and a conceptual model for defining metadata elements for records. On the other hand, ISO/TR 23081-3:2011 furnishes a self-assessment checklist in Excel format, enabling implementers to evaluate their metadata schema against the standard's requirements.

The primary objective of these standards is to define the metadata necessary to demonstrate that an electronic object has been managed as a record throughout its physical existence. This ensures that the digital object can be interpreted in the context of business operations and the individuals involved. Furthermore, it supports assertions about the characteristics of integrity, authenticity, reliability, and usability. These standards provide crucial guidance for designing technical specifications applicable in specific technological applications, supporting assertions of authenticity and reliability in various business and records environments.

Additionally, pertinent sources related to metadata include ISO 2709, which specifies an exchange format for bibliographic metadata produced by libraries and is widely supported by libraries producing machine-readable catalogs. ISO 23950, the information retrieval standard, facilitates seamless searching between bibliographic databases and is widely supported by integrated library systems, enabling the copying of catalog bibliographic records between libraries. These standards contribute to the interoperability and exchange of bibliographic information, enhancing the efficiency of library systems and supporting effective information retrieval practices.

Another critical standard is ISO 17068, which establishes a series of criteria for the suitability of digital systems generating digital records and emphasizes the need to secure these records for authenticity and legal recognition during their retention period. However, the proliferation of digital records has posed a challenge for organizations striving to ensure the authenticity of these records for crucial business activities over an extended period. To address this challenge, trusted third-party repositories (TTPRs) have emerged, providing services to verify the authenticity, reliability, and integrity of digital records according to retention schedules and policies.

ISO 14641-1 further outlines criteria for evaluating the trustworthiness of a TTPR, covering aspects such as physical security, obligations to maintain record security, standards for hardware and software systems, user authentication, authorization, record integrity, and accessibility. Compliant TTPRs must also have disaster recovery policies, backup procedures, and mechanisms for monitoring and auditing to ensure ongoing compliance. And, ISO/TR 21972:2019 offers additional guidelines for implementing trustworthy digital repositories, addressing organizational infrastructure, digital object management, technologies, technical infrastructure, and security measures.

In addition to these standards, TTPR providers often adhere to the standards set by the open archival information system (OAIS). OAIS, a widely adopted reference model, defines best practices for creating, managing, and preserving digital archives. The OAIS model specifies functional requirements and responsibilities for a compliant TTPR system, including metadata standards for descriptive, administrative, and preservation metadata. It recommends the use of open, nonproprietary file formats, guidelines for long-term storage and preservation, and access controls to protect digital objects' CIA. Overall, these standards play a crucial role in ensuring the trustworthy management and preservation of digital records for all types of organizations.

Privacy

Why Is Privacy a Business Issue?[21]

The significance of privacy extends beyond personal considerations; it is a critical business issue. Strong privacy practices form an integral part of corporate governance and accountability, reflecting a key business imperative in today's landscape. As business systems and processes grow in complexity, organizations find themselves accumulating vast amounts of personal information. This increasing complexity exposes personal information to various risks, including loss, misuse, unauthorized access, and disclosure, raising concerns for organizations, governments, and the public at large.

Organizations are striving to strike a delicate balance between the proper collection and use of customers' personal information, navigating the challenge of managing the growing cache of data. Governments are concurrently working to protect the public interest while managing the personal information gathered from citizens. Consumers express heightened concerns about the security of their personal information, feeling a loss of control over it. Identity theft and inappropriate access to sensitive data, particularly financial and medical records, and information about children, are significant worries.

In this landscape, individuals demand that organizations respect their privacy and safeguard their personal information. There is a shift in sentiment, with individuals no longer willing to overlook an organization's failure to protect their privacy. Consequently, businesses must proactively address privacy as a risk management issue, considering the following specific risks associated with inadequate privacy policies and procedures:

- Damage to the organization's reputation, brand, or business relationships.
- Legal liability and potential industry or regulatory sanctions.
- Accusations of deceptive business practices.
- Erosion of customer or employee trust.
- Rejection of consent by individuals for the use of their personal information in business operations.
- Loss of business, leading to a subsequent reduction in revenue and market share.
- Disruption of international business operations.
- Liability resulting from identity theft.

These risks underscore the necessity for businesses to prioritize robust privacy measures. Failing to do so not only jeopardizes individual privacy but also poses considerable threats to the organization's overall well-being, including its reputation, legal standing, and market position. Therefore, addressing privacy concerns effectively is not just a matter of compliance but a strategic imperative for sustainable and responsible business practices.

Generally Accepted Privacy Principles (GAPP)[22]

To create a structural understanding of these privacy risk factors, in 2009, the GAPP framework was developed via a joint consultative effort between the Canadian Institute of Chartered Accountants (CICA) and the American Institute of Certified Public Accountants (AICPA) through the AICPA/CICA Privacy Task Force. These principles can be summarized as follows:

- Management: The entity defines, documents, communicates, and assigns accountability for its privacy policies and procedures.
- Notice: The entity provides notice about its privacy policies and procedures, identifying the purposes for which personal information is collected, used, retained, and disclosed.
- Choice and Consent: The entity describes the choices available to the individual and obtains implicit or explicit consent regarding the collection, use, and disclosure of personal information.
- Collection: The entity collects personal information only for the purposes identified in the notice.
- Use, Retention, and Disposal: The entity limits the use of personal information to the purposes identified in the notice and for which the individual has provided implicit or explicit consent. The entity retains personal information only as long as necessary or as required by law and appropriately disposes of such information.
- Access: The entity provides individuals with access to their personal information for review and update.
- Disclosure to Third Parties: The entity discloses personal information to third parties only for the purposes identified in the notice and with the implicit or explicit consent of the individual.

- Security for Privacy: The entity protects personal information against unauthorized access, both physical and logical.
- Quality: The entity maintains accurate, complete, and relevant personal information for the purposes identified in the notice.
- Monitoring and Enforcement: The entity monitors compliance with its privacy policies and procedures and has procedures to address privacy-related complaints and disputes.

For each of these principles, specific criteria have been specified to guide the development and evaluation of an entity's privacy policies, communications, procedures, and controls. Privacy policies convey management's intent, objectives, requirements, responsibilities, and standards. Communications refer to the organization's communication to individuals, internal personnel, and third parties about its privacy notice and commitments, along with other relevant information. Procedures and controls encompass the actions the organization takes to achieve the specified criteria.

GAPP serves various purposes for organizations, including:

- Designing, implementing, and communicating privacy policies.
- Establishing and managing privacy programs.
- Monitoring and auditing privacy programs.
- Measuring performance and benchmarking.
- Establishing and managing a privacy program involves activities such as:
  - Strategizing: Performing privacy strategic and business planning.
  - Diagnosing: Conducting privacy gap and risk analyses.
  - Implementing: Developing, documenting, introducing, and institutionalizing the program's action plan, including establishing controls over personal information.
  - Sustaining and Managing: Monitoring activities of a privacy program.
  - Auditing: Internal or external auditors evaluating the organization's privacy program.

Data Protection and Privacy Policies[23]

Data Protection Policy Versus Privacy Policy

A data protection policy sometimes referred to as a "data protection statement," is primarily an internal document for organizational compliance with data protection legislation. Certain laws such as the EU GDPR require organizations to provide privacy notices to individuals during personal data processing.

A data protection policy serves as an internal declaration outlining how your organization safeguards the personal data it processes. With current data protection legislation, nearly all organizations are mandated to have a data protection policy, subject to periodic reviews.

A well-crafted policy clarifies how your organization intends to manage specific issues, with data being the focal point in this context. The policy elucidates how your organization aligns with the principles set forth in the GDPR, which is principle-based rather than rule-based, allowing flexibility in compliance approaches.

Following is a summary of the general terms that should be included in a typical privacy policy:

- Responsibility: The policy should designate the individual (e.g., the data protection officer or DPO) within the organization responsible for data protection.
- Review: The policy should specify how often it is reviewed and should include the date of the most recent review.
- Data Definition: The policy should clearly and completely define the scope of data that it covers including the relevant laws governing that data.
- Breach Reporting: The policy should outline the organization's procedures in the event of a data breach.
- Data Audit: The policy should detail how the organization monitors and audits stored data.
- Disclosure: The policy should clarify the process when individuals request access to their data.
- Justification: The policy should state the lawful reason for why you are collecting the data and should provide contact or tracking mechanisms for consent.

- Collection Control: The policy should outline how you are seeking to ensure that you collect the minimum amount of data necessary to process it lawfully.
- Data Review: The policy should explain how you periodically review the data and ensure its accuracy.
- Retention Policy: The policy should specify what data will be retained, for how long, and the rationale as well as your data removal procedures and timelines.
- Security Measures: The policy should highlight the security measures that you have in place to protect data within your organization's systems, including backup frequency and duration.

Privacy Programs[24]

Organizations seeking to develop and improve their privacy law compliance should employ a comprehensive approach to data privacy compliance programs that integrates and embodies certain structures. These programs should include (without limitation):

- Data mapping guidelines including mandates to:
  - Conduct data mapping exercises to keep track of products, services, and systems.
  - Ensure that all data mapping exercises address privacy law compliance, processing methods, storage locations, usage details, and retention periods.
  - Implement automated data inventories for real-time tracking and compliance.
- Understanding data privacy obligations including provisions to enable:
  - The development of a documented, defensible, and repeatable data privacy model.
  - The movement beyond basic compliance to view privacy as a business enabler.
  - The adoption of privacy-by-design principles, considering data protection controls from the outset.
  - The development of robust and meaningful privacy training programs.

o The encouragement of staff in all business units to understand and assess data necessity, access, storage, and security measures.

- The creation of an effective steering committee with representatives from privacy-impacted business units, including IT, legal, HR, marketing, and other important units.

- Ensuring effective audit processes including the appointment of an internal auditor who is active in the organization's privacy steering committees and ensuring that there is regular communication between internal audit, privacy program management, and business stakeholders.

- Establishing and cultivating broad board and senior leadership support for privacy and data protection compliance including resources and effectively communicating the ramifications of noncompliance.

- Ensuring defined periodic and role-specific data privacy training and encouraging personnel engagement.

- Actively promoting cultural awareness of privacy as a business advantage, not just a regulatory obligation.

In summary, a holistic approach to data privacy, including strategic mapping, robust compliance understanding, clear ownership, effective internal audit involvement, leadership support, cost considerations, and targeted training, is critical for any organization seeking to achieve an effective and meaningful data privacy compliance program.

Privacy Law Compliance

Privacy law compliance is an essential component of IG. These laws protect the personal information of customers, clients, employees, and supply chain members. Organizations of all types also collect and maintain sensitive information including, for example, social security numbers, personal health information, and details, subject to additional legal protections. Adhering strictly to privacy laws helps organizations ensure that this information remains confidential and is not subject to unauthorized access, use, or disclosure.

The United States

Important U.S. laws include:

The U.S. Privacy Act of 1974

The Privacy Act of 1974 regulates how government agencies that receive federal funding collect, use, and disclose personal information. The Act impacts organizations that receive federal funding and includes various sectors such as public, academic, public sector, and research organizations.

Most importantly, the Act provides specific limitations and instructions on how organizations can collect, use, and disclose personal information. Personal information is defined in the function as any information that identifies an individual, including their name, address, social security number, and other identifiable details.

Organizations covered by the Act must:

- Inform individuals when their personal information is collected and how it will be used.
- Keep accurate records and adequately safeguard the personal information they collect.
- Allow individuals to access and amend their personal information.
- Obtain individuals' consent before disclosing their personal information to third parties.
- Provide individuals with the ability to file a complaint if their privacy rights are violated.

The provisions of this Act are generally consistent with the general principles of most comprehensive privacy laws. While these laws can differ in substance, the primary elements of these laws are as follows:

Gramm-Leach-Bliley Act (GLBA)[25]

The GLBA is a federal law enacted in 1999 and is also known as the Financial Services Modernization Act of 1999. Privacy professionals often focus on Title V, Subtitle A of the GLBA (15 U.S.C. 6801 et seq), which addresses the crucial topics of "Privacy" and the "Disclosure of Nonpublic Personal Information." Generally, GLBA applies to financial institutions, brokers, dealers, and individuals providing insurance services, including investment companies and investment advisors.

Following is a summary of these critical principles:

- Protection of Nonpublic Personal Information (Section 501): Each financial institution must continually respect the privacy of its customers and safeguard the security and confidentiality of their nonpublic personal information.
- Disclosures of Personal Information (Section 502): Financial institutions must share their privacy policies and practices with consumers in writing. If a financial institution intends to share consumer nonpublic personal information with nonaffiliated third parties, consumers must be given the right to opt out of such information sharing.

Fair Credit Reporting Act (FCRA)

The federal FCRA safeguards the accuracy, fairness, and privacy of consumer information held by reporting agencies. FCRA outlines crucial rights for consumers regarding the accuracy and privacy of information held by reporting agencies. Individuals have the right to be informed if adverse actions are taken based on their credit report, and they can access their files with free disclosure in specific circumstances. Requesting a credit score is possible, but usually involves a fee. Consumers can dispute inaccurate information, and reporting agencies must correct or delete such data.[26]

Negative information generally cannot be reported after seven years (10 for bankruptcies). Access to files is limited to entities with a valid need, and consent is required for employer reports. Individuals can limit prescreened offers and impose a security freeze on their credit reports. Damages may be sought for FCRA violations, and additional rights exist for identity theft victims and military personnel. States may enforce the FCRA, and more rights may be available under state laws.[27]

A closely related rule, the Red Flags Rule was issued in 2007 under Section 114 of the Fair and Accurate Credit Transaction Act of 2003 (FACT Act), which amended the FCRA.[28]

The Red Flags Rule applies to "financial institutions" and certain "creditors." Financial institutions include banks, savings associations, credit unions, and entities holding transaction accounts. Creditors, determined by conduct, are businesses that regularly defer payment, grant credit, or participate in credit-related decisions.

The Red Flags Rule provides guidelines for the development, implementation, and administration of an identity theft prevention program. This program is crucial in addressing the threat of identity theft and must include four fundamental elements to create an effective framework:

- Identification of Red Flags: A comprehensive program must incorporate reasonable policies and procedures to identify red flags associated with identity theft during day-to-day operations. Red Flags are defined as suspicious patterns, practices, or specific activities indicating the potential occurrence of identity theft. For instance, a suspicious or fake ID presented by a customer during an account-opening process serves as a red flag.
- Detection of Red Flags: The program should be designed to detect the red flags that have been identified. For example, if fake IDs are recognized as red flags, procedures must be in place to identify possible forged, fake, or altered identifications.
- Response to Red Flags: Clear and appropriate actions must be outlined within the program for when red flags are detected. It is essential to have a well-defined response plan to mitigate the risk of identity theft promptly.
- Program Maintenance: The program must specify how it will stay current to address evolving threats. Regular updates are necessary to reflect new red flags and emerging risks related to identity theft.

However, merely documenting the program on paper is insufficient. The Red Flags Rule emphasizes the integration of the program into the daily operations of the business. While the rule provides flexibility for businesses of different sizes and risk levels, it mandates the incorporation of the program into routine activities.

The rule highlights the importance of securing customer data to reduce identity theft risks. By implementing data security practices, businesses can make it more challenging for identity thieves to access personal information. The rule adopts a dual approach: strengthening data security practices and vigilantly monitoring red flags indicating potential fraud.

Businesses subject to the rule must verify if they have "covered accounts." Covered accounts include consumer accounts for personal, family, or household purposes involving multiple payments or transactions. Additionally, any other account with a reasonably foreseeable risk of identity theft is covered. Businesses must assess the risk associated with various types of accounts, such as business accounts accessed remotely, to determine if they fall under the second category of covered accounts.

If a business does not have covered accounts, a written program is unnecessary. However, periodic risk assessments are recommended to adapt to changes in business models, services, or structures that may lead to the acquisition of covered accounts.

Health Insurance Portability and Accountability Act (HIPAA)[29]

HIPAA's Privacy Rule, which is part of the Administrative Simplification rules under HIPAA, applies to health plans, health care clearinghouses, and health care providers transmitting electronic health information. Health plans encompass various insurance entities, including employer-sponsored group health plans, while health care providers include all entities electronically transmitting health information. Health care clearinghouses process nonstandard information into standard format and are subject to certain Privacy Rule provisions. Business associates, individuals or organizations performing functions for a covered entity involving health information, are defined and must comply with specified safeguards. Protected health information (PHI), including demographic data related to an individual's health, care provision, or payment, is covered by the Privacy Rule. Deidentified health information, exempt from restrictions, neither identifies nor reasonably allows identification of an individual.

The Privacy Rule emphasizes limiting the use or disclosure of PHI, allowing such actions only as permitted or required by the rule or with written authorization from the individual. Required disclosures include providing access to individuals and reporting to Health and Human Services (HHS) during compliance investigations.

Covered entities, under the Privacy Rule, are allowed but not obligated to use and disclose PHI without individual authorization for specific purposes or situations. These include disclosing PHI to the individual, utilizing it for treatment, payment, and health care operations, obtaining informal permission for certain uses and disclosures, addressing incidental uses or disclosures with reasonable safeguards, and engaging in public interest and benefit activities.

Covered entities can rely on professional ethics and judgment for these permissive uses and disclosures. Treatment involves managing health care, payment encompasses financial aspects, and health care operations include quality assessment and business management. Obtaining consent for these activities is optional.

Other permitted uses involve situations where the individual has an opportunity to agree or object, such as facility directories or notification purposes. Incidental use or disclosure is allowed if reasonable safeguards are in place and the information shared is minimum necessary. Public interest and benefit activities cover various scenarios, including those required by law, public health activities, victims of abuse or violence, health oversight, and judicial/administrative proceedings. Decedents, organ donation, research, serious threats to health or safety, essential government functions, and workers' compensation are also permissible without individual authorization, provided specific conditions are met, and safeguards are implemented for limited datasets.

The Privacy Rule grants covered entities the discretion to use and disclose PHI for specific purposes without individual authorization. These permissible actions encompass a range of situations. First, covered entities are allowed, but not obligated, to disclose PHI to the individual it pertains to. Furthermore, PHI can be utilized for treatment, payment, and health care operations, where treatment involves the management of health care, payment pertains to financial aspects, and health care operations include activities such as quality assessment and business management.

Importantly, obtaining consent for these activities is optional, and covered entities can rely on professional ethics and judgment.

In addition to individual disclosure and internal operations, covered entities may seek informal permission for certain uses and disclosures. They also have the flexibility to address incidental uses or disclosures, provided reasonable safeguards are in place and the shared information is limited to what is deemed necessary. This reflects a balance between the need for information sharing and ensuring privacy protection.

Covered entities can also engage in public interest and benefit activities without explicit individual authorization. These activities encompass various scenarios, including instances where disclosures are required by law, participation in public health activities, addressing victims of abuse or violence, health oversight, and involvement in judicial or administrative proceedings. In these situations, covered entities are entrusted to apply professional judgment and ethical considerations.

The Privacy Rule extends permissive use and disclosure to cover various aspects of health care and beyond. This includes scenarios involving decedents, organ donation, research, addressing serious threats to health or safety, essential government functions, and workers' compensation. However, for these actions, specific conditions must be met, and safeguards are required, especially when dealing with limited datasets to ensure privacy protection. This nuanced framework allows covered entities to navigate a spectrum of situations while upholding privacy standards and ethical considerations.

The Privacy Rule mandates that covered entities, with limited exceptions, must issue a notice outlining their privacy practices. This notice must encompass details about the usage and disclosure of PHI, the covered entity's obligations to safeguard privacy, individuals' rights, and contact information for further inquiries or complaints. Covered entities are required to adhere to the terms of their notices, and the Privacy Rule specifies distribution requirements for various types of providers and health plans.

For notice distribution, a covered health care provider with a direct treatment relationship must deliver the privacy practices notice to patients in a timely manner, whether in person, electronically, or via mail, depending on the situation. Posting the notice at service delivery sites is also obligatory, and in emergency situations, the provider must furnish the notice promptly after the emergency ends. Covered entities, whether direct treatment providers or indirect treatment providers, must supply the notice upon request and make it available electronically on relevant websites. In organized health care arrangements, joint privacy practices notices are permissible.

Health plans have specific distribution obligations to enrollees, both new and existing, and must send reminders at least once every three years. Covered health care providers are encouraged to obtain written acknowledgments from patients regarding their receipt of the privacy practices notice, except in emergencies.

The Privacy Rule affords individuals the right to access their PHI in a designated record set, with certain exceptions. Individuals can request amendments to their information, and covered entities must make reasonable efforts to disseminate approved amendments to relevant parties. Individuals also have the right to request an accounting of disclosures, with some exceptions, and can request restrictions on the use or disclosure of their PHI, which covered entities may choose to accept or deny.

For communications of PHI, individuals can request alternative means or locations, and covered entities must accommodate reasonable requests to avoid endangering the individual. The administrative requirements of the Privacy Rule emphasize flexibility and scalability to accommodate the diverse nature and size of covered entities. Covered entities must establish and implement written privacy policies and procedures, appoint privacy personnel, provide workforce training, and manage sanctions for policy violations.

The rule specifically prohibits retaliation against individuals for exercising their rights and mandates that covered entities do not require individuals to waive any right under the Privacy Rule as a condition for obtaining treatment, payment, enrollment, or benefits eligibility. The fully insured group health plan exception outlines specific administrative obligations for such plans based on their scope and nature of data handling.

The Privacy Rule under the HIPAA establishes federal requirements that take precedence over state laws that are contrary to its provisions.

"Contrary" means it is impossible for a covered entity to comply with both state and federal requirements, or that the state law is an obstacle to achieving the full purposes of HIPAA. Exceptions to federal preemption exist for state laws that offer greater privacy protections or rights, relate to reporting of specific information (e.g., disease, child abuse, birth, death, public health surveillance), or mandate health plan reporting for audits.

The determination of preemption exceptions can be made if the U.S. Department of HHS concludes, in response to a request, that the state law is necessary to prevent fraud and abuse in health care, ensure appropriate state regulation of insurance and health plans, support state reporting on health care delivery or costs, serve compelling public health, safety, or welfare needs, or primarily regulate controlled substances.

In terms of enforcement and penalties for noncompliance:

- Compliance: HHS aims for voluntary compliance and may provide technical assistance to covered entities. Compliant processes, responsibilities of covered entities to provide records, and cooperation with investigations are outlined.
- Civil Money Penalties: HHS has the authority to impose civil money penalties on covered entities for failure to comply with Privacy Rule requirements. Penalties are set at $100 per violation and may not exceed $25,000 per year for identical violations in a calendar year. There are circumstances where penalties may not be imposed, such as when violations are corrected within 30 days and were not due to willful neglect.
- Criminal Penalties: Knowingly obtaining or disclosing individually identifiable health information in violation of HIPAA can result in criminal penalties. Fines can range from $50,000 and up to one year's imprisonment. For wrongful conduct involving false pretenses, penalties increase to $100,000 and up to five years imprisonment. If the wrongful conduct involves the intent to sell, transfer, or use health information for personal gain, commercial advantage, or malicious harm, penalties can be $250,000 with up to 10 years imprisonment. Criminal enforcement is overseen by the Department of Justice.

Health Information Technology for Economic and Clinical Health Act (HITECH)[30]

The HITECH was a component of the American Recovery and Reinvestment Act of 2009, an economic stimulus package introduced during the Obama administration. The Act is considered to have played a pivotal role in promoting the meaningful use of electronic health records (EHRs) and enhancing the privacy and security provisions of HIPAA. Key aspects of the HITECH Act include its impact on business associates, the introduction of the Breach Notification Rule, and the imposition of more stringent penalties for HIPAA compliance failures.

Generally, HITECH aims to incentivize the adoption of EHRs, strengthen privacy and security regulations, and impose tougher penalties for noncompliance with HIPAA. To further this purpose, HITECH outlines five goals for the U.S. health care system:

- Improve quality, safety, and efficiency.
- Engage patients in their care.
- Increase coordination of care.
- Improve the health status of the population.
- Ensure privacy and security.

These goals are achieved through incentives for health information technology adoption, increased patient involvement, expanded health information exchanges, and enhanced privacy and security provisions.

Before HITECH, only 10 percent of hospitals had adopted EHRs. The Act addressed this by providing incentives for health care providers to transition from paper records to EHRs, fostering efficiency, care coordination, and information sharing among covered entities.

HITECH introduced tougher penalties for HIPAA violations, categorizing them based on levels of culpability. Penalties increased, with the maximum penalty per violation category reaching $2,067,813 as of December 2023. Also, in 2018, the Department for HHS published a request for information, leading to an amendment to HITECH in 2021 (HIPAA Safe Harbor law). This amendment gives the HHS' Office for Civil Rights discretion in enforcement actions for organizations implementing recognized security frameworks.

HITECH introduced a number of privacy innovations including:

- The HIPAA Breach Notification Rule, requiring covered entities to notify affected individuals and HHS of data breaches within 60 days. Business associates must also report breaches to covered entities.
- Publication of health care data breaches by the HHS' Office for Civil Rights. The breach portal, often called "The HIPAA Wall of Shame," includes summaries of breaches reported by covered entities and business associates.
- Modification of the HIPAA Privacy Rule, allowing individuals to obtain copies of their health data in electronic format. Although a right of access existed before, HITECH facilitated easier sharing of EHRs.
- Revisions to permitted uses and disclosures of PHI, restricting the sale of PHI without patient authorization, tightening language in the Privacy Rule, and introducing additional requirements for accounting of disclosures.

In summary, the HITECH Act significantly impacted the health care landscape by incentivizing EHR adoption, enhancing privacy and security measures, and introducing enhanced penalties for HIPAA noncompliance. To this end, it played a critical role in modernizing health care practices and fostering the secure exchange of health information.

Controlling the Assault of Non-Solicited Pornography and Marketing Act of 2003 (CAN-SPAM Act)[31]

The CAN-SPAM Act provides a series of requirements for organizations that send unsolicited commercial e-mails. The Act bans false or misleading header information and prohibits deceptive subject lines. It also requires that unsolicited commercial e-mails be identified as advertising and provide recipients with a method for opting out of receiving any such e-mails in the future. In addition, the Act directs the Federal Trade Commission to issue rules requiring the labeling of sexually explicit commercial e-mails as such and establishing the criteria for determining the primary purpose of a commercial e-mail. The interpretation of whether a message is commercial versus transactional depends on how the recipient would likely perceive the message based on its content (using a primary purpose test).

Organizations that send commercial e-mails must provide:

- Accurate Header Information: Header information, including "From," "To," "Reply-To," and routing details, must accurately identify the sender or business initiating the message.
- Honest Subject Lines: Organizations should not use of deceptive subject lines; they must accurately reflect the content of the e-mail message.
- Clear Identification of the Message as an Advertisement: The sender should clearly and conspicuously disclose that the message is an advertisement. While the law provides flexibility in how to achieve this, transparency is essential.
- Notice of the Sender's Location: The e-mail should include a valid physical postal address of the sender, such as a street address, a registered post office box with the U.S. Postal Service, or a registered private mailbox with a commercial mail receiving agency.
- Opt-Out Mechanism: The e-mail should clearly explain how recipients can opt out of receiving future marketing e-mails in a manner that is easy for an ordinary person to recognize, read, and understand, and should provide a return e-mail address or another simple Internet-based method for recipients to communicate their choice.
- Honoring Opt-Out Requests: Opt-out requests must be honored promptly and processed for at least 30 days after sending the message. Recipients' opt-out requests must be implemented within 10 business days. No fees or additional steps beyond a reply e-mail or a visit to a single webpage should be required for opting out. Additionally, once opt-out requests are received, the e-mail addresses cannot be sold or transferred, except to a company hired to help comply with the CAN-SPAM Act.

- Applicability to Subscribers and Members: Subscribers and members have the right to opt out of marketing e-mails, even if they are part of a subscription service or membership program. Ensure compliance by allowing them to opt out, and consider the primary purpose of the message in the context of the Act.
- Monitoring Third-Party Actions: Organizations cannot contract away their legal responsibility. Both the company whose product is promoted and the company sending the message may be held legally responsible.

Each separate e-mail violation can result in penalties of up to $51,744. Multiple parties may be held responsible. Criminal penalties, including imprisonment, may apply for specific violations.

Electronic Communications Privacy Act (ECPA)

Another important law is the ECPA, which protects the privacy of electronic communications, including e-mail and Internet usage. This Act prohibits the interception, access, and disclosure of electronic communications without a warrant or the user's consent. In contrast to the Privacy Act of 1974, the ECPA applies to all types of organizations, including those that do not receive federal funding.

The ECPA prohibits organizations from intercepting, accessing, or disclosing electronic communications without obtaining the explicit consent of the user or as authorized by applicable law. The law also includes penalties to deter organizations from engaging in the unauthorized interception or disclosure of electronic communications, including fines and imprisonment. Importantly, before disclosing the contents of electronic communications, the ECPA requires organizations to obtain a court order, except in limited circumstances, such as if the user has given explicit consent.

Children's Online Privacy Protection Act (COPPA)

The COPPA regulates how websites and online services collect, use, and disclose personal information from children under the age of 13. Although the law does not specifically target organizations, it is likely to impact many organizations, particularly those that collect personal information of children, such as names, addresses, and e-mails to register them for activities or online educational resources. Organizations subject to COPPA are likely to need to obtain verifiable parental consent before collecting personal information from children under 13 and must also provide parents with the ability to review and delete their child's personal information.

USA PATRIOT Act

The USA PATRIOT Act passed during the Bush administration presents a variety of privacy and surveillance challenges. This legislation grants the federal government expansive powers to access organizational records and monitor the activities of users in the name of national security. A significant challenge organizations face is finding a balance between providing access to information and meeting the legal obligation to furnish that information and records to authorities without the user's knowledge or consent. This compromise undermines the fundamental principles of intellectual freedom and privacy that organizations strive to uphold.

Digital Millennium Copyright Act (DMCA)

Another challenge is the DMCA, particularly in the realm of copyright infringement and digital content. The DMCA prohibits individuals from circumventing technological protection measures employed by content creators to safeguard copyrighted materials. Consequently, organizations must navigate the intricate landscape of digital rights management and fair use to ensure compliance with copyright law while simultaneously providing access to information and safeguarding the rights of their users.

To address these challenges from a compliance standpoint, organizations must prioritize providing comprehensive training for their staff regarding the requirements of these laws and any legal rights they may possess. Establishing clear policies and procedures related to these laws, specifically outlining how organizations manage stakeholders' information, is crucial. Additionally, implementing technical measures to guard against digital rights infringement becomes an important protective measure, showcasing a commitment to both IG and privacy by design.

Comprehensive Privacy Laws

U.S. State Comprehensive Privacy Laws[32]

Since the enactment of the California Consumer Privacy Act (CCPA) in 2018, the landscape of proposed U.S. state privacy bills has significantly evolved. The International Association of Privacy Professionals (IAPP) is committed to keeping privacy professionals abreast of the dynamic developments in this domain.

Following is a yearly progress recap starting in 2018:

- 2018: Two bills were introduced in the United States, and California enacted a significant privacy law.
- 2019: The United States witnessed the introduction of 15 privacy bills.
- 2020: Among 24 introduced bills, one was enacted, representing an amendment to the CCPA.
- 2021: Of the 29 introduced bills, two became laws in Virginia and Colorado.
- 2022: A notable surge occurred with 59 introduced bills, resulting in laws enacted in Utah and Connecticut.
- 2023: The trend continued, with 54 introduced bills and seven becoming laws in Delaware, Indiana, Iowa, Montana, Oregon, Tennessee, and Texas.

Common elements of these laws include:

What Do Comprehensive Privacy Laws Look Like?

1 ACCESS Allow data subjects to access their personal data.

4 PORTABILITY Allow data subjects to transmit their personal data.

2 CORRECTION Correct data at request of data subject.

5 OPT-OUT & OPT-IN Allow data subjects to opt out of processing; right to opt in to processing of sensitive personal data.

3 DELETION Delete data at request of data subject.

6 NOTICE Notice and transparency requirements.

The California Consumer Privacy Act and California Privacy
Rights Act (CPRA)

The CCPA, enacted on June 28, 2018, marks a significant shift in privacy
regulations, empowering consumers with five essential rights over their
personal information. These rights grant individuals the authority to:

- Know what data is collected;
- Opt-out of its sale;
- Access the collected information;
- Request deletion; and
- Safeguard against discriminatory practices for exercising
  privacy rights.[33]

The legislation applies broadly to businesses for which California residents are a key demographic, encompassing entities with annual gross
revenues exceeding $25 million, those dealing with data from 50,000 or
more California residents, or deriving 50 percent or more of their annual
revenues from selling such data. Additionally, the CCPA places restrictions on information related to children, requiring consent for the sale of
personal information of consumers under 17, with specific provisions for
different age groups.

Notably, the definition of "sell" under the CCPA is expansive, covering various data-sharing practices, and compliance obligations extend
not only to the primary business but also to entities that control or are
controlled by the covered business. The legislation also defines personal
information broadly, incorporating a wide range of data, from traditional
identifiers such as names and addresses to more contemporary forms
such as Internet activity and behavioral inferences. While deidentified
or anonymized data is not restricted, the CCPA sets a high standard for
achieving such status, and pseudonymized data may still be subject to the
law's provisions.[34]

In terms of compliance, the CCPA requires businesses to provide
specific privacy notices, offering consumers a clear understanding of
what personal information will be collected and the intended purpose
for each category. The law grants consumers the right to opt-out of the

sale or use of their personal information, and businesses are prohibited from discriminating against those who exercise these rights. The legislation does not directly mandate data security requirements but establishes a private right of action for certain data breaches resulting from violations of reasonable security practices. Penalties for noncompliance include fines ranging from $2,500 to $7,500, depending on the nature of the violation, with consumers having the right to seek damages for data breaches.[35]

More recently, the CPRA has emerged as a pivotal development in privacy legislation, aiming to replace the existing CCPA with a more comprehensive set of privacy rights and obligations. The CPRA, designed as a ballot initiative, is expected to be adopted, given the widespread support it has garnered among Californians. This new law, which is modeled on the EU GDPR, introduces a range of impactful provisions that redefine the landscape of data protection.[36]

One noteworthy aspect of the CPRA is its effective date of January 1, 2023, with a retrospective look back to January 1, 2022. Main CPRA innovations include:

- Creation of the California Privacy Protection Agency (CPPA), dedicated to privacy enforcement, armed with significant powers, including the authority to impose administrative fines, and a broader role encompassing public awareness and guidance for both businesses and consumers.
- Expanded obligations concerning sensitive data, introducing a comprehensive definition, and granting consumers the right to limit its use.
- Augmented breach liability by including e-mail/password combinations and emphasizing the importance of maintaining reasonable security practices.
- Annual audits and risk assessments for high-risk processing, aiming to ensure robust cybersecurity practices, with regulatory oversight from the Attorney General and CPPA.
- Automated decision making and profiling that mirror GDPR provisions, and grant consumers new rights for data correction.

- Enhanced protection of children's data, imposing heightened opt-in rights and increased penalties for violations.
- A necessity-based limitation on data retention, requiring businesses to inform consumers and prohibiting retention beyond reasonably necessary periods.
- New supply chain obligations mandating service providers, contractors, and third parties, to adhere to the same privacy protection standards described by the CPRA through binding agreements with businesses.[37]

Generally, the CPRA represents a significant evolution in privacy regulations, aligning more closely with international standards and emphasizing the rights and protections afforded to consumers in an increasingly data-driven world.

Critical International Privacy Laws and Standards

European Union General Data Protection Regulation

Extraterritorial privacy laws (i.e., those that apply to persons or entities that are located outside of the jurisdiction where the law is based) such as the EUGDPR introduce distinctive privacy challenges for organizations. These challenges include:

- Significant Penalties: The GDPR imposes higher penalties, reaching up to €20 million or 4 percent of global turnover, for serious infringements of core principles. For instance, when organizations subject to the GDPR rely on consent from individuals to use their personal information, terms and conditions must transparently explain how the information will be utilized.
- Privacy by Design: Organizations subject to the GDPR must proactively incorporate technical and organizational processes that align with data protection laws. This involves avoiding unnecessary retention of personal information and ensuring the safety of IT systems, with a strong emphasis

on encryption or pseudonymization. When introducing new processes or IT systems, organizations should assess the impact on the personal information held.

- Data Breach: In the event of personal data loss or unauthorized access, organizations subject to the GDPR must report the breach to authorities within 72 hours. Affected individuals must also be promptly informed unless the personal data is encrypted.
- Rights of Data Subjects: GDPR grants individuals using organizational systems the right to be informed about the information held on them, alongside various other rights. This includes the right to receive a copy in electronic form of their data and the ability to request rectification, removal, or deletion of their data from organizational systems.
- DPO: Public authorities and many other organizations must appoint a DPO, independent of senior management and with no conflicts of interest. This officer must not report to departments such as IT and must be registered with the national data protection authority.
- Data Transfer: Strict rules govern the transfer of personal data outside the European Economic Area (EEA), applicable to all entities, including libraries. Organizations must ensure compliance with GDPR data transfer rules, providing appropriate safeguards such as standard contractual clauses (SCCs), binding corporate rules (BCRs), or explicit consent from data subjects.

The GDPR allows for personal data transfer outside the EEA without additional safeguards if the destination country or organization has an adequate level of data protection, as deemed by the European Commission. Organizations subject to the GDPR must carefully assess the legal basis for such transfers and ensure appropriate safeguards when required. Failure to comply with these rules can result in significant fines and reputational damage.

To determine GDPR applicability, organizations, especially those outside the European Union, should consider whether they collect personal data if it pertains to EU residents, and if it is used to offer goods or services or monitor behavior in the European Union. Obtaining advice from qualified privacy counsel is crucial due to the complexity of these determinations.

LGPD (Lei Geral de Proteção de Dados)—Brazil[38]

Modeled after the GDPR, LGPD came into effect in 2020. It regulates the processing of personal data in Brazil. The LGPD defines "personal data" broadly, similar to the GDPR, encompassing information directly identifying an individual or making them identifiable. Sensitive personal data includes race, religion, health, and more. The law sets stringent requirements for processing sensitive data, reducing available legal bases. Anonymized data, with no reasonable identification, is exempt from LGPD, while pseudonymized data is considered personal data, subject to the law.

Regarding data transfer, LGPD aligns with GDPR, allowing transfers to countries with adequate protection or under specified safeguards. The ANPD (Autoridade Nacional de Proteção de Dados), which is the Brazilian National Data Protection Authority responsible for overseeing and enforcing the country's data protection laws, including the LGPD, will release the list of adequate countries. Pending ANPD's operation, cross-border transfers may rely on derogations, such as consent or contractual necessity. Companies within the European Union are likely considered adequate.

Data subjects enjoy various rights under LGPD, including access, rectification, erasure, data portability, and the right to object to automated decisions. Controllers must ensure rights' exercise, and processors can also receive requests. LGPD outlines 10 principles for processing personal data, emphasizing purpose, adequacy, necessity, transparency, and accountability.

LGPD imposes civil liability for damages caused by data processing, with penalties, such as fines and suspension of activities, determined by ANPD. Legal bases for processing, including consent, require specific criteria. Principles, such as data quality, transparency, and nondiscrimination, guide processing. Retention depends on a legal basis, aligning with business purposes, legal obligations, or defense in lawsuits. Online services must comply with Internet Act provisions.

Companies may disclose data under court order for civil or criminal matters. User data disclosure for online services follows the Internet Act, requiring substantiated evidence and justification. Legal obligations, such as disclosing data to public bodies, are lawful. Noncompliance with court orders may lead to fines, executive detainment, and temporary suspension of activities. Recurrent noncompliance can result in long-term suspension.

Personal Information Protection and Electronic Documents Act (PIPEDA)—Canada[39]

PIPEDA has been in place since 2001 and applies to the private sector. It regulates the collection, use, and disclosure of personal information. The Act outlines various key requirements for organizations in Canada. Consent is a fundamental aspect, with organizations needing permission to collect, use, or disclose personal information. Individuals have the right to access their information and challenge its accuracy. Usage of personal information is limited to the initially stated purpose, requiring renewed consent for other purposes. Adequate safeguards must protect personal information.

PIPEDA applies to private-sector organizations involved in commercial activities across Canada. Commercial activities include transactions and conduct of a commercial nature. Federally regulated organizations, such as airports and banks, are always subject to PIPEDA, including their employees' information. Certain provinces, such as Alberta, British Columbia, and Quebec, have similar privacy laws exempting them from PIPEDA. Others, such as Ontario and Nova Scotia, have comparable health information legislation.

Like the GDPR, the PIPEDA operates extraterritorially. This means that businesses operating in Canada, handling information crossing borders, fall under PIPEDA, irrespective of their base province or territory. Also, like the GDPR, PIPEDA defines personal information broadly, covering identifiable individual data in any form, including opinions, evaluations, and employee files.

Also, notably, certain types of personal data are specifically not covered by PIPEDA. These include personal information managed by federal government organizations, business contact information for employment-related communication, and personal information collected for personal purposes or journalistic, artistic, or literary activities. Not-for-profit groups, political parties, and some institutions are also generally exempt.

Businesses must adhere to the 10 fair information principles outlined in PIPEDA Schedule 1. These principles are as follows:

- Accountability: Examples of accountability include appointing a designated privacy official, protecting personal information, and developing comprehensive privacy policies and practices. Compliant companies should establish a privacy management program that includes conducting privacy impact assessments, implementing protective measures, responding to complaints, and regularly reviewing and updating privacy protocols, ensuring transparency about data transfers and protection measures when dealing with third-party service providers outside Canada.
- Defining Collection and Use Purposes: Examples include documenting specific purposes for collecting personal information, informing customers of these purposes during or before collection, and obtaining consent for any new purposes. Organizations subject to the Act should further ensure whether their personal information holdings are "necessary," maintain records of identified purposes and consents, and restrict purposes to what a reasonable person would find appropriate. They should also clearly define and narrow the purposes for collecting personal information, avoiding overly broad statements to enhance understanding of its use.
- Ensuring Consent: This means ensuring that one has meaningful consent for personal information collection, use, and disclosure, making privacy information readily available, offering clear choices, ensuring transparency about risks, periodically reminding individuals, and adopting innovative and user-friendly consent processes while adhering to best practices and standards.

- Limiting Collection: This means collecting only necessary personal information for a legitimate purpose, being transparent about collection reasons, ensuring fair and lawful means, and implementing information-handling policies that limit data to what is essential for identified purposes, while reducing risks and costs associated with data collection, storage, and management.

- Limiting Use, Disclosure, and Retention: This means using or disclosing personal information only for identified purposes, obtaining fresh consent for new purposes, document any changes, implementing guidelines for retention and destruction, monitoring employee access, establishing retention schedules, and employing effective processes for secure disposal or anonymization, ensuring compliance with legal requirements and privacy protection.

- Accuracy: This includes organizations keeping personal information accurate, complete, and up to date, considering its relevance and individual interests, and establishing policies for updating information based on a checklist that includes specific items needed for a service, the location of related information, the date of acquisition or update, and verification steps.

- Security: While PIPEDA does not mandate specific security safeguards, organizations should protect personal information appropriately based on its sensitivity and implement security policies and safeguards. These measures include physical measures, technological tools, and organizational controls and should be based on an assessment of factors such as information sensitivity, risk of harm, amount of information, distribution, format, storage type, and potential risks, while regularly reviewing and updating security measures, conducting audits, and providing staff training on the importance of maintaining security and confidentiality.

- Openness: Practically, this means that organizations must inform customers and employees about their personal information management policies and practices, ensuring that they are easily understandable and accessible, comply with guidelines on meaningful consent, and provide clear information on the accountable person, access procedures, complaint mechanisms, organizational disclosures, and relevant contact details in various formats, such as in person, in writing, by telephone, publications, and on their website.

- Access: Organizations must inform individuals about the personal information held, its source, use, and disclosure, and provide access to it at minimal or no cost, explaining any refusal in writing and offering recourse options, including the right to complain to the Privacy Commissioner. Organizations should respond within 30 days, extendable under specific conditions, and ensure understandable information, with any amendments communicated to relevant third parties when applicable. Maintaining records, conducting thorough searches, and managing access requests with caution are essential practices.

- Challenging Compliance: Organizations must establish simple complaint managing procedures, informing complainants about available recourse options, investigating all complaints promptly, and improving information-handling practices if issues are identified. Recording complaint details, acknowledging receipt promptly, and assigning reviews to impartial personnel are crucial steps. Organizations should notify individuals of review outcomes, correct inaccurate information, and update policies, accordingly, fostering awareness among employees of complaint procedures and maintaining consistent records.

Information Security[40]

Introduction

ISO/IEC 27701 sets out the prerequisites and offers advice for creating, preserving, and continuously improving an organization's information security management systems (ISMS) that extends the ISMS implementation based on the criteria of ISO/IEC 27001 and the guidance of ISO/IEC 27002.

This standard is relevant to both personally identifiable information (PII) controllers and PII processors. The additional guidelines and requirements for protecting PII can be implemented by any organization, regardless of its size or cultural context.

ISO/IEC 27701 provides information on how to align this standard with the privacy framework and principles specified in ISO/IEC 29100. Additionally, it includes mapping to ISO/IEC 27018, ISO/IEC 29151, and GDPR. The first version of ISO 27701 was published on August 5, 2019.

Purpose of ISO 27701

ISO 27701 is an extension of ISO 27001 and ISO 27002 that establishes additional requirements and provides guidance for the safeguarding of privacy as potentially affected by personal data processing. These requirements and recommendations help entities incorporate requirements regarding information security and protection of personal data into their general information security management systems (ISMS).

ISO 27701 also details what is necessary for establishing, implementing, maintaining, and continually improving organizations' personal information management systems (PIMS) and offers guidance to organizations enable the establishment, implementation, maintenance, and continual improvement of a PIMS and maintain the "CIA" of the personal data within those systems. ISO 27701 also references the privacy framework of ISO 29100.

The goal of this standard is to provide interested parties ranging from internal staff to customers and regulators with confidence that personal data is being sufficiently managed by the entity through the implementation of a PIMS. To this end, Clause 6.15 of ISO 27701 notes that reference to this standard can be used to form the basis of a customer contract, outlining an entity's privacy-related obligations as well as the potential sanctions for noncompliance.

ISO 27701 Certification

Organizations that meet the requirements of certifiable ISO standards can be certified by an accredited external certification body after successfully completing an audit against the standard as ISO does not provide certification or conformity assessments itself. The ISO has also issued various guidance regarding information systems generally as well as its standards, which include the following.

ISO 27701 is intended to apply to all types of organizations, irrespective of their industry, size, and nature. Evidence of certification can also be used as an internal tool to assess an entity's ability to meet its own requirements related to protecting the security of information.

For example, an organization using evidence of ISO 27701 certification as a tool, can demonstrate its commitment to protecting the security of information and continuously improving its security practices, which can help it to build trust with stakeholders, including employees, supply chain vendors, and investors by showing evidence of audits, commitment to security practices, controls and risk management and identification, and continuous performance monitoring.

Importantly, ISO 27701 applies to both data controllers and data processors of personal data, who are required to formulate a PIMS and who are thereby considered to be responsible and accountable for the processing of personal data. Importantly, it also considers the various well-known requirements of standards and legislation such as the GDPR and emphasizes the importance of mapping data management practices to these standards.

Structure of ISO 27701

ISO 27701 is structured into eight clauses that guide organizations on implementing controls within six annexes. The controls in the annexes are also considered to be considered relevant by default, and any deviations must be justified by organizations, typically, through evidence of a risk assessment or exemption from applicable legislation.

Following are some of the most important clauses and annexes:

Clause 5 outlines PIMS requirements related to ISO 27001, while Clause 6 outlines PIMS requirements for ISO 27002. Annex F then shows how ISO 27701 can be applied by organizations to these standards and clarifies that the ISO 27701 framework extends the information security requirements of ISO 27001 and ISO 27002 to include the protection of privacy.

Clause 7 offers PIMS guidance for personal data controllers, which is supplemented by Annex A, which contains specific controls and objectives for controllers. Clause 8 provides PIMS guidance for PII processors, and Annex B contains specific controls and objectives for processors.

Annexes A and B of ISO 27701 describe requirements and guidance for either controllers or processors, with the specific objectives broken down further into controls related to conditions for collection and processing of personal data, obligations to data subjects, privacy by design and default, and sharing, transfer, and disclosure.

Annex C provides information on how specific controls of ISO 27701 relate to the Privacy Principles of ISO 29100, while Annex E does the same for ISO 27018 and ISO 29151. Annex D informs organizations that subclauses of ISO 27701 correspond to specific Articles of the GDPR, highlighting the strong links between the two regulations. However, it is important to note that ISO 27701 does not provide certification under Article 42 of the GDPR.

Key ISO 27701 Definitions and Basic Concepts

Some of the key definitions of ISO 27701 include:

- Joint PII Controller: This is generally defined as a controller of personal data that determines the purposes and means of the processing of PII joint with one or more other PII controllers.
- Privacy Information Management System: ISMS, which addresses the protection of privacy as potentially affected by the processing of PII.
- Interested Party/Stakeholder: Person or entity that can affect, be affected by, or perceive itself to be affected by a decision or activity.
- Management System: Set of interrelated or interacting elements of an organization to establish policies and objectives and processes to achieve those objectives.

- Customer: Depending on the role of the organization, a "customer" can be understood as:
  - An organization in a contract with a PII controller;
  - A PII controller in a contract with a PII processor; or
  - A PII processor in a contract with a subcontractor for PII processing.

ISO 27701 Data Processing Requirements

The requirements of ISO 27701 outline various requirements related to policies, objectives, risk assessment, treatment, and monitoring and review requirements for a PIMS. Clause 5 also emphasizes the importance of senior management commitment, the involvement of employees, and the need for continual improvement of the PIMS. In addition to these general standards, organizations seeking to achieve ISO 27701 compliance must consider various factors, such as organization context, governance, policies and procedures, contractual obligations, and relevant legislation, which may impact that system.

In addition, for each type or act of processing, organizations subject to ISO 27701 must determine whether they are processing PII as a controller, joint controller, or processor. Where more than one role applies, the entity must establish separate role-specific sets of controls. And, finally, organizations must include requirements related to the processing of personal information within the scope of their PIMS.

ISO 27701 Retention Obligations

Once a retention schedule has been formulated, organizations should have a procedure in place to delete or deidentify logged information that contains personal data (Clause 6.9.4.2 of ISO 27701). It is also important for organizations to ensure that personal data is not stored for longer than necessary and that retention periods are clearly documented in retention schedules (Clause 7.4.7 of ISO 27701). When personal data is no longer needed, organizations should dispose of it safely according to established procedures that consider the nature of the data (Clause 7.4.8 of ISO 27701).

ISO 27701 Requirements Related to the Processing and Collection of Personal Data

- Clause 7.2 and Controls A.7.2 of ISO 27701 provide guidelines for processing personal data lawfully and for specific purposes. To comply with these requirements, PII controllers must determine and document the specific purposes, lawful basis, consent process, joint controller agreements, conduct privacy impact assessments, have contracts with PII processors, and must also maintain records of personal data processing.
- Clause 8.2 and Control B.8.2 guide ensuring that PII processors process personal data lawfully. PII processors must also keep records of their processing activities. Control B.8.2 also covers PII processor requirements for customer agreements, clarifying purposes, marketing, and advertising, complying with customer instructions, and customer obligations.

ISO 27701 Security Management System Requirements

The ISMS requirements of ISO 27701 supplement those of ISO 27001, which, generally, require organizations to:

- Conduct risk assessments at regular intervals, or whenever significant changes occur in the organization or their information systems;
- Document the risk assessment process in a manner that identifies the methodology and criteria used;
- Ensure that the assessment encompasses all data on the information assets and processing facilities including hardware, software, people, and processes;
- Evaluate risks based on their likelihood and impact, and consider potential harms including damage to the CIA of information;
- Institute appropriate controls to mitigate risks;

- Review the risk assessment regularly to ensure effectiveness and relevance; and
- Ensure management support of the risk assessment program.

In addition to the requirements of ISO 27001, ISO 27701 requires organizations to perform information security risk assessments in compliance with ISO 27001 to identify risks related to CIA, as well as privacy risk assessments to identify potential privacy risks. These assessments should be followed by an evaluation of the potential impact of such events, in addition to the requirements specified in ISO 27001 (Clause 5.4.1.2).

Organizations are required under ISO 27701 to conduct privacy impact assessments as necessary, especially when planning to initiate or modify processing activities involving personal data. Such assessments may be necessary for activities such as automated decision making, large-scale processing of sensitive data, or systematic monitoring of publicly available data (as specified in Clause 7.2.5 and Control A.7.2.5 of ISO 27701).

Management of Information Security Risks Under ISO 27701

ISO 27701 mandates that organizations under its scope must assess the effect of identified risks on personal data processing and the concerned data subjects. Based on this assessment, they should prepare a Statement of Applicability outlining which controls from Annex A would be implemented or not, along with the reasons for each decision (as per Clause 5.4.1.3 of ISO 27701).

These controls include:

- Documenting a justification for each decision on whether or not to implement each control;
- Describing any additional controls implemented to address privacy risks;
- Outlining the entity's justification for including or excluding additional controls;
- Summarizing the current status of each control, whether it has been implemented or not implemented, and any describing planned actions to address controls that have not been implemented.

Information Security Policies

According to ISO 27701, the information security policies and their review requirements of ISO 27002 are expanded to apply to the protection of information security and privacy. Additionally, organizations must establish a statement with partners, subcontractors, and any third parties, outlining their support and commitment to comply with relevant data protection laws, with clear definitions of related responsibilities (Clause 6.2.1.1 of ISO 27701).

An example of this type of statement could be:

X Organization and its partners, subcontractors, and any third parties commit to compliance with relevant data protection legislation, including GDPR. To ensure compliance, each party shall clearly define its responsibilities regarding the processing of personal data and agree to cooperate with others to protect the CIA of such data. Each party shall appoint a DPO, ensure that their personnel are aware of and trained in data protection, and maintain appropriate technical and organizational measures to protect personal data.

Roles and Responsibilities

ISO 27701 expands the applicability of ISO 27002's security requirements that detail various elements of information security compliance, including the compliant management of information security, the handling of information assets, and the protection of information through the implementation of security controls. Topics addressed in ISO 27002 include access controls, cryptography, physical security, network security, incident management, and business continuity management. ISO 27002 also emphasizes the importance of risk assessment and management for organizations, as well as the need for ongoing monitoring, review, and improvement of information security management.

Notably, ISO 27701 extends ISO 27002's information security requirements and review to address the protection of both information security and privacy. ISO 27701 also requires organizations to document the terms and conditions for the joint processing of personal data in a binding agreement, thereby clarifying their specific roles and responsibilities. This agreement should cover topics such as the purposes of the joint processing, the identities of the parties involved, and how the parties will ensure that data subject rights are respected. Additionally, organizations should appoint a point of contact for customers and responsible persons, known as DPOs in some jurisdictions.

Responsible Persons (DPOs, etc.)

Under ISO 27701, an organization needs to appoint a DPO if they are a public authority or body (except for courts acting in their judicial capacity), their core activities consist of processing that requires the regular and systematic monitoring of data subjects on a large scale, or of processing special categories of data (i.e., sensitive personal data) or data relating to criminal convictions and offenses on a large scale. This means, for example, that an entity that processes sensitive data, such as health information or political affiliations, on a large scale as part of its research activities, could potentially be required to appoint a DPO. Also, even if not required by ISO 27701, some organizations may choose to appoint a DPO voluntarily to help promote compliance with data protection laws and regulations.

Clause 6.3.1 of ISO 27701 specifies the requirements for appointing a DPO or a person in charge of data protection (PiCDP) within an organization. These include:

- Informing and advising the organization and its employees their data protection compliance (e.g., the GDPR);
- Monitoring compliance with data protection laws and regulations and drafting and updating the organization's data protection policies and procedures;
- Providing advice and guidance on data protection impact assessments (DPIAs);
- Cooperating with supervisory authorities and serving as the point of contact for data protection inquiries;
- Conducting data protection training for employees and third-party data processors; and
- Ensuring that data protection policies and procedures are up-to-date and in compliance with relevant regulations.

Additionally, a DPO should be appointed based on their professional qualifications, expertise, and ability to fulfill their responsibilities and provided with sufficient resources and independence to perform their duties effectively.

Employment Law Compliance

ISO 27701 describes the extension of various information security requirements of ISO 27002 regarding screening, disciplinary procedures, and change of employment to apply to the protection of information security and privacy. The overall purpose of these controls is to lower the risk of malicious or accidental actions by employees that could compromise the security of personal data. Specific requirements include:

- Screening and background checks on all new employees, contractors, and third-party users with access to personal data, which should include a verification of references, criminal records, and education and other relevant checks, depending on the sensitivity of the data being accessed, followed by documentation of such checks.
- A clear and documented disciplinary process that describes the consequences of violating information security policies and procedures, is communicated to all employees and includes specific consequences for repeat offenses or particularly egregious violations.
- Immediate revocation of access to personal data when employees leave the organization, which includes revoking their access to physical and electronic systems and data and data stored on third-party systems, a mandate that all such persons should return all organizational assets, including laptops, mobile devices, and other equipment, and a requirement that any personal data stored on these devices is securely erased.

Clause 6.4 of ISO 27701 also outlines the requirements for organizations to implement procedures for managing privacy-related incidents. These requirements include:

- Having a documented incident response plan that describes the procedures required to be followed in the event of a privacy-related incident.

- Complying with reporting requirements for privacy-related incidents that include reporting the incident to the relevant authorities and affected data subjects, as well as the organization's management and DPO.
- Instituting specific procedures governing the investigation and assessment of data incidents, including identifying the cause, scope, and impact of the incident.
- Enacting mitigation measures to lower the impact of data incidents and to prevent similar incidents from occurring in the future.
- Keeping records of all privacy-related incidents, including the actions taken to redress them.
- Regularly evaluating the effectiveness of the incident response plan and procedures and making necessary improvements to ensure that they remain effective and up to date.

Awareness and Training

According to Clause 5.5 of ISO 27701, organizations seeking to comply with ISO 27701 should apply the information security principles of ISO 27001 regarding support to their PIMS with additional resources, communication, and awareness of employees to the protection of personal data. These principles include:

- Confidentiality: The duty to protect personal information from unauthorized disclosure.
- Integrity: The obligation to ensure the accuracy and completeness of personal information processed.
- Availability: The requirement that organizations ensure that personal information is accessible when needed.
- Authentication: The obligation to verify the identity of individuals who access personal information.
- Authorization: Ensure that individuals have the necessary permissions to access personal information.
- Accountability: The creation of systems, policies, and procedures to hold relevant persons accountable for protecting personal information.

- Nonrepudiation: Ensuring that actions related to personal information cannot be denied. For example, through the use of an electronic signature that provides a record that can be used as evidence to prove that the person agreed to the action or transaction.
- Compliance: Monitoring and ensuring legal, regulatory, and contractual obligations related to personal information.
- Risk management: Identifying and managing risks to personal information.
- Continual improvement: Continually improving the effectiveness of the entity's PIMS.

In addition to the requirements of ISO 27002, Clause 6.4.2.2 of ISO 27701, organizations must implement measures to ensure that employees are aware of the impact of data breaches and policy breaches for themselves and for the data subjects, for example, through training, awareness programs, and regular reminders. Clause 6.5.2.2 of ISO 27701 further requires organizations to ensure that employees can correctly identify personal data.

Examples of these measures could include training sessions for all staff members on how to identify and report a data breach or policy violation, as well as regular reminders of the importance of safeguarding personal information provided by supply chain partners. Additionally, the organization could create an incident response team to manage and determine the validity of reported incidents, and to create a methodology for increasing the likelihood that necessary remedial actions are promptly taken.

Data Asset Management

Clause 6.4 of ISO 27701 states that the information security requirements of ISO 27002 regarding the management of assets extend to the protection of information security and privacy. This includes a requirement to identify the type of personal data processed, its location, the data subject's rights associated with that data, and the various risks associated with processing that data. The organization must also ensure that the data is adequately protected against unauthorized access, use, disclosure, modification, destruction, or accidental loss.

Clause 6.5.2 of ISO 27701 further requires organizations to implement an information classification system that explicitly considers how and where personal data is processed, stored, and transferred. For a research organization, this type of classification system can help ensure the proper handling and protection of personal data collected from organization users, such as their names, contact information, and borrowing history. For example, the organization can classify the personal data of its employees based on its sensitivity, the level of risk associated with its processing, and the applicable legal requirements. The organization staff can then apply appropriate security controls based on these classifications (and document those controls), such as access controls and encryption, to the personal data based on its classification. And, finally, the organization can institute access controls that help to ensure that personal data is only stored and transferred to authorized recipients in a manner that complies with applicable data protection laws and regulations.

Information Backups

Clause 6.9.3 of ISO 27701 requires organizations to create a policy that covers their requirements for the backup, recovery, restoration, and erasure of personal data as required by ISO 27002, for data, generally. These requirements include (without limitation): regularly backing up personal data based on criticality, storing personal data securely offsite to protect against data loss due to loss or disaster, encryption of backup data, assessing the integrity and completeness of personal data backups (and also to ensure confidentiality), regularly testing data restoration measures, and securely erasing personal data when no longer required.

Privacy Risk Assessments

ISO 27701 requires organizations to conduct privacy risk assessments and/or privacy impact assessments to incorporate the outcomes into a Privacy by Design approach. Moreover, when conducting data testing, in cases where fake personal data cannot be used, organizations should conduct risk assessments to identify and deploy the level of suitable control for managing and mitigating related privacy risks.

A use case for a pharmaceutical company can include, for example, the facilitation of research that involves collecting personal data from research subjects, such as names, addresses, and contact information. In this case, a privacy risk assessment could help organization management identify potential risks to the privacy of the research subjects and determine appropriate controls to mitigate those risks. These measures can include technical safeguards such as encryption or access controls that are supplemented by organizational measures such as training staff on proper data handling procedures, drafting and updating policies and procedures, and verifying that consent is obtained from research subjects before their data is collected.

Continuous Improvement

ISO 27001 requires organizations to establish, implement, maintain, and continually improve an ISMS that promotes the CIA of information. This analysis should include a performance evaluation, internal auditing, and management review.

The analysis should be supplemented by an auditing process that requires organizations to conduct regular and systematic audits of their ISMS to ensure that the system is operating as intended and to continually identify areas for improvement. Further, senior management should review this system at regular intervals to ensure its continued suitability, adequacy, and effectiveness.

These requirements apply to the protection of personal data as per Clause 5.7 of ISO 27701. Specifically, this clause organizations to establish, implement, maintain, and continually improve a PIMS that is designed to protect personal data. The performance evaluation, internal auditing, and management review processes should be applied to the PIMS to verify that it is operating effectively and efficiently to protect personal data including the controls used for personal data protection, regular audits of the PIMS, and reviewing the system at regular intervals to ensure its continued suitability, relevance, and effectiveness.

In the context of organization management, the organization can use the results of a performance evaluation, internal auditing, and management review to ensure that its personal data management system used for managing contracts protects the privacy of the data subjects. The organization can then use this analysis to identify and diagnose any weaknesses or gaps in its current system and take corrective actions to address them.

Mobile Devices and Remote Work

Clause 6.3.2 of ISO 27701 requires organizations to implement appropriate measures to ensure that personal data is not at risk when accessed or processed on mobile devices or when employees are working remotely. Compliance with this requirement can include measures such as implementing access controls, mandating the use of encryption and secure connections such as virtual private networks (VPNs), and ensuring that data is not stored locally on mobile devices.

Practically, this could mean requiring employees who work remotely or who access personal data on mobile devices to use secure connections and encryption technologies when accessing the organization's systems or databases. The organization could also implement policies requiring that data be not stored locally on mobile devices, and access controls that access to personal data is restricted based on the employee's role and level of authorization. The organization could also conduct risk assessments to identify potential vulnerabilities and implement appropriate controls to mitigate those risks, such as requiring the use of secure VPN connections or multifactor authentication.

Encryption

Clause 6.5.3 of ISO 27701 requires organizations that process personal data to document their use of removable devices such as USBs. These devices can be a risk since they can leave the organization's premises. As a measure to mitigate this risk, an organization could verify that removable devices capable of encrypting personal data are used whenever possible. Also, the organization must document any personal data from removable devices that are disposed of or physically transferred. To prevent unauthorized access, the organization must implement secure disposal procedures for the former and an authorization procedure for the latter.

Access Controls

Clause 6.6 of ISO 27701 stipulates that the access control requirements of ISO 27002 must also consider the protection of information security and privacy. These requirements include:

- Limiting personal data access to personal data to authorized individuals and preventing their unauthorized access, alteration, or destruction.
- Instituting and maintaining personal data access rights controls for employees, contractors, and third parties to personal data.
- Using multifactor authentication or other forms of best-practices authentication for accessing personal data and regularly reviewing such access controls and audit logs to identify and redress any unauthorized access attempts.
- Having updated procedures that enable the entity to manage access requests, access rights changes, and revoke access rights when an employee leaves the organization or changes roles.
- Ensuring that access to personal data is only granted on a need-to-know basis.
- Establishing controls to prevent the accidental disclosure of personal data via tools such as screen filters or password-protected screensavers.
- Establishing procedures for granting temporary access to personal data to individuals outside of the organization, such as auditors or regulators.

In addition, ISO 27701 indicates specific requirements regarding registration and deregistration to ensure the protection of personal data. For example, organizations must ensure that registration and deregistration processes for system administrators or operators should cover procedures for potential compromise of access control. Also, Clause 6.2.2 of ISO 27701 mandates that deactivated or expired user accounts should not be reused, states that customer responsibilities for the protection of their user

ID should be outlined, and, where applicable, checks of unused authentication credentials should be conducted as frequently as necessary.

Clause 6.2.2 also requires organizations to maintain an accurate and up-to-date record of any individual user access profiles and the related personal data so that the individuals, organizations, and potentially the customers where applicable, are aware of the personal data that has or has not been processed.

Finally, organizations must implement policies, procedures, or mechanisms allowing them to meet their obligations to data subjects regarding the access to and correction of their personal data (Clause 7.3.6 and Control A.7.3.6 of ISO 27701).

As a practical example, Clause 6.6 of ISO 27701's access control requirements could be applied to the protection of personal data by limiting access to organization users' personal information to authorized staff members and preventing unauthorized access, alteration, or destruction of such data. Such a system would limit the access to the personal information of organization users to staff with a need-to-know and would inform staff of their obligations through procedures for managing access requests and changes to access rights and the inclusion of information regarding these procedures within staff training sessions. The organization should also implement multifactor authentication or other forms of secure authentication to enable secure access to personal data, and institute procedures for revoking personal data access rights when staff members leave the organization or change roles.

The organization should also enact and maintain specific registration and deregistration processes governing the conduct of system administrators or operators related to a potential compromise of access control. And, the organization should also maintain an accurate and up-to-date record of individual user access profiles and related personal data, so organization users are aware of their personal data that has or has not been processed. Finally, the organization must have policies and procedures in place to allow organization users to access and correct their personal data as required by ISO 27701.

Secure Disposal or Reuse of Equipment

To ensure personal data on a device that will be reused is no longer accessible, an organization should follow the guidelines outlined in Clause 6.8.2.7 of ISO 27701. One way to achieve this goal is by implementing technical measures such as data encryption and/or data wiping to erase the personal data on the device. For example, the organization can use software that can securely wipe data on the device to ensure that unauthorized persons cannot recover it. If erasure is impractical due to performance issues, the organization must implement other technical measures, such as isolating the device from the network and applying access controls, to ensure that the personal data on the device is not accessible by unauthorized persons. The organization should also document the measures taken to ensure that personal data is no longer accessible on the device, to demonstrate compliance with the requirements of Clause 6.8.2.7 of ISO 27701.

Accountability and Recordkeeping

Organizations must ensure that they maintain accurate and up-to-date records to support their requirements for processing personal data. This requires appointing an individual responsible for ensuring the accuracy of the record of processing activities, which might include the type and purposes of processing, categories of personal data and recipients involved, and relevant reports from privacy impact assessments (Clause 7.2.8 and Control A.7.2.8 of ISO 27701).

Organizations must also keep records of the personal information being processed including the categories of processing, any transfers of data to third countries or international organizations, and the relevant technical and organizational measures (Clause 8.2.6 and Control B.8.2.6 of ISO 27701). They must also inform their data subjects of any legally binding requests for disclosure of personal data to third parties, such as law enforcement, and must reject nonlegally binding requests after consulting with the data subject (Clauses 8.5.4–8.5.5 and Control B.8.5.4–B8.5.5 of ISO 27701).

Finally, organizations must identify and record the specific purposes for which the personal data will be processed (Control A.7.2.1 of ISO 27701).

Cross-Border Transfers of Data

The requirements in ISO 27002 and ISO 27701 related to cross-border transfers are important for organizations of all types, especially those that operate internationally and are regulated by comprehensive and extraterritorial privacy laws.

Cross-border transfers of personal data involve transferring this data to another country where different privacy and data protection laws may apply. From a privacy perspective, the primary concern is that the laws within the recipient country may not offer the same level of protection as the laws of the country where the data was collected. As a result, the transfer of personal data may be at risk of unauthorized access, use, or disclosure, which could lead to identity theft, fraud, or other harmful outcomes.

ISO 27002 and ISO 27701 guide how to protect personal data during cross-border transfers. They require organizations to implement appropriate safeguards, such as encryption, access controls, and contractual agreements with third-party service providers, to ensure that personal data is protected during these transfers.

Some of the main guidance elements of these standards include:

- The duty to perform a risk assessment to identify the risks associated with cross-border transfers of personal data that includes identifying the types of personal data that will be transferred, the countries to which the data will be transferred, and the potential risks to the data during transfer.
- The obligation to understand relevant legal requirements related to cross-border transfers of personal data by the organization and to ensure that appropriate safeguards are maintained to protect the transferred data.
- The requirement to obtain appropriate consent from data subjects before transferring their personal data across borders

and to ensure that they are informed about the transfer and the risks involved.

- The duty to maintain appropriate technical and organizational measures to protect personal data during cross-border transfers including encryption, access controls, and secure transmission methods (especially when the personal data is transmitted over untrusted networks such as the Internet or external facilities).
- The obligation to monitor and review cross-border data transfer practices to ensure that they remain effective and compliant with applicable laws and regulations.
- The duty to ensure that personal data is transferred solely to authorized individuals.
- The establishment of contractual agreements with third-party service providers involved in the transfer of personal data to ensure that they comply with applicable data protection laws and regulations.
- The duty to enter into confidentiality agreements with employees and contractors to ensure the protection of personal data throughout its life cycle (and specifying the time period for privacy obligations).
- The duty to account for and record the legal basis for international data transfers and any jurisdiction-specific requirements, and to take into account whether data can be transferred to the jurisdictions with or without review from supervisory authorities.
- The duty to record the nature, recipient, and time of transfers or disclosures of personal data to third parties.

Management of Third-Party Processors

ISO 27701 outlines various requirements that organizations must adhere to when engaging third-party service providers in handling personal data, emphasizing appropriate controls, defined roles, and contractual stipulations. The principles of Privacy by Design and Privacy by Default must be applied to outsourced information systems, and contracts with personal data processors should mandate compliance with selected controls. Processing personal data on behalf of another party requires the processor to follow documented instructions, notify customers of contract infringements, and demonstrate compliance.

Moreover, organizations must align with ISO 27002 and regional privacy regulations, clarifying responsibilities and procedures for preventing, identifying, and documenting data breaches. Breach notification procedures should be outlined in contracts, and ISO 27701 emphasizes the continuous review of event logs to identify and address issues, emphasizing the implementation of monitoring processes.

PART 3

How Information Governance Can Improve ESG Framework Compliance

Governance Overview in the Context of ESG Frameworks

In the realm of ESG reporting, IG becomes a critical driver for managing an enterprise's people, process, and technology. Emphasizing risk, legal compliance, information management, and business intelligence, IG intersects with disciplines crucial for ESG compliance, including e-Discovery, data privacy, big data, architecture, operations, organizational continuity, and audit.

The overarching goal of an ESG-aligned governance strategy and framework is to ensure that the organization comprehends and collaboratively executes strategic ESG goals. The focus is on fostering a harmonious operation where all facets of the enterprise, including employees and resources, work judiciously toward ESG objectives. This approach envisions the organization not merely as a collection of disparate parts but as a cohesive mechanism, aligning its functions to meet ESG standards and expectations.

Leadership and Regulatory Influence

In the context of ESG, leadership plays a pivotal role in setting the tone and strategy, establishing the organizational culture needed for ESG adherence. Depending on the industry and location, enterprises may be subject to varying degrees of ESG-related regulations. These regulations influence the governance frameworks, privacy requirements, best practices, and infrastructure adopted by the organization. Leaders guide the establishment of technology, third-party systems, and operational structures that align with ESG goals, ensuring compliance and enabling the extraction of metrics vital for ESG reporting.

According to an analysis by McKinsey and Co., data governance excellence is contingent upon the effective implementation of six critical practices, providing a comprehensive framework for organizations to derive a value from their data. The first priority noted by McKinsey is to secure the attention of top management. This involves proactive engagement between the data management office (DMO) and the C-suite to grasp business leadership needs, articulate existing data challenges, and elucidate the role of data governance. The formation of a data governance council within senior management, possibly including C-suite leaders, is crucial. This council steers governance strategies toward business requirements and oversees initiatives, fostering collaboration with the DMO.[1]

Success Metrics and Strategic Alignment for ESG

Success in ESG reporting is measured not only by financial performance but also by the organization's ability to achieve strategic alignment across leadership, budgeting, technology, operations, and legal compliance. Program management becomes instrumental in planning, executing, and resourcing executive leadership's core ESG strategies. Organizations drive specific requirements and core competencies aligned with ESG standards, while IT and operations build the necessary processes and infrastructure. Legal and compliance functions outline and enforce policies, mitigating ESG-related risks to maintain the organization's standing with regulators, shareholders, and the public.

As a result, it is not surprising that the second priority noted by the McKinsey study is to integrate data governance efforts with the organization's primary transformation themes. Aligning data governance efforts with priorities such as digitization or enterprise resource planning (ERP) modernization ensures synchronization with CEO objectives. This integration shifts the responsibility for data governance toward product teams, emphasizing the importance of governing data at the point of production and consumption.

Another critical practice is to effectively secure data assets. The DMO, in collaboration with the data governance council, should prioritize data domains based on transformational efforts, regulatory demands, and other inputs. Rapid deployment of priority domains, starting with two to three initially, ensures functional domains within a few months.[2]

Another core practice is to emphasize applying the right level of governance. Organizations should adopt a needs-based approach, aligning governance sophistication with their unique regulatory landscape and data complexity. This tailored approach prevents unnecessary constraints on data use and ensures a balanced strategy between risk management and innovation.[3]

In addition, organizations should tailor their governance priorities to specific domains, using an iterative approach to swiftly adapt to evolving needs. This includes daily review and reprioritization of known data-quality issues, focusing on maximizing business benefits, and enabling priority use cases, even if the solution is not perfect. The emphasis is on demonstrating value quickly and refining solutions over time.[4]

Finally, organizations should generate excitement for data. Successful organizations invest in change management to foster support for data enablement. Motivating employees to use and share data is achieved through various interventions such as role modeling from leadership, recognizing high-quality data sources, and implementing training programs or data-related events to create a positive data culture. This practice acknowledges the human element in data governance, recognizing that enthusiastic involvement is crucial for the success of data initiatives.[5]

Using IG Principles to Promote and Sustain ESG Principles and Sustainability Frameworks

Addressing ESG issues requires organizations to take a comprehensive approach that allows them to adequately tackle problem areas. Organizations grapple with challenges such as data archival and availability and the implementation of measures to align activities with ESG goals. Examples include enhancing waste management, promoting transparency in supply chains, and fostering net-zero initiatives.[6]

IG plays a pivotal role in ensuring organizations can successfully meet these challenges. Focused on efficient governance, IG best practices align with ESG objectives, providing secure, available, and transparent information to meet organizational obligations.

Put simply, IG and RIM allow organizations to obtain the right information at the right time. This is critical for the successful implementation of ESG initiatives and aligns with organizations' overall needs to ensure transparency and accountability of the information that they collect and maintain.

In the context of ESG compliance, success in these areas can ensure the compilation of reporting on social data (e.g., antislavery law compliance), accident information, and environmental impact data.

Having robust IG compliance practices also helps organizations to successfully maintain disaster recovery programs, which, in turn, allow businesses to be resilient in the face of natural disasters or environmental challenges. Another benefit is legal compliance—a cornerstone of the Governance aspect of ESG, which includes privacy compliance, retention compliance, and good governance, generally. And, in the realm of litigation, IG not only reduces the need for paper storage but also puts-in-place the mechanisms for reducing personnel document review hours and improves organizations' ability to find and present the right information quickly. RIM also acts as a defense against risks associated with data degradation, veracity, and authenticity. In the context of ESG, this ensures the integrity of environmental and social data, contributing to the overall effectiveness of compliance.

Following is a summary of 10 ways that we believe IG best practices can foster IG compliance:[7]

- Life-Cycle Tracking: Employing IG practices enables companies to monitor the entire life cycle of ESG data, contributing to a reduction in environmental impact.
- Data Transparency: IG practices play a crucial role in ensuring transparency and compliance with regulations, such as the California Consumer Privacy Act, by providing a robust system for tracking and managing data.
- Continuous Progress Reporting: Companies benefit from IG practices as they aid in the systematic collection and reporting of data, showcasing progress toward meeting the UN Sustainable Development Goals.

- Audit Preparedness: By adhering to IG practices, companies secure accurate and comprehensive ESG data, ensuring readiness for audits mandated by regulations such as the Sarbanes–Oxley Act.
- Enhanced Collaboration: IG practices foster collaboration among various departments and stakeholders, aligning with recommendations from the TCFD.
- Data Privacy Assurance: IG practices guarantee compliance with privacy regulations, such as the EU and UK GDPR, safeguarding data privacy and integrity.
- Compliance Monitoring: Companies ensure adherence to ESG reporting standards established by the Sustainability Accounting Standards Board through robust IG practices.
- Risk Mitigation: IG practices aid companies in identifying and mitigating ESG-related risks, including those associated with conflict minerals, as mandated by the Dodd–Frank Act.
- Data Accuracy Assurance: Sound IG practices guarantee precise and consistent data collection, storage, and analysis, aligning with regulations such as the GRI's Standards.
- Transparency: IG practices serve as the linchpin for companies to possess accurate data, fulfilling reporting obligations on policies and performance as mandated by ESG regulations such as the EU Nonfinancial Reporting Directive.

Intersection of Responsible IG and ESG Compliance

Phases of Compliance

Responsible records retention compliance creates a comprehensive framework that spans the entire life cycle of organizational records. This multifaceted approach required by IG best practices is grounded in three key pillars:

- Identification and retention
- Preservation and safekeeping
- Destruction and disposal

By diligently adhering to these principles, businesses align themselves with the various ESG frameworks and goals and demonstrate a clear commitment to responsible and sustainable practices.

The first aspect of this compliance strategy involves the meticulous identification and retention of records. From an IG perspective, this means that organizations must maintain and undergo a systematic process of categorizing and organizing information, which enables pertinent records to be identified and preserved based on legal and regulatory requirements.

To fulfill the second prong, organizations must adopt measures to protect and safeguard records throughout their life cycle. This includes implementing secure storage systems, robust data encryption, and resilient backup mechanisms. By prioritizing the preservation of records, businesses enhance their resilience against potential risks while reinforcing their commitment to sustainable operations and accurate sustainability reporting.

Finally, IG helps organizations to develop, benchmark, and quantify data disposal practices in a way that is both economically and environmentally conscious and that complies with applicable laws, rules, and standards. This process not only has a demonstrable impact on lowering organizations' carbon footprint but also improves organizations' governance, compliance, efficiency, and stakeholder engagement.

Importance of IG to ESG Reporting

Organizations seeking to comply with various ESG standards must be able to accurately access diverse data on an organizationwide basis. With reporting standards moving toward requiring reasonable assurance, the necessity for complete, accurate, and reliable supporting data becomes evident. Data analytics tools and IG best practices become indispensable, aiding organizations in aggregating information from internal systems, external suppliers, and diverse databases where sustainability-related data are stored. In addition, centralizing ESG data in a repository streamlines the reporting process, facilitating comprehensive consideration of all relevant data.[8]

Once collected, ESG data requires thorough organization, normalization, cleaning, and analysis. Data analytics techniques play a crucial role in identifying and correcting errors, inconsistencies, and missing values. And, data standardization becomes increasingly important as data is likely to be aggregated from different sources. This process ensures the accuracy and reliability of reported ESG metrics. ESG analytics further calculates and tracks key metrics such as carbon emissions, water usage, waste generation, employee diversity, and human rights records. This robust reporting allows companies to monitor progress toward ESG goals and benchmark their performance against industry peers, regulatory standards, and best practices.[9]

In addition, given the evolving nature of ESG reporting standards, an organization's internal audit teams must focus on their organization's reporting and disclosure processes. Accurately leveraging data analytics, which requires organizations to access "good data" uncovers patterns and trends, providing auditors with insights to evaluate the effectiveness of internal controls related to data gathering and analysis. It also addresses fraud risks, such as greenwashing, and verifies the accuracy of reported information through traceability to source systems. This meticulous approach ensures compliance with ESG reporting standards and guards against misleading information.[10]

An analysis from PwC suggests that organizations should ask themselves a series of questions when analyzing the quality of existing data collection and their data assessment processes for ESG reporting. These include:

- What are the known ESG data sources? Have all data sources been identified?
- How are ESG data captured in your organization today? What processes and internal controls exist? How long does it take to gather the information?
- How does your company assess its ESG disclosures?
- How comfortable are you with the reliability of those data sources? Are the data complete and accurate?

- What's your company's desired future state? How does that compare with your company's current state?
- How prepared is your company to have its ESG reporting audited under limited or reasonable assurance?[11]

Following this analysis, organizations should ensure that they collect ESG data in a manner that allows them to properly leverage the benefits of IG to benefit their ESG reporting efforts. Specific steps include:

- Ensuring that the organization has C-suite level support and approval for your IG processes.
- Implementing a centralized data management system that collects and consolidates data from diverse departments to ensure both consistency and accessibility.
- Developing standard operating processes to enable ESG data collection that include detailed methodologies, tools, and techniques for gathering ESG data, define the required frequency of data collection, and align data collection with ESG reporting timelines and strategic goals.
- Assigning responsibilities for specific aspects of your ESG documentation program to ensure accountability.
- Auditing the program by promoting mechanisms for regular quality checks, data verification, and remaining dynamic to adapt to evolving ESG reporting standards.
- Promoting the consistent engagement of diverse departments, including IT, facilities, HR, operations, and finance. The rationale behind this inclusion is that each department or division can provide unique insights into different dimensions of ESG, fostering a holistic understanding and management of an organization's ESG performance.
- Regularly training staff to instill a compliance culture that understands and prioritizes ESG data.
- Leveraging surveys, audits, and business reports.
- Using tools such as surveys and internal audits for collecting ESG data and using the data presented within business

reports, sustainability disclosures, and previous ESG reports enriches the data sources.[12]

Following are a series of strategies that companies and, in particular, public companies can use when seeking to ensure that they comply with ESG reporting requirements.

- Monitor Internal ESG Disclosures and Commitments: Designate a team to oversee the company's ESG disclosures and commitments, spanning various formal channels such as SEC filings, sustainability reports, and informal communication methods such as social media, employee communications, media interviews, and website postings.
- Identify existing ESG commitments to establish a baseline and implement a monitoring procedure for both the company's ESG disclosures and those of peer firms.
- Treat ESG Statements Like All Other Public Statements: Subject publicly made ESG statements to the same vetting process for factual accuracy and context as any other public statement.
- Qualify forward-looking commitments, similar to other forward-looking statements, with aspirational qualifiers and appropriate disclaimers.
- Consider extending the internal disclosure controls and procedures process to ESG statements, as they may find their way into SEC filings.
- Educate Employees on ESG Disclosure Risks: Sensitize employees responsible for ESG disclosures to the risks associated with public disclosures. Emphasize the importance of ensuring that ESG statements align with the company's business description, management discussion and analysis, and risk factors in annual and quarterly reports, even when those disclosures seemingly lack explicit ESG themes.
- Encourage coordination among relevant internal constituencies for all material statements included in public disclosure.

- Measure ESG Performance: Establish procedures within the ESG team to assess whether the company's actions align with its public ESG goals, industry standards, and frameworks set by third parties.
- Audit Performance: Regularly evaluate ESG performance against commitments and standards, aiding in the identification of potential vulnerabilities and the mitigation of associated legal and reputational risks.[13]

By implementing these considerations, companies can better navigate the complexities of ESG disclosures, align their commitments with actions, and proactively address legal and reputational challenges.

As discussed in detail, in Part 1, the proper use of metadata (or data about data) is a critical element of the IG process and "tool chest." Using metadata helps to promote ESG compliance by enabling precise tracking, management, and retrieval of environmental, social, and governance data, enhancing transparency, accountability, and regulatory adherence. The following paragraphs illustrate this connection.

In the ESG context, when tracking carbon emissions, possessing detailed metadata associated with emission-related documents, such as source, date of creation, and stakeholders involved, allows organizations to possess a transparent audit trail of critical information that needs to be maintained, benchmarked, and reported. It also allows the information to be presented in a manner that allows stakeholders to readily grasp the accuracy and reliability of emission data, fostering trust and demonstrating the organization's commitment to ESG compliance.

Another example is the use of clear metadata indicating legal hold status, which allows stakeholders to easily identify constrained documents, offering transparency into the organization's commitment to legal compliance. As with the previous example, this practice allows companies to deploy and present a comprehensive ESG narrative, that aligns core IG best practices of effective document retention and management with their commitment to maintaining legal and regulatory compliance.

Metadata use also enables the proper creation, capture, and version control of records to ensure accurate documentation of environmental, social, and governance activities. By maintaining precise records of when and how documents are created, organizations can demonstrate account-ability and transparency in their operations, which are key components of good governance practices and they can also support social responsi-bility by ensuring that all collaborative efforts are well-documented and changes are tracked, fostering an environment of trust and integrity.

The practice of organizing and classifying records using a structured taxonomy and retention schedule likewise ensures that data is managed, retained, and disposed of in accordance with relevant laws and regula-tions, which with ESG goals by minimizing legal risks and ensuring that environmental and social data is preserved and accessible for reporting and compliance purposes.

Moreover, from an audit and compliance perspective, having an estab-lished mechanism to review and proactively destroy of records helps orga-nizations to reduce unnecessary storage costs and improve operational efficiency, which directly supports sustainability goals within ESG frame-works. Specifically, through the structured and defensible elimination of outdated or redundant information, organizations can reduce their envi-ronmental footprint associated with physical and digital storage.

Additionally, in the ESG space, maintaining an accurate inventory of data that tracks diversity-related documents, including contributors, creation dates, and updates, allows companies to accurately present their diversity metrics. This, in turn, allows stakeholders to track changes over time, gaining insight into the evolution of organizational practices. Through precise metadata management, the organization enhances the credibility of diversity and inclusion reporting, showcasing a commitment to social responsibility. In these illustrated examples, strategic metadata management throughout the records management life cycle contributes significantly to the quality of ESG reports, ensuring transparency, accu-rate data tracking, and a comprehensive understanding of organizations' compliance and governance progress in the ESG landscape.

Moreover, having an accurate inventory that allows organizations to hedge against resignation in the form of the "'keep everything'" approach supports the governance aspect of ESG by ensuring a structured and com-pliant approach to information management. For instance, consider a scenario where a company, as part of its governance commitment under the "G" (Governance) pillar of ESG, is required to maintain accurate and transparent records of board meetings, decision-making processes, and policy implementations. The record inventory, meticulously linked to retention schedules, becomes a critical tool in upholding governance standards.

Another benefit of maintaining an accurate records inventory is that it ensures that a company's records are systematically managed and retained for the required duration and creates a clear link between records and retention schedules, allowing the organization to confidently dispose of outdated records by established governance guidelines. This not only streamlines data management but also reduces the risk of retaining unnecessary information, aligning with efficient and transparent governance practices.

Furthermore, the reduced legal liability and monetary risk associated with avoiding spoliation (intentional destruction of evidence) showcase a commitment to ethical governance. In the context of ESG, this supports the organization's efforts to uphold high ethical standards and mitigate risks associated with noncompliance or legal challenges. For example, in regions with stringent antislavery legislation, companies are required to maintain accurate and transparent records related to their supply chain activities that verify that they are not inadvertently involved in human rights abuses or forced labor.

The record inventory, connected to retention schedules, becomes a key instrument in demonstrating compliance with these laws. It allows organizations to systematically track and retain records related to supplier due diligence, audits, and assessments aimed at identifying and addressing any potential instances of modern slavery in the supply chain. Metadata associated with these records, such as supplier agreements, labor practices assessments, and corrective action plans, provides a detailed trail of the organization's commitment to ethical business practices.

In addition to the effective use of metadata and records inventories, from an ESG perspective, it is critical to align records and retention schedules with ESG goals in a manner that enables effective data management, reduced redundancies, lower storage costs, minimized legal liability, and mitigation of cybersecurity risks.

Following are a number of process steps and practices that organizations should use to align their records management life-cycle activities with their ESG goals:

- Clearly Identify ESG Goals: Clearly identify organization-specific ESG goals. Examples include measuring environmental impact (e.g., carbon emissions), promoting social responsibility (e.g., community engagement), and enhancing governance practices (board oversight quality).
- Assess Impact: Conduct a comprehensive ESG impact assessment to understand how and where records management activities intersect with ESG considerations, such as energy consumption, waste reduction, diversity and inclusion, and ethical governance.
- Integrate ESG Criteria Into Record Classification: Improve the organization's classification criteria and records taxonomies by incorporating ESG considerations by, for example, classifying certain records based on their relevance to ESG goals, and ensuring that this taxonomy is managed and updated throughout the records' life cycle.
- Map ESG Records: Align the IG-based management life-cycle stages (creation, storage, retrieval, retention, and disposal) to the organization's ESG-relevant activities and establish clear processes for the effective and accurate creation, capture, and retention of records that document the organization's adherence to ESG principles and frameworks.
- Incorporate ESG-Based Metadata Tagging: Tag records that have a specific ESG impact to capture ESG attributes (e.g., energy consumption, diversity) within the organization's records management system to ensure that ESG records are discoverable and traceable.
- Ensure That Retention Policies Align With ESG Compliance Goals: Review and enhance retention policies to apply to ESG standards and reporting requirements and verify that records and nonrecord business data related to subjects such

as environmental reporting, social impact assessments, and governance practices are kept for and disposed of based on the required minimum and maximum retention periods.

- Integrate ESG Concepts Into Record Disposal Processes: Use disposal methods that align with (and, hopefully improve) your ESG metrics. Examples include decreasing the paper-records footprint of the organization through digitization, using secure disposal methods, and deploying energy-efficient disposal technologies.
- Training: Institute comprehensive and relevant training programs to raise awareness of the integration of ESG goals and promote staff commitment to ESG goals.
- Monitoring and Continuous Improvement: Audit and track the organization's progress in aligning records management with ESG goals, for example, by creating reports highlighting ESG KPIs. Also, regularly review IG processes to verify alignment with ESG goals (and sanity-check these processes periodically with relevant stakeholders such as investors, board members, and employees). Also, compile ESG data in a way that accords with transparency goals and that demonstrates a commitment to commonly adopted ESG principles.

Aligning ESG With Metadata Management Activities

IG-based metadata management principles play a pivotal role in the effective functioning of organizations of all types and sizes. These principles are not only essential for internal information management but also function as a catalyst for sharing and reusing information, influencing decision making, research, analytics, and information sharing. The evolving landscape of technology, coupled with the increasing volume and variety of information, underscores the critical role of metadata in providing reliable content, context, and information quality.

In the broader scope of organizational governance, these standards can guide metadata creators, information asset custodians, information management specialists, and various other stakeholders involved in the information life cycle.

In the realm of complying with ESG frameworks, effective metadata management takes on heightened significance. Metadata, as the key to identifying, cataloging, and governing information, is integral to providing accurate, reliable, and transparent data, aligning with the principles of responsible business practices set forth by ESG standards. Accurate and well-managed metadata not only aids in meeting compliance requirements but also enables organizations to demonstrate their commitment to environmental sustainability, social responsibility, and effective governance.

Processes required to achieve this goal include:

- Assessing ESG Requirements: Thoroughly evaluate the specific ESG requirements relevant to the organization. This involves understanding the ESG factors that impact the business. Identify KPIs and data elements crucial for ESG reporting.
- Identifying Relevant Metadata: Identify the core metadata elements that are critical for cataloging and governing information related to environmental impact, social responsibility, and governance. Examples include data related to energy consumption, emissions, diversity initiatives, community engagement, and governance practices.
- Aligning Approach With Management Principles: Align the identified metadata elements with metadata management principles, particularly the standardized, contextualized, and managed principles to promote a consistent approach to metadata that enhances its reliability, accuracy, and usefulness in supporting ESG compliance.
- Developing Standardized Metadata Schemas: Create or adopt standardized metadata schemas that align with industry best practices and ESG reporting standards and verify that these schemas cover the identified metadata elements and facilitate interoperability across different data repositories within the organization. Also ensure that metadata incorporates information such as collection methods, data sources, approvals, and timestamps.
- Integrating Schemas With IG Framework: Integrate the standardized metadata schemas into the broader

IG framework of the organization. Ensure that metadata management is embedded in IG policies, procedures, and practices, emphasizing the importance of accurate and well-managed metadata for ESG compliance.

- Creating and Refining Data Dictionaries and Business Glossaries: Develop data dictionaries and business glossaries specific to the identified ESG-related metadata elements. These glossaries should provide clear, organization-specific, and contextual definitions and explanations, supporting a common understanding of terms and promoting accurate data usage in ESG reporting.

- Effectively Managing the Metadata Life Cycle: Organizations should implement a comprehensive metadata life-cycle management approach and ensure that metadata is captured accurately during information creation, actively maintained, updated with changes, and monitored for accuracy and consistency over time. This aligns with the managed principle.

- Publishing Metadata for Transparency: The next step is to publish relevant metadata to external discovery tools and platforms, following the principles of transparency outlined in ESG frameworks. This enhances the visibility of information related to ESG factors, contributing to transparent and accountable reporting.

- Automating Metadata Processes: Organizations should adopt a cross-functional approach to implementing suitable automated processes in metadata capture, modification, and management. The goal of these solutions should be to enhance efficiency, reduce resource intensity, and improve the overall quality of metadata, aligning with the automated principle.

- Continuous Improvement and Monitoring: Organizations should establish defined mechanisms for continuous improvement and monitoring of metadata practices. They should also review and update metadata schemas, data dictionaries, and business glossaries to ensure that they remain aligned with evolving ESG requirements and organizational priorities.

- Training and Awareness: Organizations should develop, provide, and update training and awareness programs for relevant stakeholders, including metadata creators, data analysts, and ESG reporting teams. Ensure that personnel understand the importance of metadata in ESG compliance and how to adhere to standardized metadata practices.

The Environmental Impact of Overstorage and How IG Can Help

Overstoring data is both an IG and an ESG issue. In previous parts, we discussed some of the main IG problems with overstorage. Here, we discuss some of the environmental issues. These include data discovery costs, data center consolidation issues, and other associated environmental costs. IG best practices.

Data Discovery

Unstructured data makes up roughly 80 percent of all enterprise data and can represent high costs and risks if not managed properly. By eliminating ROT, which can represent as much as 30 to 50 percent of storage, across an enterprise, companies can reduce their carbon footprint in cloud migration efforts by two metric tons of CO_2 per terabyte of data.[14]

Data Center Consolidation

Defensible deletion and the consolidation of data centers wield a considerable influence on sustainability initiatives. In the context of a carbon price of ~US$51 per metric ton, a petabyte of data translates to a carbon footprint of 4,000 metric tons of CO_2, amounting to an annual cost of $500,000 for server operation. The financial advantages of data deletion are noteworthy; eliminating every terabyte equates to potential savings of approximately ~$3,300 in primary storage costs. Integrating practices aligned with ESG principles and robust data security measures not only mitigates risks and safeguards critical data but also contributes to substantial cost savings, fostering a shift toward more sustainable and ethically driven business practices.[15]

Employing data minimization strategies, characterized by the collection and retention of only the essential information for specific purposes, offers an avenue to diminish the environmental impact associated with data processing. Recent estimations reveal that a substantial portion—up to 30 percent—of servers in data centers are essentially dormant, consuming energy and resources without performing significant tasks.[16]

Encryption

While organizations heavily rely on data analytics for business insights, the associated risks of data misuse, loss, or theft are substantial. Privacy-preserving techniques, such as deidentification or anonymization, enable the utilization and analysis of data without compromising sensitive information about individuals. However, certain privacy-preserving technologies, including homomorphic encryption, may demand additional resources and energy.[17]

Impact of Cloud Adoption

The transition of enterprise workloads and data to the cloud, particularly through major cloud service vendors, presents an opportunity to reduce carbon emissions. A 2019 report from 451 Research underscores the operational efficiencies and carbon footprint reduction achieved by moving enterprise workloads to a major cloud service vendor. The industrywide commitment of major cloud service vendors to renewable energy, energy-efficient servers, and improved server utilization can result in substantial benefits. Calculations in the report indicate that migrating a 1-megawatt enterprise data center to a major cloud service vendor, for example, can reduce carbon emissions by 400 to 1,000 metric tons annually. As these vendors progress rapidly toward its renewable energy goals, further potential savings in carbon emissions are anticipated.[18]

Relevant IG strategies include:

- Implementing data cleanup and hygiene, targeting ROT data.
- Reducing carbon footprint in cloud migration by eliminating ROT.

- Executing defensible deletion strategies to reduce the carbon footprint associated with server operation costs.
- Using IG data quality strategies to consolidate information to create the business case for deletion including data related to the financial advantages of data deletion and the environmental impact of privacy-preserving technologies, such as homomorphic encryption (a cryptographic technique that allows computations to be performed on encrypted data without decrypting it), considering additional resources and energy.
- Deploying privacy and security controls to ensure that data minimization strategies lead to the collection and retention of only essential information for specific purposes. Also, employ privacy-preserving techniques such as deidentification or anonymization to enable secure data utilization and analysis.
- Deploy data management tools to accurately calculate the operational efficiencies and carbon footprint reduction achieved by moving enterprise workloads to cloud-based services.

Aligning IG With Environmental Sustainability Goals

According to a study published by the World Economic Forum,[19] organizations seeking to develop a robust environmentally sustainable strategy must define the issues that matter most to the entity and its stakeholders. To accomplish this, organizations need to understand which business activities have the greatest potential impact on environmental sustainability, which, in turn, requires a framework in which leadership can access the right information at the right time and update that information as and when needed. The following chart highlights various core goals and activities that promote this process together with their IG analogs.

Process	Environmental Data Priorities	IG Strategies	Goals
Assess Risks	Highlight the environmental risks and opportunities that have the greatest strategic significance.	Establish clear metadata standards for environmental data, ensuring data quality and accuracy, and implementing robust data management practices. Promoting collaboration among different departments and stakeholders through effective information sharing and communication channels contributes to a holistic understanding of environmental factors.	Integrate IG strategies into environmental impact analysis to strategically assess, prioritize, and respond to environmental risks and opportunities in a well-informed manner and align corporate actions with broader sustainability goals and ESG frameworks.
Monitor	Monitor environmental risks and opportunities, tracking trends in regulatory landscapes, media dialogues, and external factors such as climate disruptions.	Implement data-driven technological tools to track dynamic regulatory trends that can exert an impact on carbon emissions. Use metadata tools to track those records that correlate to the broader environmental impact trends. Maintain centralized and integrated repositories for environmental data and verify that these repositories incorporate metadata standards and promote effective information sharing across departments.	Enhance the organization's ability to comprehensively analyze and respond to emerging environmental trends and risks.

Measure the Impact of Risks	Evaluate the environmental effects of operations throughout the life cycle of products and services to pinpoint areas where the most substantial influence can be exerted on the overall environmental performance of the entire value chain.	Implement a robust metadata standardization process to facilitate and prioritize the accurate tracking and analysis of environmental impacts. Ensure cross-functional collaboration (i.e., a diverse working group) that includes diverse incorporates diverse perspectives for collecting data related to environmental compliance.	Improve the precision and comprehensiveness of measuring and addressing environmental impacts throughout the product and service life cycle.
Establish Environmental Sustainability Strategy	Define and communicate a comprehensive, long-term environmental sustainability strategy with clear targets, allocated resources, and the integration of digital technology. Implement metrics, KPIs, and dashboards to facilitate ongoing management oversight and track performance against established goals. Integrate the oversight of environmental issues into broader business processes, encompassing risk management, product design, long-term business strategy, leaders' respective areas of responsibility and incentives, while leveraging the synergy between digital and environmental initiatives.	Integrate environmental data management into broader information management processes. Ensure that the organization's IG steering committee verifies that investment in information management allows the organization to adequately track environmental data. Ensure C-suite level support for documentation activities. Continuously monitor environmental data tracking metrics, enabling real-time insights and adaptive strategies. Conduct training programs to enhance employees' awareness and understanding of environmental issues, fostering a culture of sustainability throughout the organization.	Define and communicate a comprehensive, long-term environmental sustainability strategy with clear targets, allocated resources, and digital integration. Implement metrics, KPIs, and dashboards for ongoing oversight, integrating environmental concerns into broader business processes. Ensure that information management processes align with environmental data tracking, gaining C-suite support and continuous monitoring for adaptive strategies. Conduct training programs for enhanced employee awareness, fostering a culture of sustainability.

(Continued)

Process	Environmental Data Priorities	IG Strategies	Goals
Maintain Clearly Defined Governance Structures	Align digital transformation and environmental sustainability goals. Achieve broad (both higher and lower level) buy-in throughout the organization. Create use cases that translate environmental sustainability goals into value propositions and efficiencies (both internal and external).	Establish and maintain a comprehensive data analytics strategy to systematically collect environmental sustainability data across business units. Incorporate IG by design structures to proactively integrate best practices into technologies and governance strategies while promoting environmental sustainability goals. Address systemic issues related to collecting environmental compliance data through the IG steering committee. Assess and track data from the organization's vendor and supply chain network in alignment with the organizational IG structure.	Align the organization's digital transformation and environmental sustainability goals by harmonizing the IG framework, ensuring broad organizational buy-in, and creating compelling use cases that translate sustainability objectives into value propositions and efficiencies.

Improve the Environmental Sustainability of Digitization Efforts	Develop capabilities for adopting digital business models that enhance environmentally sustainable resource use through intelligent provisioning and optimization. Enable cross-organizational data-sharing to optimize and track the environmental and economic benefits of digitally enabled business models, fostering aggregated impact understanding. Real-time Analytics and Resource Efficiency: Facilitate a data-sharing digital economy with real-time analytics to align supply and demand, leading to improved resource utilization and waste reduction in supply chains or urban transportation. Customer-Centric Digital Innovation: Centralize customer data with API interoperability and security by design, enhancing customer experience while maintaining trust.	Implement defined IG action items to develop and enforce data governance protocols specifically tailored for the adoption of digital business models that focus on ensuring data accuracy, security, and compliance with environmental sustainability goals. Ensure that the IG framework enables and governs cross-organizational data-sharing, emphasizing security, privacy, and compliance including providing guidelines for optimizing and tracking environmental and economic benefits derived from digitally enabled business models. Incorporate IG controls for real-time analytics, ensuring that data used for vendor and supply chain analysis is properly governed including monitoring data stewardship, access controls, and ethical data management considerations. Ensure that managed data is properly centralized API interoperability and security by design, for example, by creating policies that define data storage, access, and sharing protocols.	Establish and enhance digital capabilities for environmentally sustainable resource use through intelligent provisioning and optimization, coupled with the implementation of IG measures to ensure accurate, secure, and compliant data management, encompassing cross-organizational data-sharing, real-time analytics governance, and centralized customer data management with application programing interfaces (APIs) interoperability, ultimately fostering a data-driven, environmentally responsible digital ecosystem.

(Continued)

Process	Environmental Data Priorities	IG Strategies	Goals
Use Technology to Drive New Digitally Enabled Business Models	Develop the necessary capacities to embrace digital business models enhancing environmentally sustainable resource utilization, encompassing materials, energy, and water, achieved through intelligent provisioning, coordination, or optimization.	Promote collaboration by enabling data-sharing among distinct organizational units to optimize and monitor the environmental and economic benefits derived from digitally enhanced business models. Promote a data-sharing ecosystem and digital economy with real-time analytics and optimization to align supply and demand, leading to enhanced resource utilization and reductions in waste, such as perishable supply chain waste or urban transportation inefficiencies. Centralize all customer data in a secure, API-interoperable location to elevate the customer experience while upholding trust and security. Utilize digital platforms and channels to gather diverse and widespread customer feedback, fostering innovation in environmentally sustainable digital business models.	Leverage IG best practices to allow the organization to embrace environmentally sustainable business models through seamless data-sharing, real-time analytics, and centralized customer data frameworks to ensure the security and interoperability of environmentally sustainable digital business models.

Improve Sustainability Operating Models	Create a strategic plan for investing in IT capabilities that enhance transparency and incorporate data-driven efficiency enhancements across diverse organizational units. Integrate environmental factors into operational decision-making processes, prioritizing areas with substantial impact, such as evaluating the carbon intensity of the local grid for facility site selection.	Implement intelligent information management workflows and process automation to achieve quantifiable efficiency improvements and enhance resource utilization.	Develop and implement a comprehensive strategic plan to invest in IT capabilities, fostering transparency, and integrating data-driven efficiency enhancements across diverse organizational units. Incorporate environmental factors into operational decision-making processes, with a focus on areas of significant impact, such as evaluating the carbon intensity of the local grid for facility site selection and implementing intelligent information management workflows and process automation to achieve measurable efficiency improvements and optimize resource utilization.
Optimize Supply-Chain Management	Create end-to-end supply-chain visibility and traceability to enable real-time, traceable, and data-backed supply-chain management decisions.	Implement a centralized data "control tower" solution that integrates real-time data across the supply chain and external sources, enhancing visibility and resilience for improved delivery, environmental sustainability, and overall customer experience.	Establish a robust supply-chain visibility system for real-time decisions that include mechanisms such as a centralized data "control tower" to enable enhanced visibility, resilience, and improved delivery, sustainability, and customer experience. Embrace IG principles to reduce environmental impacts.

(Continued)

Process	Environmental Data Priorities	IG Strategies	Goals
		Adopt IG principles by designing a data model that integrates both internal and external data sources to identify and mitigate exposure to acute and chronic environmental risks, ensuring better performance tracking against environmental goals.	
		Embrace IG by partnering with industry associations, peers, and suppliers to establish secure data-sharing and tracking platforms. This collaboration aims to enhance visibility and accountability, ultimately reducing environmental impacts.	
		Integrate IG best practices by collaborating with environmental certification providers to incorporate certifications directly into traceability data flows. Additionally, support digital solutions that streamline reporting challenges for improved efficiency.	
		Leverage IG strategies to evaluate the potential of enabling technologies such as the industrial Internet of things (IIoT), AI, or digital twins. Explore how these technologies can optimize operational efficiencies, minimize environmental impact, and reduce costs.	

Incorporate Fact-Based Environmental Decision-Making Processes	Embed quantifiable environmental sustainability considerations into corporate decision making to ensure that environmental sustainability is a critical factor (e.g., when comparing a set of manufacturing processes). Transparently inform organizational and value chain stakeholders of the environmental considerations used to make business decisions.	Use data analytics-based strategies together with AI technology, to monitor changes in strategic environmental considerations. Regularly audit data sets to enable accurate scenario analyses that accurately depict environmental costs. Establish companywide KPIs and reporting standards and collaborate with IT to create user-friendly dashboards and similar visuals.	Leverage best-practice IG and data analytics technologies to enable the development and analysis of fact-based sustainability insights.
Accurately Assess Financial Impact of Environmental Targets	Create and deploy tools for measuring environmental impacts, assessing progress toward company targets, and determining return-on-investment.	Establish and utilize measurement tools aligned with IG protocols to ensure the accuracy, security, and reliability of data collected through measurement tools and impact assessment frameworks to measure environmental impact, monitor progress toward company targets, and evaluate return-on-investment. Integrate digital tools into financial assessment procedures to ensure comprehensive evaluations of environmental sustainability impacts under predefined future scenarios.	Develop and implement tools for measuring environmental impacts, assessing progress toward company targets, and determining ROI, while aligning with IG protocols to ensure data accuracy and security.

(Continued)

Process	Environmental Data Priorities	IG Strategies	Goals
		Centralize and integrate data to facilitate reporting on environmental KPIs based on global sustainability reporting standards, such as the GRI or the SASB.	
Obtain and Promote Organizational Buy-In	Inform and engage employees by effectively communicating the organization's long-term growth plans, including its environmental goals. Continuously enhance KPIs that integrate digital transformation and environmentally sustainable goals. Align incentives and acknowledge employees for their contributions to the convergence of digital transformation and environmentally sustainable goals. Minimize the company's travel footprint through the implementation of digital solutions for remote work, collaboration, training, and client engagement, while adhering to IG protocols to protect sensitive data.	Empower employees with digital and data tools, incorporating IG practices, such as design thinking or agile project management, to drive innovation aligned with the company's purpose and advance environmental sustainability-related KPIs in their roles. Create effective work-from-home protocols that enable home workers to maintain data in line with IG processes and goals.	Create and maintain organizational structures that both inform employees of environmental priorities and ensure their continual buy-in through IG best practices and organizational culture.

Alignment of IG With Social Goals

The first part of this book addressed, among other topics, the various components of some of the most widely used ESG frameworks. As discussed in that part, one of the critical components (and also, possibly, the most elusive) is "Social," and particularly, how to measure social development using objective metrics.

One important ISO standard that establishes clear priorities for organizations seeking to align their social goals with ESG practices is ISO 26000. The ISO 26000 standard serves as a comprehensive guide for organizations in understanding and implementing social responsibility. It defines seven core subjects, outlined in Clause 6, which organizations need to consider fulfilling their societal obligations. These subjects cover a broad spectrum, ranging from organizational governance and human rights to labor practices, environmental concerns, fair operating practices, consumer issues, and community involvement and development.[20]

In the realm of organizational governance (6.2), ISO 26000 emphasizes decision making aligned with societal expectations, integrating factors such as accountability, transparency, ethics, and stakeholder considerations. The standard also addresses human rights (6.3), promoting fair treatment, and the elimination of discrimination, torture, and exploitation. Labor practices (6.4) highlight the importance of preventing unfair competition through ethical employment relationships, conditions of work, and social protection.[21]

Environmental responsibilities (6.5) underscore the need to reduce unsustainable production patterns, prevent pollution, and contribute to climate change mitigation. Fair operating practices (6.6) advocate for systems of fair competition, anti-corruption measures, and responsible political involvement. Consumer issues (6.7) focus on ensuring fair marketing, protecting consumer health and safety, and promoting sustainable consumption. Community involvement and development (6.8) stress the role of organizations in creating sustainable social structures and contributing to education, employment, technology development, and overall well-being.

ISO 26000 also encourages social responsibility reporting, suggesting that organizations periodically report on their performance to stakeholders. This reporting should cover core subjects, stakeholder involvement, a comprehensive performance overview, and plans for addressing short-comings. To enhance the credibility of reports, ISO 26000 recommends adhering to reporting guidelines from external organizations. The GRI and CSRWire are two such entities offering reporting frameworks and resources to organizations aligning their practices with ISO 26000. GRI G4, in particular, provides guidance for organizations using GRI guidelines as the reporting framework for ISO 26000 implementations. By embracing these principles and reporting practices, organizations can effectively demonstrate their commitment to social responsibility and sustainable business practices.[22]

Another critical ISO standard is ISO 37001, related to antibribery. ISO 37001 outlines a set of measures aimed at assisting organizations in preventing, detecting, and addressing bribery, emphasizing a reasonable and proportionate approach. The key measures include the implementation of an antibribery policy and supporting procedures, ensuring top management's commitment and leadership, effectively allocating compliance responsibilities throughout the organization, and appointing an individual or team to oversee antibribery compliance. Additionally, controls over decision-making processes, resource allocation, vetting of personnel, antibribery training, and appropriate documentation are crucial components.[23]

The standard emphasizes the importance of periodic bribery risk assessments, due diligence on transactions and business associates, and the implementation of financial and nonfinancial controls. Organizations are required to extend antibribery measures to entities under their control, ensuring proportionate measures based on the nature and extent of bribery risks. When dealing with business associates posing higher bribery risks, organizations should encourage the implementation of antibribery controls and obtain relevant commitments. Controls over gifts, hospitality, and donations, along with reporting procedures for whistleblowing, are crucial to prevent these avenues from being exploited for bribery purposes.[24]

Ongoing monitoring, evaluation, and improvement of the antibribery management system (ABMS) procedures are integral, including internal audits, reviews by the compliance function and top management, and rectification of identified issues. The standard, ISO 37001, not only provides a framework for addressing bribery but also emphasizes the need for a comprehensive and systematic approach, aligning with international best practices and promoting a culture of ethical conduct within organizations.[25]

Following is a summary of certain critical areas in which IG best practices can help organizations realize their social compliance goals.

Goal	ESG "Social" Priorities	Relevant IG Strategies
Education and Skill Development	Support educational initiatives and skill development within the communities in which the organization is located.	Use IG strategies around metadata and categorization to find the information needed to provide data-driven insights on the education programs that cater to the specific needs of the community and then analyze the data to create insights that allow the organization to tailor programs for maximum social development impact. Promote the ethical and secure management of educational data by remaining aware of the various laws requiring the organization to protect the privacy and confidentiality of individuals participating in educational programs. Train employees to comply with these standards.
Customer Engagement/ Satisfaction and Data Privacy	Protect the privacy and confidentiality of customer, shareholder, personnel, and other stakeholder data.	Implement a data classification system to categorize data based on sensitivity and confidentiality levels for personally identifiable information. Conduct regular security risk assessments to identify potential vulnerabilities and threats to the privacy of customer, shareholder, personnel, and stakeholder data. Maintain robust data encryption mechanisms to safeguard sensitive information during storage, transmission, and processing as well as stringent access controls to restrict unauthorized access to sensitive data based on a system of role-based permissions.

(Continued)

Goal	ESG "Social" Priorities	Relevant IG Strategies
		Defensibly and securely delete personal data when no longer needed for a legitimate purpose.
		Develop and enforce comprehensive and legally compliant data privacy and retention policies that align with relevant regulations, industry standards, and best practices.
		Establish robust disaster preparedness and vital records programs.
		Provide relevant and role-specific employee training.
Social Innovation and Product/ Service Impact	Promote innovation for social impact through products and services. Examples: A company that creates products that prioritize inclusive design to ensure that their use is accessible to persons with disabilities. A company that optimizes its website to ensure access by people with a hearing disability.	Use IG strategies to track and manage data related to the social aspects of product development. Implement technical systems to assess and report on the sustainability metrics of each product, ensuring alignment with ESG goals. Ensure that the organization collects and analyzes data from community interactions in a way that is both effective and complies with privacy and confidentiality laws. Deploy IG best practices related to metadata classification to track data related to product safety and inclusiveness. Audit data quality to ensure the accuracy and consistency of social impact messaging.
Adapt to Societal Challenges	Build and improve the organization's ability to adapt to societal challenges (e.g., improving diversity, equity, and inclusion (DEI) efforts boosting philanthropic efforts).	Use of metadata and other IG tools to find data faster. Develop robust and meaningful analytics. Incorporate IG priorities into the goals of the DEI steering committee. Protect important personal data using ISO 27701 standards.

| Promote Ethical Supply Chain Management | Ensure that sourcing and procurement practices prioritize environmental sustainability, social responsibility, and governance, thereby fostering fair labor conditions, preventing human rights violations, and promoting overall ethical conduct within the supply chain. | Develop and enforce a comprehensive supplier code of conduct that outlines clear expectations regarding ethical and sustainable practices covering areas such as fair labor practices, environmental responsibility, anti-corruption measures, and respect for human rights.

Utilize technology, such as blockchain or other tracking systems, to provide visibility into the origins of raw materials, manufacturing processes, and distribution channels.

Establish mechanisms for real-time reporting and investigation of ethical concerns, enabling timely corrective actions to mitigate risks and uphold ethical standards. |
| Improve Investment in Employee Training | Invest in employee training and development for long-term career growth. | Develop and implement structured IG training programs that specifically address ethical supply chain management and align with ESG goals.

Use IG tools to monitor and assess employee progress in understanding and implementing ethical supply chain practices. |

Taking an IG-Centric Approach to Diversity, Equity, and Inclusion Metrics

Diversity is recognized as a critical factor for increasing performance within organizations. Chief diversity officers face challenges, however, when attempting to take a data-driven approach to DEI. One significant issue involves the risks of relying on DEI data and metrics—for example, the use of sensitive personal information.[26]

According to a McKinsey study, there is a compelling profit argument for gender diversity, as well as ethnic and cultural diversity, within corporate leadership, and underscores the ongoing enhancement of this business case. Presently, the most diverse companies exhibit a higher likelihood of surpassing less diverse counterparts in terms of profitability. The analysis conducted in 2019 reveals that companies positioned in the top quartile for gender diversity on executive teams demonstrated a 25 percent higher probability of achieving above-average profitability compared to those in the fourth quartile, indicating a positive correlation between diversity and superior financial performance.[27]

Given this backdrop, it has become increasingly clear that organizations seeking to benefit from DEI must be able to rely on good data and clear and meaningful metrics (i.e., not just a body count of people from different groups). This means, for example, that they need to go beyond the "outcome" metrics of body count, but combine them with broader process metrics, to correlate them with and identify problems related to personnel management processes. Examples of this approach include examining the rate at which individuals from diverse backgrounds progress within the corporate hierarchy or analyzing salary differentials between genders in similar roles serves as illustrative process metrics, guiding efforts to effect meaningful change.[28]

From an IG perspective, this requires organizations to develop and become aware of their "data practice maturity" level. It also requires organizations to support the development of data practice maturity at their highest levels and as a consistent exercise.

Generally, data practice maturity can be broken down into five core levels:

- Unaware: Individuals lack comprehension and endorsement of established data practices.
- Aware: Individuals comprehend and endorse the formal exertion of authority and control over data.
- Define: Definite responsibilities are outlined, and associated activity metrics are recorded formally.
- Manage: Individuals recognize optimal practices, enhance performance, automate processes, and employ metrics for outcome management.
- Enhance: Individuals recognize optimal practices, enhance performance, automate processes, and employ metrics for outcome management.[29]

Characterizing an enterprise as "data-driven" implies that it has optimized sound and developed data practices throughout the entire company.

On a practical level, this signifies that the organization has realized that sound data management is considered "everyone's job," implying that each individual utilizes data daily to propel actions, achieve outcomes, and discern "how can we make it happen?"[30]

From an IG perspective, this requires the existence of clearly defined roles outlined in formal policies and procedures. These advanced data practices stand in stark contrast to less mature organizations categorized as "data-aware," where solely executives employ reports to ascertain "what happened." They also differ from moderately mature organizations labeled as "data-informed," where functional experts analyze data to discern "why did it happen." Gaining insight into your organization's position in terms of data maturity is a crucial step in evaluating the type of risk that can and should be embraced.[31]

It also requires the development of data life-cycle management processes hallmarked by sound stewardship and robust involvement (i.e., not top-down) so that staff understand how to properly collect, process, and use DEI data. Following is a summary of some of the IG principles that can and should apply to this effort:

- Collection: Only collect DEI data for the specific purposes outlined in the notice given to the individual supplying the data, also referred to as the "data subject."
- Use: Restrict the use and processing of DEI data to the purposes specified in the notice and for which the individual has granted implicit or explicit consent.
- Retention: Retain DEI data solely for the duration necessary to fulfill the stated purpose.
- Disclosure: Disclose DEI data to third parties exclusively for the purposes identified in the notice and with the consent of the individual.[32]

Achieving DEI data maturity success also requires organizations to develop a robust and clearly defined roadmap, which should involve many of the following steps:

- Understand Leaders' Risk Tolerance: Gauge leaders' tolerance for risks associated with a metrics-driven DEI approach as well as for DEI endeavors, generally (i.e., do they believe in the value of DEI?). Consider both outcome and process metrics in alignment with diversity goals.

- Evaluate Process Maturity: Assess the maturity of underlying processes for managing DEI-related risks. Ensure that processes are well-defined, documented, and capable of addressing potential challenges associated with data-driven DEI.
- Study Legal Implications: Acquire a thorough understanding of laws relevant to DEI data including the risks of overstorage and improper collection. Also, when collecting data related to DEI, be aware of potential risks associated with interview questions related to national origin, race, age, disability, sexual orientation, or gender identity. Also, scrutinize the antidiscrimination implications of diversity targets and, as necessary, laws related to education records.
- Navigate Privacy Laws: Ensure that your collection and use of data complies with federal, state, municipal, and international privacy laws related to employee data.
- Acknowledge Accountability: Realize that DEI staff may have certain residual legal risks that cannot be mitigated through administrative or technical controls and understand the importance of accountability in the context of legal compliance.[33]

Recognizing diversity as a critical driver of organizational performance underscores the importance of a data-driven approach to DEI. However, the inherent risks in relying on DEI data and metrics, particularly sensitive personal information, necessitate organizations to prioritize the development of robust data practices and meaningful metrics. This requires a strategic IG-centric focus on "data practice maturity," spanning five levels from unawareness to enhancement. Being truly "data-driven" implies optimized data practices across the organization, emphasizing that effective data management is everyone's responsibility. This maturity contrasts with less advanced organizations categorized as "data-aware" or "data-informed." A pivotal aspect of this maturity is the development of sound data life-cycle management processes, emphasizing bottom-up involvement and robust stewardship.

Moreover, key IG principles, such as purpose-specific data collection, restricted data use, appropriate retention, and controlled disclosure, play a vital role in achieving DEI data maturity. The journey toward success also involves understanding leaders' risk tolerance, evaluating process maturity, comprehending legal implications, navigating privacy laws, and acknowledging accountability for residual legal risks. And, finally, establishing a clear roadmap incorporating these steps is essential for organizations committed to fostering a data-driven, mature, and compliant approach to DEI.

IG Best Practices and Governance Goals

Governance, while lacking a universal definition, is fundamentally about making informed decisions for an organization in, both the short and long terms. Examining governance through the lens of credit risk provides a narrower perspective, emphasizing aspects such as how an enterprise is managed, its relationships with various stakeholders, its ownership structure, and the impact of internal procedures on risk creation or mitigation.[34]

Weak governance can significantly influence a corporation's outlook, as it forms the bedrock for sound business decisions. Governance failures have historically led to corporate collapses, exemplified by the 2022 case of FTX where insufficient reserves to meet customer demands were admitted by the CEO. The impact of poor governance often outweighs the positive effects of good governance, highlighting the critical importance of assessing governance.[35]

ESG analysts aim to gain a deeper understanding of the alignment between leadership incentives and stakeholder expectations, the perspective and adherence to shareholder rights, and the presence of internal controls fostering transparency and accountability in leadership.[36] Important components of "Governance" include tracking executive pay, bribery and corruption, political lobbying and donations, board diversity and structure, tax strategy, and data breach compliance.[37] Several of these concepts, such as addressing bribery and corruption and data breach compliance overlap with the social goals of ESG.

Following is a chart addressing how IG best practices can be leveraged to address some of the challenges facing entities seeking to promote and improve their ESG governance practices.

Concept	ESG "Governance" Priorities	Relevant IG Strategies
Executive Pay	Link executive pay to ESG goal achievement.	Regularly review and audit organizational data and decision-making processes to identify and rectify any biases.
	Establish and maintain fair and equitable executive compensation structures, by, for example, addressing gender and diversity pay gaps and ensuring that executive pay aligns with broader societal expectations of fairness and equality.	Augment classic IG analysis with technology tools that can analyze and flag potential disparities in executive pay based on gender, ethnicity, or other factors.
		Solicit broad-based IG steering committee input when determining methods for improving data uniformity and quality as it relates to executive compensation.
	Accurately report on executive pay fairness to ensure stakeholder transparency.	Regularly update and verify the data used for performance evaluations, enabling executives and stakeholders to make informed decisions based on reliable information.
	Create accountability structures such as clawback measures that allow the organization to reclaim excess executive compensation following a financial restatement or unethical behavior.	Incorporate ESG concepts, workflows, and use cases into IG training.
		Maintain and tag accurate and well-documented records of executive performance and conduct, ensuring that the necessary data is readily available when needed.
Bribery and Corruption	Ensure that the organization abstains from corrupt practices internally and also proactively develops policies and programs addressing corruption within its supply chain.	Develop a comprehensive data governance policy that includes specific guidelines for preventing and detecting corruption. Establish protocols for secure data storage, access controls, and encryption to safeguard sensitive information related to anti-corruption measures. Regularly update and communicate these policies to employees, ensuring awareness and adherence.

		Create standardized templates for reporting on anti-corruption initiatives, ensuring clarity and consistency in the data presented. Leverage metadata management to provide context to the reported data, enhancing transparency and accountability.
		Maintain a stakeholder engagement data strategy that includes secure communication channels, data-sharing protocols, and regular reporting mechanisms.
Political Lobbying and Donations	Promote transparency, accountability, and ethical conduct in the organization's engagement with political activities to ensure that its political involvement aligns with responsible business practices and respects the principles of good governance.	Create data stewardship, access controls, and metadata standards for information related to political lobbying and donations that align with IG metadata practices generally, promote the secure and effective tracking of political donations, and are a combination of suitable technologies and IG best practices.
		Integrate political donation records into organizational retention policies specifying how long this data should be retained and when it should be securely disposed.
		Incorporate training on political donation compliance requirements, ethical considerations, and policies related to political lobbying and donations into general information management training programs.
		Develop protocols to ensure that political donation data is stored and shared securely and in line with privacy laws.
		Create a centralized repository for storing documents related to political activities, including communication records, reports, and compliance documentation.

(Continued)

Concept	ESG "Governance" Priorities	Relevant IG Strategies
Board Diversity and Structure	Promote diversity within the organization's corporate board to promote adaption to changing business environments, promote diverse thinking and problem solving and improve objective decision-making processes.	Utilize data analytics tools and HR information systems that focus on diversity metrics to analyze workforce demographics, track trends over time, and provide insights into needed improvements. Ensure that document management systems (DMS) are configured to store and manage documents related to diversity policies, internal promotion tracks, and management programs so that relevant information is easily accessible, supporting transparency and accountability in diversity initiatives. Train board members how to use or access these systems.
Tax Strategy	Ensure that the organization conducts its tax affairs in a responsible and sustainable manner and aligns tax practices with ethical, social, and environmental considerations.	Use IG best practices on data management to ensure that information on tax positions, payments, and contributions to tax authorities is properly maintained and reported. Use IG best practices to manage tax data and to ensure both its accuracy. Ensure that tax records are maintained in accordance with the organization's defensible retention policy. Train staff on how to retain tax records. Implement automated compliance checks to ensure that tax practices align with the latest legal requirements. Use analytics tools to assess the fairness of the organization's contribution to public finances, considering economic activities in each region and to measure the environmental and social implications of tax strategies.

		Establish a governance structure within the IG framework that includes oversight mechanisms for tax practices. Implement role-based access controls to ensure that only authorized personnel have access to sensitive tax-related information.
Data Breach Strategy	Develop and maintain a comprehensive approach to prevent, detect, respond to, and recover from data breaches while considering the broader impact on environmental and social responsibilities.	Implement and enforce robust data governance policies that define data handling, access controls, encryption, and retention practices and that are based on accepted standards such as ISO 27701.
		Clearly define the stewardship-responsibility for ESG data within the organization and assign roles and responsibilities that promote managing ESG data to ensure accountability.
		Incorporate privacy-centric principles into data governance policies to highlight the needs for the protection of personal information, access controls, and regular auditing of data management practices to prevent privacy violations.
		Align data breach training content with ESG goals, emphasizing the social and ethical responsibilities associated with data handling.
		Leverage environmentally sound AI and machine learning technologies to promote advanced threat detection.
		Ensure that the organization's incident response plan is adequately updated and includes predefined processes for detecting and responding to data breaches.

(Continued)

Concept	ESG "Governance" Priorities	Relevant IG Strategies
		Ensure that the data breach incident response team is adequately trained to address both legal data breach obligations and the social environmental considerations related to data breach. These considerations can include the erosion of trust, emotional harm, potential discrimination (why were only some customers impacted?) and others.
		Use IG best practices to accurately collect and manage data related to the breach including metadata-based categorization, secure central repository storage and other tools to track this data so that it can be made available (and align these practices with ESG sustainability concerns).

Leveraging IG Best Practices to Mitigate Legal and Regulatory Liability

A well-structured IG program also helps organizations to effectively mitigate legal and regulatory liabilities while simultaneously reducing discovery costs.

For example, an organization that suffers a data breach or other adverse data event is likely to face both legal and regulatory scrutiny. Typically, the first question asked by regulators is: "What did you do to prevent it?" Organizations that can demonstrate and document well-organized and thought-out records management programs that closely integrate both state-of-the-art technology and legally defensible records management practices (such as an updated retention schedule and effective policies, procedures, and training) are far more likely to avoid compensatory damages arising from litigation or regulatory fines.

This commitment to effective record management directly aligns with the governance pillar of the ESG framework, showcasing a dedication to legal compliance and regulatorily sound thinking.

A very closely related element is the impact of IG on minimizing the potential impact of litigation. Organizations that adhere to IG best practices can streamline their e-discovery processes through well-organized data management and minimize the expenses associated with legal discovery, including document retrieval, review, and analysis. Additionally, implementing data retention policies facilitates the systematic disposal of unnecessary data, diminishes the legal exposure of "bad" but disposable data, and vastly reduces the costs associated with storing and managing excess information.

When faced with legal discovery requests, the streamlined retrieval of information from an efficiently managed IG program not only expedites the response time but also substantially reduces the expenses tied to e-discovery, document review, and legal analysis.

The efficiency gains are particularly important in the e-discovery process. Having a well-organized records program helps organizations create a quicker, more accurate, and more targeted response to legal inquiries. Moreover, by integrating best practices IG with the right suite of technological tools, an organization's teams can swiftly identify and assess relevant records, leading to more accurate and expedited reviews. The end result is a reduction of the time and resources traditionally spent on navigating through a cluttered data landscape, which translates into both increased efficiency and reduced costs.

How IG Impacts ESG Risk Management

ESG risk management has become a pivotal element in global business strategy. According to a 2023 IBM IBV study, companies recognized as ESG leaders are 43 percent more likely to outperform their peers in terms of profitability. Despite the potential benefits, 57 percent of CEOs acknowledge the challenges in defining and measuring the ROI of sustainability efforts. Prioritizing ESG risk management is touted as a strategy for enhancing profitability, and organizations are urged to embark on this journey promptly.[38]

ESG initiatives can significantly impact the bottom line. The shift in customer preferences toward sustainability is evident, with 68 percent expressing a high level of interest in environmental sustainability. Nearly half of consumers have willingly paid premium prices for socially responsible or environmentally sustainable products in the past year. IBM's research indicates that ESG leaders can boost revenue through innovative approaches, such as implementing QR codes on packaging, resulting in an 8 percent increase in sales for a consumer-packaged goods brand in Europe.[39]

To effectively manage ESG risk, organizations are advised to follow key steps. First, conducting thorough ESG assessments, akin to cybersecurity assessments, helps identify potential risks and opportunities across operations and the supply chain. Once identified, organizations should develop implementation plans to remediate these risks and seize opportunities. Monitoring and tracking ESG performance through metrics such as carbon emissions, human rights violations, and labor practices, along with collaborating with suppliers, who play a crucial role in ESG goals, are additional strategies. The integration of ESG metrics into supply chain operations is highlighted, emphasizing the importance of clear goals, standards, and collaboration to drive sustainability and financial performance. Overall, adapting existing risk management techniques is essential for businesses to navigate ESG challenges effectively.[40]

Vital records programs play a crucial role in helping organizations seeking to manage ESG risks by identifying and categorizing critical ESG-related data that is essential for the organization's sustainable practices. These programs help organizations to ensure that vital information related to environmental impact, social responsibility, and governance is recognized as vital and receives appropriate attention in risk assessments. In addition, by performing a data severity level classification exercise, organizations can prioritize variant types of ESG data based on its significance and potential impact on the business. In addition, vital records programs often include provisions for disaster recovery and business continuity planning, which are crucial aspects of ESG risk management. And, given the long-term nature of ESG goals, vital records programs facilitate the secure and compliant retention of historical ESG data.

Vital records programs also align with governance policies by establishing guidelines for the creation, maintenance, and disposal of critical ESG records, which promotes consistency in managing information and minimizes the risk of overlooking key data elements.

Another core IG overlap is in the area of metadata classification. Metadata classification is integral to ESG risk management as it enables organizations to systematically categorize important ESG data by assigning specific metadata tags to various ESG information categories, such as environmental impact metrics and governance documents, organizations can efficiently locate, analyze, and assess relevant data during risk assessments. The traceability function of metadata-based systems help organizations to effectively audit their data, which, in turn, enhances the quality and transparency of ESG reporting data. Metadata-based systems also support data quality by indicating accuracy levels and assists in establishing interconnected relationships between different ESG datasets, promoting a holistic view of potential risks and opportunities. This approach contributes to effective ESG risk management, aiding compliance with reporting standards, and informing informed decision making in sustainable business practices.

Another essential IG-related component of ESG risk management success is the successful deployment of long-term digital archival programs, which can provide a structured and secure framework for preserving critical ESG data over extended periods. These programs enable organizations to securely and systematically archive historical ESG records, so that stakeholders can access them for trend analysis, regulatory compliance, and informed decision making. Effectively using long-term digital archival programs also enables organizations to promote data integrity by safeguarding the authenticity and reliability of archived ESG records, which can mitigate the risk of data degradation or loss over time.

Additionally, long-term digital archival programs contribute to data security by ensuring the secure storage and retrieval of intellectual property related to sustainable practices. These programs help organizations protect their intellectual capital, maintain the integrity of ESG data, and comply with legal requirements, which can reduce the risk of unauthorized access or loss of valuable intellectual property over time.

IG's Role in Enhancing Transparent Compliance Efforts

IG plays a pivotal role in enhancing transparency for companies striving to meet ESG compliance requirements. Most importantly, a robust IG framework ensures that data is systematically managed and accessible, creating a transparent organizational compliance culture. By implementing comprehensive records management processes, companies can streamline data collection, storage, and retrieval, reducing the risk of inaccuracies or omissions in ESG reporting. For instance, effective IG controls enable companies to track and trace their environmental impact by maintaining accurate records of emissions, waste management, and resource consumption. This transparency not only satisfies ESG criteria but also helps build trust both internally and externally by allowing stakeholders to confidently rely on the accuracy and completeness of the disclosed information.

In addition, in the social responsibility domain, IG can be instrumental in tracking and reporting on diversity and inclusion initiatives, employee welfare programs, and ethical supply chain practices. This level of transparency allows companies to clearly demonstrate their tangible efforts in compiling accurate information regarding their social standards goals and achievements, which can then be transmitted quickly and effectively to investors, customers, and regulatory bodies.

Importance of Integrating Cybersecurity Programs Into ESG

In the contemporary landscape of corporate responsibility, companies are being called upon to view cybersecurity through the lens of ESG compliance. Cyber risk emerges as the most pressing and financially impactful sustainability challenge faced by organizations today. The absence of effective governance in cybersecurity, characterized by the utilization of suitable tools and metrics, not only diminishes a company's resilience but also compromises its sustainability. This deficiency in cybersecurity governance can have a cascading effect, impacting the stability of interconnected organizations, communities, and even governments that rely on one another.[41]

To underscore the urgency of integrating cybersecurity into ESG strategies, it is important to consider factors such as the following:

- The current landscape in which 90 percent of the asset value in most organizations is comprised of intangible assets, which are subject to cybersecurity threats. As organizations increasingly digitize their assets, data emerges as a pivotal intangible asset, and a cybersecurity breach could have far-reaching consequences.
- The pervasive adoption of digital transactions across sectors introduces heightened cybersecurity risks, impacting society at large. The surge in identity theft during the COVID-19 pandemic exemplifies the potential societal fallout of data breaches, particularly in healthcare and utility sectors.[42]
- The fact that reliance on insurance alone is recognized as an inadequate strategy, as courts progressively narrow the scope of coverage and regulatory fines loom large—a shift toward a standardized framework for measuring cyber risk is advocated to enhance comprehension and management, aligning it seamlessly with broader ESG strategies.

This imperative underscores not only the potential consequences for individual companies but also the broader societal impact, emphasizing the need for a comprehensive and proactive approach to cybersecurity within the ESG framework.[43]

IG best practices play a critical role in improving and maintaining a strong cybersecurity stance by providing a structured and proactive approach to managing an organization's information assets.

For example, the establishment of clear data classification policies is fundamental to IG. An organization following IG best practices will typically categorize its data assets based on relative sensitivity, ensuring that confidential and critical information is identified and treated with the appropriate security measures. By doing so, the entity can prioritize cybersecurity efforts, directing resources toward safeguarding the most valuable and vulnerable data, thereby reducing the risk of unauthorized access or data breaches.

In addition, IG best practices involve implementing robust access controls and user permissions. Strict access policies ensure that only authorized personnel have the necessary permissions to access, modify, or share sensitive information. This not only lowers the risk of insider threats but also acts as a crucial defense against external cyber threats.

Another best practice aimed at improving organizational cybersecurity is the provision of regular security training and awareness programs for employees and consultants. Educated and aware staff members are less likely to fall victim to social engineering tactics or inadvertently compromise security measures, contributing to an overall more resilient cybersecurity posture.

Finally, organizations exhibiting robust IG practices tend to conduct routine data audits and assessments. Regularly reviewing and evaluating the organization's data landscape allows executives to identify vulnerabilities and potential weaknesses in security protocols. This proactive approach enables swift remediation of any issues before cyber adversaries can exploit them. These practices also support compliance with data protection regulations, fostering a culture of accountability and adherence to industry standards. Ultimately, by implementing comprehensive IG measures, organizations can establish a robust IG framework that not only enhances cybersecurity but also promotes a holistic and sustainable approach to managing data securely.

How IG Helps Organizations Comply With Antimoney Laundering Laws

The year 2023 was a banner year for antimoney laundering (AML) fines.

By far, the largest fine was Binance Holdings Limited, operator of the world's largest cryptocurrency exchange, which pleaded guilty to various violations, including breaches of the Bank Secrecy Act and failure to register as a money transmitting business. Binance's founder and CEO Changpeng Zhao, a Canadian national, also pleaded guilty to inadequate AML practices and resigned. The $4 billion settlement with the U.S. Justice Department, Financial Crimes Enforcement Network (FinCEN), OFAC, and CFTC underscores the repercussions of noncompliance in the crypto industry.[44]

In Australia, Crown Resorts faced a $450 million penalty from AUSTRAC for past Australian AML infractions at its casinos. AUSTRAC acknowledged the disregard for risks, including money laundering and terrorism funding. While awaiting final court sanction, Crown Resorts' CEO Ciarán Carruthers committed to rectifying transgressions and ensuring AML law adherence, highlighting the significance of compliance in the gaming sector.[45]

Another significant event involved Deutsche Bank, which was fined $186 million for insufficient efforts in remedying money laundering control issues and other shortcomings. Emphasizing potential future fines, the U.S. Federal Reserve urged Deutsche Bank to enhance risk and data management systems. Stemming from consent orders in 2015 and 2017, connected to interactions with Danske Bank's Estonian branch, Deutsche Bank committed to swiftly addressing weaknesses and has allocated funds from earlier quarters for penalties.[46]

An AML compliance program aids various businesses, encompassing traditional financial institutions and entities specified in government regulations, such as money-service businesses and insurance companies, in identifying suspicious activities related to criminal acts, including money laundering and terrorist financing.[47]

In the United States, the mandate for firms to establish AML compliance programs is rooted in the Bank Secrecy Act (BSA), which mandates that financial institutions formulate policies and procedures to detect suspicious activities and report them to the government through suspicious activity reports (SARs). The USA PATRIOT Act broadened the scope of entities required to engage in suspicious activity reporting.[48]

Various countries have enacted similar legislation such as the United Kingdom's Money Laundering Regulations, the European Union's AML Directives, Canada's Proceeds of Crime Act, Australia's AML/CTF Act, and similar frameworks in Singapore and Hong Kong, all aimed at combating money laundering and terrorist financing through mandated policies, reporting obligations, and preventive measures. These international counterparts reflect a collective commitment to establishing comprehensive legal frameworks tailored to the unique needs of each jurisdiction.

Beyond uncovering money laundering and terrorism financing, SARs are utilized by the U.S. government to investigate various criminal activities such as fraud, bribery, corruption, tax evasion, and organized crime.

Effective AML compliance programs, as outlined by the Federal Financial Institutions Examination Council (FFIEC) in April 2020, necessitate a system of internal controls, independent compliance testing, appointment of a BSA compliance officer, ongoing employee training, a risk-based customer identification program (CIP), and techniques for continuous customer due diligence (CDD) and compliance with beneficial ownership requirements issued by the FinCEN.[49]

AML compliance is intricately tied to ESG success (primarily, the Social component) as it addresses social responsibility and ethical business practices by combating financial crimes such as money laundering and terrorist financing. Compliant AML programs help organizations to achieve legal compliance, mitigate reputation risks, and enhance transparency in financial operations. By actively participating in global AML efforts, companies also align with the principles of international collaboration, promoting financial stability and risk management.

IG best practices can play a significant role in promoting and developing the controls necessary for AML compliance.

One area, for example, where IG impacts AML law is in the area of records retention. Multinational companies, in particular, must be apprised of the various AML record retention periods, which vary among jurisdictions. This is illustrated by the following chart.

How Long do you keep AML Data?

5 Years	7 Years	10 Years
5	**7**	**10**
US Bank Secrecy Act (some data 3 years) **EU** Anti-Money Laundering Directive	**Hong Kong** Money Laundering and Terrorist Financing (Prevention) Ordinance **Australia** Anti-Money Laundering and Counter-Terrorism Financing Act 2006 **Canada** Proceeds of Crime (Money Laundering) and Terrorist Financing Act	**Japan** Anti-Money Laundering Law Some specific cases US/EU/Australia

In addition to this, and as described in the following chart, IG best practices can significantly aid organizations seeking to realize their AML compliance goals.

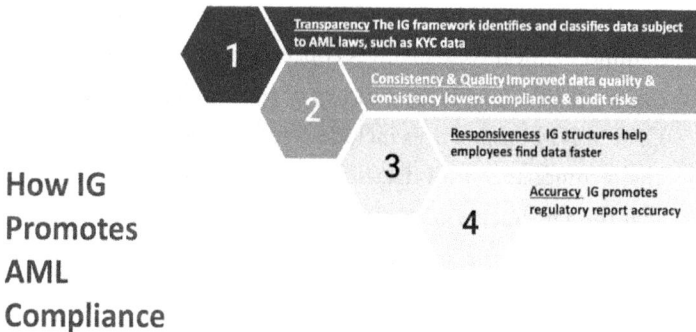

How IG Promotes AML Compliance

1. **Transparency** The IG framework identifies and classifies data subject to AML laws, such as KYC data

2. **Consistency & Quality** Improved data quality & consistency lowers compliance & audit risks

3. **Responsiveness** IG structures help employees find data faster

4. **Accuracy** IG promotes regulatory report accuracy

In addition to measures that we have addressed in prior sections such as metadata management and the development of project-specific data taxonomies, specific best practices related to AML IG include:[50]

- Data Ethics Training: Having effective and relatable training that includes instruction on ethical data considerations allows organizations to empower their workforce to comprehend the implications of data-related decisions, ensuring compliance and cultivating a culture of responsible data usage.

An example of this type of practice is a bank that implements mandatory training programs that include information on handling sensitive data responsibly and the proper retention of AML records.

- Data Breach Response Training: Another example is data breach literacy training. For example, a company that experiences a data breach compromising sensitive customer information needs to decide whether to disclose the breach immediately, potentially causing reputational damage, or delay disclosure to investigate and minimize immediate fallout. Organizations that implement a robust incident response plan that includes legally defensible instructions for notification, transparency, and corrective action, ensure that their contractual data breach notifications reflect their current practices, and provide regular (organization and role-specific) incident training to their employees are more likely to make the right, legally defensible decisions.

- Third-Party Data-Sharing Policies and Auditing: Another common ethical issue involves concerns over the use of sensitive data by external partners or supply chain members. Critical IG best practices include regularly auditing supply chain compliance with data-sharing agreements, ensuring that the agreements are reviewed and vetted by all required internal parties (i.e., not just Legal), training personnel on restrictions (and red flags), and regularly monitoring compliance with retention laws, including retention schedule requirements.

Information Governance and Supply Chain Compliance

Effective IG is essential for organizations aiming to attain supply chain transparency and responsibility. Achieving success in this area requires a deep understanding of business, political, regulatory, and stakeholder factors. This understanding should be guided by a firm dedication to ensuring the availability of "accurate data at the appropriate time."

On the other hand, neglecting to supervise supply chain partners is frequently rooted in a series of data access and accuracy lapses. In the most severe instances, such lapses can lead to significant market consequences and regulatory scrutiny. This scenario has been observed in cases where reliance on suppliers with substandard conditions adversely affected major companies.

One example of good supply chain management practice aligning with IG best practices, is exemplified by findings in the General Motors Sustainability Report in which the company detailed and substantiated its robust corporate commitment to supply chain compliance. Measures referred to in this report included:

- Enforcing ethical practices via a supplier code of conduct and contract terms and conditions, which aligns with IG strategies such as documentation frameworks, training sessions, and attestations ensuring supplier adherence and commitment to ethical standards.
- Conducting annual surveys involving over 3,000 suppliers to verify ethical practices, with IG strategies such as automated tracking, risk-based sampling, and continuous monitoring streamlining the process and ensuring real-time insights.
- Requiring Tier I suppliers to uphold environmental, safety, and quality standards, monitored through BIQS aiming for Level V compliance. IG strategies, including centralized data repositories, automated certification checks, and IR, can provide a comprehensive view of Tier I supplier compliance.[51]

Companies looking to enforce or improve their ethical supply chain standards should take concrete steps including:

- Actively searching out partners with shared ethical practices, such as sustainable working practices, use of conflict-free minerals, and fair labor practices using predefined criteria, policies, and procedures;
- Implementing an identity and access management platform to assign digital identities to trading partners;

- Digitizing the supply chain that accurately connects and tracks trading partners' compliance, ideally using a cloud-based, data-integration environment that can scale and that includes authentication controls to prevent data falsification;
- Leveraging modern technologies such as blockchain, robotic process automation (RPA), and other forms of AI to track the movement, condition, temperature, and location of shipments and ensure traceability;
- Actively participating in collaboration platforms to maintain up-to-date contact details and survey supplier communities for insights; and
- Gathering ethical insights using advanced analytics, AI, and machine learning tools as well as AI dashboards that can consistently monitor the ethical performance of trading partners and make strategic business decisions based on measurable outcomes.[52]

Other solutions include:

- Deploying data quality and authentication tools to ensure the accuracy and reliability of supplier data;
- Continually monitoring and updating systems security standards to ensure compliance with common ISO standards such as ISO 27701;
- Implementing digital DMS to successfully digitize and manage supply chain documents, reducing the risk of document falsification and improving data quality;
- Maintaining detailed access logs and conducting regular audits of trading partner interactions to ensure compliance with security protocols and clearly defining and documenting ethical criteria and policies and procedures for supplier selection, creating a record of the organization's commitment to ethical practices;
- Tagging and indexing records evidencing ethical supply chain compliance and instituting version control protocols; and
- Effectively training staff on their ethical supply chain responsibilities including responsibilities related to privacy,

security, records management, and documentation requirements.

By integrating robust IG strategies into the supply chain management process, companies can proactively find the correct information that they need to ensure and quantify adherence to ethical standards, which, in turn, can mitigate risks, and build resilient, responsible supply chains that resonate with stakeholders and stand the test of scrutiny.

Information Governance and Modern Slavery Law Compliance

Year 2016 inquiries into the supply chains of major retailers have revealed widespread human rights violations. In one report, online fashion merchant ASOS, British luxury retailer Marks and Spencer, and Japanese casual wear retailer Uniqlo were implicated by the BBC in investigations revealing exploitative practices in Turkish textile factories, where child labor was prevalent, with seven- and eight-year-old children working 60-hour weeks and Syrian refugees being underpaid. In a related report, advocacy group War on Want highlighted Uniqlo's Chinese suppliers for imposing conditions such as excessive overtime, low wages, hazardous workplaces, and oppressive management on workers. The findings underscore the need for heightened scrutiny and ethical sourcing practices within the global supply chain.[53]

Globally, modern slavery manifests in various forms, representing a contemporary institutionalized type of slavery and encompassing a range of human rights violations. Predominant among these violations are forced or coerced labor, child labor, sexual exploitation, and forced marriage. This risk briefing will focus primarily on forced or coerced labor and child labor, as defined by the ILO:

- Forced Labor—According to the ILO, it encompasses "all work or service which is exacted from any person under the threat of a penalty and for which the person has not offered himself or herself voluntarily." Coercion can take diverse forms, including direct methods like violence and intimidation, or subtler means such as withholding identity cards, engaging in work to repay an unattainable debt (known as bonded labor), or threats of deportation or disciplinary actions from immigration authorities.

- Child Labor—ILO defines child labor as work that deprives children of their childhood, potential, and dignity, and is harmful to their physical and mental development. While definitions of child labor may vary among countries due to differences in regulations on minimum working age requirements, ILO advocates for the eradication of the worst forms of child labor and has established minimum age standards.[54]

Modern slavery represents a lucrative enterprise for perpetrators. A 2014 ILO study estimated that it generates approximately $150 billion annually in illicit profits. However, this industry imposes a significant burden on public funds. A 2018 study by the Government of the United Kingdom revealed that the cost incurred by the country due to modern slavery is up to £4.3 billion per year, with a single incident of the offense costing over £300,000. This financial burden includes victim support, law enforcement expenses, and lost earnings. Beyond the monetary aspect, the emotional toll on victims is immeasurable, as individuals who have experienced slavery often find themselves among the most economically deprived and socially marginalized.[55]

Modern slavery compliance is gaining increased attention among U.S.-based and global corporations. The landscape of compliance is swiftly evolving, marked by significant developments in recent months. Some of these changes necessitate immediate action, while others will unfold over an extended period.[56]

Examples of relevant laws include Australia's federal Modern Slavery Act, the UK Modern Slavery Act and, in the United States, the Federal Acquisition Regulation's antihuman trafficking rule. The presence of modern slavery in supply chains is posing trade compliance risks. In addition to these risks, however, it is not uncommon to find shareholder proposals related to modern slavery.[57]

In addition, certain of these laws such as Section 54 of the Modern Slavery Act mandate that specific commercial entities with an annual global turnover exceeding £36 million (plus a connection to the United Kingdom) release an annual modern slavery statement that details the measures taken throughout the year to prevent modern slavery and human trafficking in both their business operations and supply chains.

From an ESG perspective, complying with modern slavery laws aligns with Principle 5 of the UN Global Compact ("Social part of ESG"), which focuses on the effective abolition of child labor, recognizing it as a grave violation of human rights universally condemned by international instruments. Under this framework, businesses are urged to prioritize eradicating these worst forms of child labor to mitigate ethical risks and potential damage to reputation, especially for multinational companies with extensive supply chains. Moreover, to combat child labor effectively, companies should adopt a comprehensive approach involving regional awareness, identification of high-risk areas, and the swift implementation of context-specific policies and procedures.

One of the tool sets involved in this process is IG. Specific IG tasks and practices that can help organizations comply with these reporting requirements include:

- Conducting a thorough data mapping and inventory exercise to identify and categorize data related to supply chains, business operations, and potential modern slavery risks.
- Aligning the data mapping and inventory exercise with a comprehensive risk assessment to identify areas within the organization and its supply chains where modern slavery and human trafficking risks may exist.
- Utilizing tools such as metadata and records taxonomies to verify the accuracy and quality of data by implementing measures to verify and update information related to suppliers, contractors, and other relevant entities.
- Implementing clear modern slavery policies and procedures that can be reviewed against those of supply chain members.
- Establishing training sessions to raise awareness among employees about modern slavery risks and their role in compliance.
- Ensuring that modern slavery law compliance is integrated into the organization's IG working group and that records management best practices inform decisions about how to compile, assess, and audit records establishing compliance with these laws.

IG's Role in Promoting the Alignment of AI Practices With ESG Goals

IG plays a critical role in ensuring that the AI that organizations develop is created and used in a compliant and responsible manner that is consistent with ESG compliance efforts. These include:

- Data Quality Management: Companies using AI models must ensure that the data they use to train these models are accurate, complete, and reliable—and failing to do this can create both legal and practical risks. IG tools such as uniform categorization of data, data quality controls, and eliminating excess "junk" data help to promote the use of high-quality data.
  o This promotes a variety of ESG Social goals including stakeholder inclusiveness and the need to prevent adverse impacts on society.
- Data Protection and Security: IG can help ensure that sensitive data used for AI analysis is appropriately protected and secured. IG includes implementing access controls to suppress sensitive information or personal data that you no longer need (but are required to keep because of retention laws), which can help to shield you from potential liability.
  o This supports various ESG Governance goals such as the need to mitigate risks associated with data breaches and unauthorized access.
- Ethical and Legal Compliance: IG is a lifestyle that includes regular maintenance and data quality, privacy, and retention obligation audits. In the context of AI, these tools help to promote and sustain the success of AI models by ensuring that the information that they use complies with applicable law.
  o Conducting regular maintenance, audits, and compliance checks aligns with ESG Governance goals such as those established in ISO 26000, promoting ethical behavior.
- Privacy: IG helps to protect records throughout their entire life cycle and can help ensure that personal data used for AI analysis is managed (and disposed of) in accordance with applicable privacy laws and regulations.

- Protecting personal data aligns both Social and
     Governance ESG Goals by ensuring that organizations
     manage personal information responsibly in a manner that
     respects individuals' privacy rights and promotes high-
     quality corporate governance structures.
- Transparency: IG tools can help companies to create the types
  of policies and training mechanisms that help to ensure that
  AI decisions are transparent and explainable and help ensure
  that AI models are properly documented, understood, and
  communicated.
    - Creating policies, training, and documentation practices
       that emphasize transparent decision making and adherence
       to ESG reporting standards creates a framework for
       ensuring that AI policy decisions are understandable,
       documented, and communicated transparently, supporting
       both the Social and Governance aspects of ESG.
- Risk Management: IG can help companies to ensure that
  AI-related risks are identified and managed appropriately.
  Relevant IG tools include implementing risk management
  and disaster recovery processes, such as risk assessments
  and risk mitigation plans, to ensure that AI-related risks are
  properly identified and addressed.[58]
    - Ensuring that AI-related risks are identified, assessed, and
       managed appropriately contributes to the Governance
       aspect of ESG.

Using IG to Improve RPA Outcomes in the Realm of ESG

RPA is a software technology used to automate basic, repetitive tasks across applications by mimicking human actions through the use of software robots (bots) or AI/digital workers that perform tasks such as extracting data, filling in forms, and moving files.

RPA, consistent with technological innovation, generally plays a mission-critical role in driving economic growth and development. In one recent academic study, investigators measured the extent to which RPA positively impacted ESG outcomes. The research team examined the usage of

RPA and its impact based on data gathered from the 300 largest companies in terms of market capitalization and then assessed whether these companies used RPA and obtained their corresponding ESG ratings, which were chosen based on the information listed within companiesmarketcap.com as of March 23, 2023. The investigation focused on determining the utilization of RPA technology among these chosen companies and was based on information from their official websites and vendor platforms as well as on whether the companies had posted job listings related to RPA roles such as RPA developer, RPA analyst, or RPA engineer, or had personnel with titles such as RPA developer, RPA architect, RPA analyst, or engineer. Through this process, they found that out of the top 300 global companies, 256 incorporate RPA in their operations. [59]

To investigate the relationship between RPA and ESG, the researchers further employed a contingency table analysis, which involved categorizing the data based on ESG ratings, revealing that RPA, representative of modern technologies, likely influences the achievement of a sustainable future and the promotion of entrepreneurship. [60]

The research team noted, importantly, that, based on its findings, RPA positively impacted the Governance aspect of ESG, and specifically, the social aspect of providing clear explanations and that RPA as a tool can bring a higher level of transparency into organizations to help manage all legal activities.[61]

Not surprisingly, IG best practices can and do play a role in RPA success. Potential strategies include:

- Efficiently capturing and analyzing data used within sustainability reports is a key aspect of IG best practices by enforcing uniformity to derive accurate insights from the data, contributing to more reliable and consistent sustainability reporting.
- Promoting data security, especially concerning the handling of personal data by bots within both supply chains and internal operations to ensure compliance with data protection laws so that organizations can maintain the integrity and confidentiality of sensitive information used in DEI analysis processes.

- Improving the overall sustainability stance of RPA programs by managing RPA bots in compliance with applicable laws and regulations, addressing ethical considerations, and fostering responsible automation practices to align with broader sustainability goals.
- Implementing continuous monitoring and auditing processes ensures ongoing compliance with data quality standards. Regular audits help identify and rectify issues promptly, maintaining the reliability of data processed by automation technologies.
- Establishing clear ethical guidelines for the development and deployment of AI and automation technologies, including RPA, ensures responsible and ethical practices. This involves addressing biases, promoting transparency, and aligning automation processes with ethical considerations.
- Engaging with data stewards and incorporating their expertise in data governance processes enhances the overall effectiveness of RPA initiatives who can then provide insights into data quality, security, and compliance, contributing to better decision making.
- Aligning RPA programs with established ESG frameworks to ensure that automation processes contribute directly to the organization's sustainability goals.
- Incorporating proactive risk management strategies specific to RPA and automation technologies helps identify potential risks and vulnerabilities including assessing the impact of automation on ESG outcomes and implementing mitigation measures to address any identified risks.
- Providing IG training to employees involved in RPA processes on automation ethics and responsible AI usage fosters a culture of awareness and responsibility to equip those employees to understand the ethical implications of RPA and contribute to ethical decision making.
- Implementing a robust data life-cycle management strategy ensures that data used by RPA systems is managed appropriately throughout its life cycle including data creation,

usage, storage, archiving, and disposal in compliance with
regulatory requirements.

- Facilitating collaboration between IT, legal, compliance,
  and sustainability teams ensures a holistic approach to IG in
  RPA initiatives to promote a comprehensive understanding
  of the legal, regulatory, and sustainability implications of
  automation processes.

IG's Role in Enhancing ESG Blockchain Technology Use

Blockchain enables secure and direct business transactions among participants, eliminating the need for intermediaries such as lawyers, banks, brokers, or governments. It ensures trust through identity confirmation, transaction validation, and rule enforcement. The technology's potential extends to a wide range of assets and participants, including machines, fostering substantial commercial opportunities. When fully matured and integrated with AI and IoT, blockchain could enable autonomous agents to negotiate insurance rates directly with multiple providers using sensor data.[62]

According to Sustainalytics, companies that adeptly employ blockchain for ESG risk management are poised to attract increased investments. Such firms are perceived as better equipped to handle forthcoming challenges and opportunities, thereby fostering investor trust. The report also indicates that investors engaged in the blockchain market encounter marginally lower overall ESG risks compared to those in the broader global equities market, emphasizing the potential of blockchain to bolster investor confidence.[63] Ultimately, this confidence is rooted in the abilities of blockchain technology to enhance operational efficiency, fortify supply chain resilience, and improve product governance.

On a functional level, blockchain encompasses distribution, encryption, immutability, tokenization, and decentralization. Distributed participants, encryption through public and private keys, cryptographic immutability of completed transactions, secure exchange of value through tokenization, and decentralized governance collectively define true blockchain. This framework aids CIOs in explaining the technology to executives, distinguishing complete blockchain solutions from partial implementations, and showcasing the transformative potential of blockchain in diverse business scenarios.[†]

Gartner projects that by 2030, blockchain is poised to generate $3.1 trillion in new business value. The adoption of blockchain technologies is particularly crucial as major multinational corporations and digital giants have actively integrated blockchain components, such as distributed ledger technology, to strengthen a centralized business approach and expand market shares.[‡] Moreover, according to the Association for Intelligent Information Management's (AIIM) Industry Watch report on Automating Governance and Compliance, nearly 10 percent of budgets allocated for information management and governance will be dedicated to blockchain implementation.[64]

Deploying blockchain technology can help to improve ESG reporting by establishing a clear, unchangeable, and verifiable record of ESG data. By establishing a decentralized and unalterable ledger for ESG data, blockchain ensures the accuracy and integrity of the information. This transparency and immutability contribute to making ESG reporting more dependable and trustworthy. According to Ernst & Young (EY), blockchain can facilitate the attainment of comprehensive sustainability goals by fostering radical transparency and verifiability. It also aligns seamlessly with real-time regulatory changes throughout the value chain, aiding organizations in complying with evolving global transparency standards.[65]

That said, it is critical for organizations seeking to obtain that data to use of IG best practices and standards to help them minimize the risk of bad data, find relevant data quickly, and ensure that their data is secure. Relevant processes include:

- Deploying IG practices such as homographic encryption, role-based access controls, consensus mechanisms (e.g., proof of work, proof of stake) inherent to blockchain technology, multisignature wallets, and smart contracts, to prevent

---

[†] www.gartner.com/smarterwithgartner/the-cios-guide-to-blockchain
[‡] Id.

tampering to enhance the security of sustainability data stored on blockchain, safeguarding against unauthorized access or tampering.

- Implementing regular data backups of sustainability information stored on the blockchain to facilitate recovery in the event of data corruption or tampering.
- Using data quality management principles established by IG frameworks such as applying data validation checks, ensuring consistent data formats, and establishing protocols for error resolution, to promote the accuracy and reliability of sustainability information recorded on the blockchain.
- Developing and enforcing robust data management policies as part of IG, addressing the life cycle of sustainability data from collection to archival including defined protocols governing the collection of sustainability data on the blockchain and blockchain consensus mechanisms to establish agreement among network participants regarding the validity of sustainability data.
- Establishing mechanisms for continuous monitoring of sustainability data on the blockchain and implementing reporting processes to keep stakeholders informed of progress and compliance such as deploying real-time analytics, audit trails, and anomaly detection, ensuring ongoing scrutiny to detect any irregularities, and implementing reporting processes.
- Conducting training and awareness programs to educate employees and stakeholders about the importance of IG in supporting sustainability goals and maintaining transparency.
- Integrating data privacy compliance measures within IG practices prioritizing encryption, anonymization techniques, and adherence to regulatory frameworks to address privacy concerns related to sustainability data stored on the blockchain.
- Incorporating scalability considerations within IG plans to accommodate the growth of sustainability data and ensure the continued effectiveness of blockchain solutions over time and that anticipate increased transaction volumes, growing data size, and network expansion.

Dark Data Minimization Through IG Best Practices

"Dark data" refers to digital information that is stored in the cloud but is rarely accessed or reused. This type of data takes up server space, contributing to increased electricity consumption and, consequently, a higher carbon footprint. Despite common assumptions that digital data is environmentally benign, the process of digitization itself was responsible for 4 percent of global GHG emissions in 2020, challenging the perception of its carbon neutrality.[66]

The environmental impact of dark data is rooted in the energy required to store and maintain this information on servers, typically housed in large data centers. Even if the data is never retrieved or reused, it continues to occupy space and demand energy resources. This energy cost is often overlooked within organizations, and the challenge lies in balancing the need for an effective organizational memory with the environmental consequences of maintaining extensive digital archives.[67]

While efforts toward achieving net-zero goals have primarily focused on traditional sources of carbon production, the processing of digital data has emerged as a substantial contributor to GHG emissions. In 2020, digitization was responsible for 4 percent of global emissions, a figure expected to rise significantly as the world generates an estimated 97 zettabytes (97 trillion gigabytes) of data in 2024, with projections indicating a near doubling to 181 zettabytes by 2025. Despite this significant impact, there has been a notable lack of policy attention on reducing the digital carbon footprint of organizations.[68]

The rapid growth of dark data raises concerns about the efficiency of current digital practices. To address this issue, the concept of "digital decarbonization" was introduced, emphasizing the need to reduce the carbon footprint associated with digital data. It highlights that while digitization itself is not an environmental problem, the ways in which digital processes are utilized in daily workplace activities have substantial environmental implications. To quantify the impact, data centers, which are responsible for 2.5 percent of human-induced carbon dioxide, exhibit a larger carbon footprint than the aviation industry (2.1%).[69]

Calculations based on the carbon cost of data reveal that a typical data-driven business with 100 employees may generate nearly 3,000 gigabytes of dark data daily. Keeping this data for a year would result in a carbon footprint comparable to flying from London to New York six times. As companies collectively produce vast amounts of dark data daily, efforts to reduce its production are crucial for the broader digital decarbonization movement. Individuals are encouraged to contribute by managing their digital footprint, such as deleting unnecessary files, to mitigate their personal impact on the digital carbon footprint.[70]

Robust IG practices play a crucial role in minimizing the environmental impact of dark data through strategies such as data minimization and adherence to a retention schedule.

Data minimization involves identifying and retaining only essential data, reducing overall storage needs. This reduction in unnecessary data storage contributes to lower energy consumption and a smaller carbon footprint associated with maintaining extensive data storage infrastructure, including servers and data centers.

Adherence to a well-defined and legally defensible retention schedule further ensures that data is retained only for as long as necessary, based on legal, regulatory, and business requirements. This facilitates the timely disposal of obsolete data, preventing unnecessary storage and reducing the environmental impact associated with data storage infrastructure.

Regular audits of data holdings are a crucial aspect of IG. These audits help identify and eliminate ROT data, which can constitute a significant portion of dark data. Removing such data contributes to more efficient storage practices and a smaller environmental footprint.

Efficient data management practices, such as structured archiving and optimized backup strategies, further help minimize the need for excessive data duplication. By segregating essential information from dark data, organizations can manage their data more effectively, reducing the environmental impact associated with maintaining unnecessary data.

Finally, effective education and employee engagement are vital components of a sustainable IG strategy both generally, and as it pertains to the need to minimize ROT or dark data. Employee awareness programs and training on data retention policies foster a culture of responsible data stewardship. When employees understand the environmental implications of data storage, they are more likely to actively contribute to data minimization efforts.

Selected Case Studies

Cisco Systems, Inc.

Under the leadership of CEO Chuck Robbins, Cisco Systems Inc. has established an ambitious objective of reaching net-zero emissions by 2040, with interim milestones to achieve net-zero emissions for both global scope 1 and scope 2 emissions by 2025.[71]

In the social realm, Cisco consistently ranks among the best places to work. The company's CSR initiatives, encapsulated in its "Conscious Culture" framework, prioritize inclusivity and positive impacts on people, society, and the planet. Cisco's CEO has prioritized mental health destigmatization, and policies such as a companywide 10-day shutdown at the end of December underscore its commitment to employee well-being.[72]

With respect to diversity, equity, and inclusion efforts, while Cisco has faced lawsuits in these areas, they also instituted remediation programs to actively address these issues such as programs to mentor, retain, and support diverse employees. Cisco's CSR report provides transparent data on gender and ethnicity diversity, showcasing the company's commitment to full-spectrum diversity and inclusion.[73]

In the arena of Governance, Cisco publishes annual CSR reports guided by the GRI Standards and also conducts a comprehensive materiality assessment every two years, reinforcing the importance of CSR through dedicated orientation sessions for new employees. Finally, in line with comprehensive privacy laws, Cisco actively promotes privacy as a fundamental human right and advocates for legislation respecting this right.[74]

We believe that the following IG strategies are critical to the above-mentioned profile:

- Data Transparency and Reporting:
  - Implementing a robust data transparency framework to track and report on environmental metrics, such as emissions data for scope 1 and scope 2.
  - Aligning standardized reporting processes with sustainability standards such as the GRI for transparent and effective communication.

- Environmental Impact Assessment:
  - o Utilizing IG best practices for data management including metadata tagging to promote data quality, ease access to critical data, and effectively assess the information needed for conducting regular assessments of the environmental impact of business operations.
  - o Establishing protocols for data collection and analysis to measure progress toward net-zero emissions goals.
- Inclusive Work Culture Data Management:
  - o Employing IG data management strategies to manage data related to workplace inclusivity, employee well-being, and mental health initiatives.
  - o Promoting data privacy and confidentiality while collecting and analyzing information about employee experiences and well-being.
  - o Developing data-driven strategies to monitor and improve diversity, equity, and inclusion efforts within the organization.
  - o Leveraging data quality management strategies that track progress, identify areas for improvement, and implement targeted initiatives to address diversity challenges.
- Legal Compliance and Remediation Programs:
  - o Implementing IG frameworks to ensure compliance with privacy laws and regulations throughout the company's sphere of operations including retention laws and laws related to personal data that is no longer needed for its processing purpose.
  - o Combining classical IG strategies with data analytics technologies to address and track legal challenges and actively monitor progress in addressing diversity-related issues.
- Materiality Assessment Data Management:
  - o Using IG information management principles to effectively and compliantly manage data collected during comprehensive materiality assessments and create relevant and specific data management protocols to promote the

accuracy, reliability, and consistency of information used for materiality assessments.

- Employee Orientation and Training:
  - o Incorporating IG training into the employee and contractor orientation process for new personnel to emphasize the importance of CSR and privacy as it applies to the company's overall ESG objectives.
- Continuous Improvement Through Data Analysis:
  - o Establishing compliant data analysis frameworks to effectively monitor and evaluate the effectiveness of CSR initiatives and to deliver data-driven insights that refine ESG goals.

Boston Properties

Boston Properties (BXP) is a leading real estate investment trust (REIT) that owns and manages 196 properties, encompassing office, retail, residential, and mixed-use spaces. As the largest publicly held developer of high-end Class A office space in the United States, the company focuses its building portfolio on key markets: Boston, Los Angeles, New York, San Francisco, and Washington, DC.[75]

Environmental

BXP is a leader in eco-friendly building practices, with 24.3 million square feet of LEED-certified buildings, constituting half of its portfolio. The company mandates LEED Silver certification or higher for all new developments. To further environmental commitments, BXP aims for LEED Zero certification, emphasizing carbon-neutral buildings. The company addresses criticisms by implementing strict procurement policies, limiting material toxicity, waste output, and supply shipping distances.

The company's environmental targets include a 75 percent waste diversion rate, 32 percent energy use reduction, 39 percent reduction in scopes 1 and 2 GHG emissions, and a 30 percent water use reduction, aligning with a 1.5°C global warming trajectory as per the Science-Based Targets initiative (SBTi).[76]

Social

BXP engages in social impact through:

- Offering favorable lease conditions to positive social actors.
- Investing in affordable housing, with 412 qualifying units among its 2,852 housing units.
- Allocating $124.7 million to public realm improvements in 2019, enhancing community spaces and amenities.
- Creating mixed-use, transit-oriented developments such as The Hub on Causeway in Boston, fostering inclusivity and walkable urban environments.
- Implementing green roofs for environmental and social benefits, including urban beekeeping initiatives.
- Prioritizing employee benefits, volunteer programs, and Fitwel-certified buildings promoting well-being. Diversity and inclusion efforts include transparent reporting of employee demographics and board composition.[77]

Governance

BXP emphasizes sustainable corporate governance through:

- A high rate of independent board directors (as of 2021, 82%).
- Ensuring that independent board committees oversee audit, nomination, and remuneration.
- Maintaining an employee training and whistleblower hotline to reinforce ethical practices.

However, as of 2021, CEO compensation is 103.4 times the median employee's compensation, surpassing industry peers. Also, BXP did not disclose the political donations of its board members.

We believe that the following IG strategies are relevant to the above-mentioned profile:

- Data Quality Management: Implementing uniform data categorization, quality controls, and comprehensive reporting, for example, as embodied in BXP's commitment to LEED certification, which aligns with data quality management principles by using common standards to ensure accuracy and reliability in environmental data.

- Data Protection and Security: Implementing strict and secure procurement policies that reflect a commitment to responsible sourcing.
- Ethical and Legal Compliance: Conducting regular audits and compliance assessments in line with the Science-based initiative to promote alignment with legal standards, scientific standards, and ethical principles.
- Privacy: Privacy impact assessments and controls to safeguard personal data in line with privacy regulations related to building management.
- Transparency: Promoting data quality through providing clear and defensible documentation, defined reporting mechanisms, and stakeholder communication strategies.
- Training: Regularly training personnel related to data handling, privacy, and security, contributing to ethical and responsible data management.

Toyota Motor Corporation[78]

Toyota Motor Corporation, a Japanese multinational automotive entity, engages in the design, manufacturing, and sale of both passenger and commercial vehicles. Complementing its automotive operations, the company operates a financial services branch providing financing options to both vehicle dealers and customers. Globally recognized, Toyota holds the position of the second-largest car manufacturer globally and is ranked as the 11th largest company by Forbes. The company boasts a diverse vehicle lineup, featuring brands such as Toyota, Hino, Lexus, Ranz, and Daihatsu. Toyota also has collaborative partnerships with Subaru, Isuzu, and Mazda.

Environmental

- GHG Emissions: Toyota, as the second-largest car manufacturer globally, recognizes the impact of motor vehicles on GHG emissions. Despite being a significant contributor to climate change, Toyota has taken initiatives to lead in reducing emissions. These include:

o Pioneering Hybrid Vehicles: The pioneering of hybrid vehicles began with the release of the Prius in 1997. In 2018, 58 percent of Toyota's sales were hybrids, surpassing industry standards for CO_2 emissions. The company aims for a 30 percent reduction in CO_2 emissions by 2025 and 90 percent by 2050, with plans to offer electric versions of all Toyota and Lexus models by 2025.

o Smog and Air Quality: Toyota is conscious of pollutants affecting air quality and has excelled in addressing emissions and fuel efficiency. The company has introduced green bonds, with the latest $750 million bond focusing on developing vehicles with hybrid or alternative fuel powertrains and better smog ratings.

o Plant Emissions and Water Usage: Toyota aims to achieve zero plant emissions by 2050 by utilizing renewable energy and optimizing equipment. The company has also focused on reducing water usage in manufacturing, with a goal of a 34-percent reduction from 2001 levels by 2025.

o Supply Chain and Waste Management: Toyota addresses the environmental impact of its supply chain through Green Purchasing Guidelines. The Global 100 Dismantlers Project aims to establish proper treatment for end-of-life vehicles, promoting battery collection and car recycling. Toyota seeks to have 15 vehicle recycling facilities by 2025.

Social

• Safety: Recognizing the inherent risks in driving, Toyota has set a goal of zero casualties from traffic accidents. The company invests in traditional safety features and autonomous vehicle development, including a $500 million investment in Uber for autonomous ride sharing.

• Recall Scandal: Toyota faced significant financial repercussions and damage to its reputation in 2009 due to unintended

acceleration issues. Recalling millions of vehicles, the
company settled with the Justice Department and NHTSA
for over $5 billion. This incident negatively impacted sales
and stock prices.

- Human Rights: Toyota's extensive supply chain makes it
  susceptible to human rights abuses. The CSR addresses
  concerns, but historical reports accuse Toyota of human
  rights abuses, including exploitation of foreign workers.
  The company partners with NGOs to promote fair working
  conditions but needs further development in labor and
  human rights policies.
- Discrimination: In 2016, Toyota Motor Credit Corporation
  agreed to pay $21.9 million in restitution for charging higher
  interest rates on auto loans to African American, Asian,
  and Pacific Islander customers. Toyota has since updated its
  pricing and compensation system.

Governance

- Transparency and Reporting: Toyota demonstrates strength
  in transparency, preparing its CSR according to various
  reporting agencies. The CSR is verified by a third party, and
  starting in 2021, it will be updated as necessary for timely
  disclosure.
- Board Composition: Toyota's board of directors lacks
  independence, and the chair is not independent. The
  report suggests that Toyota needs to strengthen its board
  composition, aligning it with corporate governance standards
  and the Japanese Corporate Governance Code.
- Lobbying and Regulatory Influence: Toyota's lobbying efforts,
  particularly related to fuel economy standards, have been
  noted. The company's association with lobbying groups that
  oppose climate change regulation contradicts its public stance
  on emissions. The report raises concerns about potential
  influence over regulatory agencies.

We believe that the following IG strategies are critical to the above-mentioned profile:

- Data Classification: Implementing a robust system for classifying information based on its sensitivity and importance that includes data related to vehicle designs, manufacturing processes, and financial transactions.
- Information Security Policies: Comprehensive information security policies to safeguard customer data, financial information, and intellectual property.
- Regularly updating and communicating security protocols to employees to ensure compliance.
- Implementing processes to ensure compliance with data privacy laws, especially when handling customer information and financial data.
- Developing a clear document retention policy outlining the duration for which different types of information will be retained and regularly reviewing and securely disposing of outdated or no longer necessary information to minimize data risks.
- Implementing role-based access controls to restrict access to sensitive information, ensuring that only authorized personnel can view or modify critical data and regularly auditing and monitoring access permissions to mitigate the risk of unauthorized access.
- Establishing and maintaining processes for managing the entire life cycle of information, from creation and usage to archival and disposal and providing appropriate training to personnel.
- Implementing IG practices within the collaboration process for partners and vendors, especially those involving data sharing and verifying that third-party entities adhere to information security and privacy standards.
- Implementing measures to maintain the accuracy and integrity of data, especially in systems related to financial services, manufacturing, and customer information.

- Regularly conducting data quality assessments and addressing any issues promptly.
- Developing and regularly assessing incident response plans to address data breaches or information security incidents promptly.

Verizon Communications, Inc.[79]

Verizon, based in New York City, is a global provider of voice, data, and video services and solutions through its acclaimed networks and platforms. As of the fourth quarter of 2022, Verizon's mobile network was the second-largest wireless carrier in the United States, serving 143.3 million subscribers.

Environmental

- Green Initiatives: Verizon is actively involved in green initiatives, aiming to be carbon neutral by 2035. The company has invested in renewable energy projects through green bonds and plans to purchase over 2.5 GW of renewable energy by the end of the year.
- Energy Efficiency: Verizon's fiber-delivered broadband services are highlighted as being at least 100 times more energy-efficient per gigabyte than copper-delivered broadband services.
- E-Waste Management: In 2021, Verizon reused or recycled approximately 35.5 million pounds of e-waste, showcasing a commitment to responsible electronic waste management.
- Certifications: The company has received various certifications, including ISO 14001 and 45001 certifications for its Environmental Health and Safety (EHS) department.

Social

- Gender Disparity: A weakness identified is the gender disparity in the company's workforce.

- Employee Engagement: Verizon aims to enroll 50 percent of its workforce as Green Team members by the end of 2026, showing a commitment to engaging employees in sustainability efforts.
- Supplier Sustainability: Verizon recognizes and rewards supplier sustainability efforts, as seen in the Supplier Sustainability Award given to Corning for a return-and-recycle program.

Governance

- Compliance and Certifications: Verizon adheres to various standards and frameworks, including the TFCD, SASB, and ISO certifications. This indicates a commitment to governance and transparency.
- Green Financing Framework: The issuance of green bonds, with a focus on diversity and alignment with the UN Sustainable Development Goals, reflects Verizon's commitment to sustainable financing.
- Targets and Progress Reporting: The company sets ambitious targets, such as achieving net-zero operational emissions by 2035. While some progress has been made, there are reported gaps, indicating a transparent approach to reporting.

Relevant IG strategies include

- Implementing a data classification system to manage information related to green initiatives, tracking progress toward carbon neutrality by 2035 and renewable energy projects facilitated through green bonds.
- Enforcing data security measures to safeguard information concerning energy-efficient technologies, especially in the deployment of fiber-delivered broadband services.
- Ensuring that the records policy specifically addressing the management of e-waste, ensuring responsible handling

and disposal practices align with Verizon's commitment to recycling electronic waste.

- Using IG concepts and controls such as metadata classification, strategies related to improving version control, and strategies related to records retention and privacy to ensure that the information collected to inform audits of gender pay gaps within the organization are timely and accurate to take corrective actions to address any disparities.

- Developing the records taxonomies related to mentorship and development information to capture both objective and subjective or qualitative data to more accurately track the success of mentorship and leadership development programs designed to support and advance women, minorities, and other underrepresented groups (e.g., socioeconomic) in the workplace and the rate at which the organization has encouraged such personnel to take on leadership roles and provide mentorship opportunities for career growth.

- Taking a comprehensive and interactive approach to developing the supplier code of conduct outlines expectations for sustainable practices including environmental responsibility and social equity. Use IG best practices to collect the data used to inform audits that are conducted to assess supplier sustainability practices.

- Ensuring a broad base of voices within the governance committees responsible for overseeing diversity and inclusion, sustainability, and compliance, and ensure that these committees seek the input of IG colleagues to ensure that they are relying on the right datasets to inform their decisions.

Merck and Co[80]

Merck and Co, headquartered in Rahway, New Jersey, is a multinational pharmaceutical company with a focus on health care solutions, including medicines, vaccines, biologic therapies, animal health, and consumer care products. The company has positioned itself as a key player in the pharmaceutical industry, leveraging its global reach and commitment to sustainability.

Environmental

- Renewable Energy: Merck is actively pursuing environmental sustainability, sourcing 41 percent of its electricity from renewables in 2021. The company has set the goal of becoming a sustainability champion, aiming to achieve net-zero emissions and implement circular economy practices.
- Waste Management: Merck's commitment to reducing environmental impact is evident in its efforts to manage waste responsibly. In 2021, the company produced 82,000MT of waste, with 28 percent recycled and 26 percent recovered for energy, showcasing a comprehensive waste management strategy.
- Certifications: The company has secured various certifications, including LEED Gold, Silver, and Fitwel for its facilities globally. Additionally, Merck adheres to ISO 14001:2018 for energy management, reflecting a commitment to high environmental standards.

Social

- Global Health Impact: Merck's core mission involves positively impacting global health. The company's products reach millions of people, and it actively contributes to initiatives such as providing rabies vaccines to eliminate human deaths from dog-mediated rabies.
- Employee Development: Merck invests in its workforce with various development programs, including the General Management Acceleration Program (GMAP), Business Leadership Program, and Women's Leadership Program. These programs aim to empower employees and contribute to a diverse and inclusive workplace.

- Community Engagement: Merck engages in social initiatives, as seen in its partnerships with organizations such as UNICEF and Gavi to provide HPV vaccines to those in need. The company's involvement in programs such as the Medical Outreach Program underscores its commitment to humanitarian assistance and disaster relief.

Governance

- Sustainability Reporting: Merck's commitment to transparency and governance is evident in its comprehensive sustainability scorecard. The company reports on various aspects, including progress toward sustainability goals, achievements, weaknesses, and setbacks, providing stakeholders with a clear understanding of its performance.
- Certifications and Standards: Merck adheres to a multitude of external charters, principles, and initiatives guiding its work in ESG focus areas. This includes participation in initiatives such as the SBTi, CEO Action for Diversity and Inclusion, and the UN Global Compact, showcasing a commitment to global standards and best practices.
- Financial Commitment: The issuance of a $1 billion sustainability bond in December 2021 exemplifies Merck's financial commitment to sustainability, signaling a dedication to responsible and impactful investments.

Relevant IG Strategies

- Implementing a holistic IG strategy by establishing standardized metadata protocols, developing a comprehensive records taxonomy, defining defensible deletion policies, and enforcing robust data security measures for environmental data to ensure consistency, accuracy, streamlined retrieval, and compliance in tracking renewable energy sources, waste management, and certifications.

- Fostering employee engagement in environmental data stewardship through awareness programs, encouraging responsible data handling and reporting for sustainability initiatives including providing targeted training on the proper handling and documentation of environmental data, and incorporating policies and procedures to guide employees in maintaining data integrity.
- Implementing metadata governance practices and specific taxonomies for social impact data, ensuring accurate tracking of global health initiatives, employee development programs, and community engagement efforts.
- Establishing defensible deletion policies to ensure that data related to global health, employee development, and community engagement is systematically reviewed and deleted when appropriate and ensuring the maintenance of robust data security measures for social impact data, safeguarding information on global health initiatives, employee development, and community engagement to protect sensitive information.
- Enhancing data security measures for governance-related data, safeguarding sensitive information on progress, achievements, weaknesses, and setbacks to maintain the integrity of sustainability reporting.
- Promoting employee engagement in governance-related data stewardship, encouraging responsible data handling and reporting for sustainability reporting and compliance.

Additional Slides and Illustrations

How IG Supports ESG Compliance

IG Goals: Environmental Compliance

Improve management & tracking of environmental sustainability efforts

Ensure that ESG reports are transparent, accurate, and consistent

Comply with environmental regulations and standards

Reduce environmental risks

Improve stakeholder engagement

Use Cases: Environmental Compliance

01
Carbon Footprint

Accurately collect and report carbon footprint

02
Energy Efficiency

Track and report on their energy efficiency and identify & track improvement needs

03
Water Use

Accurately track and report water use

Case Studies: Environmental Compliance

amazon

In addition to creating a company-wide environmental compliance database, Amazon implemented robust information governance practices, such as data management, privacy, and security controls, to ensure that its sustainability efforts were transparent and well-documented and created metrics and KPIs for tracking and reporting on their environmental performance.

Unilever

Unilever established a centralized environmental database & implemented data management processes to ensure data accuracy & consistency.

Use Cases: Social Compliance

Accuracy & Consistency

Create & maintain policies and procedures to promote accuracy & consistency of ESG data related to social issues, such as diversity and inclusion, human rights, and labor practices

Stakeholder Engagement

Engage stakeholders to address social issues help companies create holistic ESG programs that generate a positive societal impact

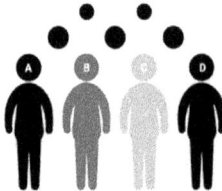

Data Analytics

Use data analytics to track diversity and inclusion metrics, such as gender and ethnic diversity, to ensure that companies are meeting their social obligations

Data Security

Maintain policies and procedures to promote the security of sensitive data, such as employee and financial data, help companies protect the privacy and rights of their workers and reduce data breach risk

IG Goals: Social Compliance

Improve social impact reporting by promoting accurate and consistent data	Understand and comply with labor regulations and anti-corruption and human rights law compliance	Increase stakeholder engagement and improve response to stakeholder initiatives and improve employee data access	Identify and assess social risks stemming from labor abuses or human rights violations	Improve privacy controls

Case Studies: Social Compliance

Walmart implemented a data governance program to ensure the accuracy and consistency of its ESG data related to social issues, such as labor practices, diversity and inclusion, and human rights. The company also leveraged data analytics to monitor its performance on these issues and identify improvement areas.

The Coca Cola Company leveraged data analytics to monitor its ESG performance and identify areas for improvement, including its social performance. As part of its information governance program, Coca-Cola established policies and procedures to ensure the accuracy and consistency of its ESG data and used data analytics to track its progress on social issues.

Proctor & Gamble implemented a comprehensive information governance program to improve its data management and regulatory compliance, including its social performance. As part of this program, Procter & Gamble established policies and procedures to ensure the accuracy, completeness, and consistency of its ESG data, and leveraged data analytics to monitor its ESG performance and identify needed improvements.

IG Goals: Governance

Improve governance practices through transparent, accurate, and consistent data	Comply with applicable laws including retention laws and defensibly govern records lifecycle including email	Provide relevant data to stakeholders including governmental entities and improve periodic reporting compliance	Identify, assess & address legal and regulatory risks related to the management of data	Improve protection of confidential and personal data

Case Studies: Governance

JPMorganChase

Establishment of data management processes and technologies to promote the secure and compliant handling of sensitive data.

Efforts supported by regular employee training and awareness programs for employees to promote familiarity with relevant regulations and understanding of information management obligations.

Pfizer

Creation of records management processes and technologies to maintain accurate, compliant, and complete operational records.

Support processes through regular monitoring & audit to promote ongoing compliance.

Notes

PART 1

1. PWC (2023).
2. Ibid.
3. Bergman, Deckelbaum, and Karp (2020).
4. PWC (2023).
5. Ibid.
6. Ibid.
7. Henisz, Koller, and Nuttall (2019).
8. Ibid.
9. PWC (2023).
10. Ibid.
11. Royal (n.d.).
12. Henisz, Koller, and Nuttall (2019).
13. Ibid.
14. Ibid.
15. Ibid.
16. Ibid.
17. IBM (n.d.).
18. Ibid.
19. Ibid.
20. Ibid.
21. Ibid.
22. Ibid.
23. Ibid.
24. Ibid.
25. Ibid.
26. PWC (n.d.).
27. KPMG (2023).
28. SASB (n.d.).
29. Ibid.

30. Ibid.

31. Ibid.

32. KPMG (2023).

33. Ibid.

34. Ibid.

35. Guidance and regulation (2023).

36. IBM (n.d.).

37. Ibid.

38. Ibid.

39. Ibid.

40. Ibid.

41. Deloitte UK (n.d.).

42. IBM (n.d.).

43. Ibid.

44. Invest Europe (n.d.).

45. CDP (n.d.).

46. Invest Europe (n.d.).

47. Invest Europe (n.d.).

48. CDP (n.d.).

49. Ibid

50. United Nations Global Compact, Principles (n.d.).

51. ISO (2017).

52. Sustainanalytics (n.d.).

53. Ibid

54. Ibid

55. Ibid

56. Ibid

57. Yahoo! Finance/Morningstar (2016).

58. Ibid.

59. Social Value International (n.d.).

60. International Integrated Reporting Council (n.d.).

61. Fernando (2023).

62. S&P Global (n.d.).

63. Nora Hahnkamper-Vandenbulcke (2021).

64. European Commission (n.d.).

65. Davis, Quinn, Shaw, Sandhu, and Este (2022).

66. U.S. Securities and Exchange Commission (2022).
67. Ibid.
68. Ibid.
69. Davis ,Quinn, Shaw, Sandhu, and Estes (2022).
70. U.S. Securities and Exchange Commission (2022).
71. Ibid.
72. Ibid.
73. Ibid.
74. Ibid.
75. U.S. Securities and Exchange Commission (n.d.).
76. KPMG (2023).
77. Davis ,Quinn, Shaw, Sandhu, and Estes (2022).
78. Ibid.
79. Cheng, Zilberberg, and Roberts (2023).
80. Ibid.
81. Ibid.
82. KPMG (2023).
83. IBM (n.d.)
84. Ibid.
85. Ibid.
86. Ibid.
87. Ibid.
88. Ibid.
89. Crowe, UK (2020).
90. Hong Kong Stock Exchange (2022).
91. Principles for Responsible Institutional Investors (2020).

PART 2

1. Elin and Rapaport (2023).
2. Fasching, McCarroll, Ragan, Redgrave, LLP, Emory, and Kearney et al. (n.d.).
3. United Nations, Archives and Records Management Section (n.d.).
4. ARMA Magazine (2017).
5. Ibid.
6. Ibid.

7. Ibid.

8. Ibid.

9. United Nations, Archives and Records Management Section (n.d.).

10. Ibid.

11. Ibid.

12. Peck, Feldman, and Kiker (2021).

13. Ibid.

14. Ibid.

15. Ibid.

16. Ibid.

17. Ibid.

18. Ibid.

19. Ibid.

20. Elin and Rapaport (2023).

21. AICPA and Canadian Institute of Chartered Accountants (CICA) (2009).

22. Ibid.

23. Pearson (n.d.).

24. Jaeger (2018).

25. Liu (n.d.).

26. Federal Trade Commission (n.d.).

27. Ibid.

28. Federal Trade Commission (n.d.).

29. U.S. Department of Health and Human Services (n.d.).

30. HIPAA Journal (2023).

31. U.S. Federal Trace Commission (n.d).

32. IAPP (2024).

33. Diamond (2019).

34. Ibid.

35. Ibid.

36. IAPP (2020).

37. Ibid.

38. IAPP (n.d.).

39. Office of the Privacy Commission of Canada (2020).

40. Elin and Rapaport (2023).

PART 3

1. Petzold, Roggendorf, Rowshankish, and Sporleder (2020).
2. Ibid.
3. Ibid.
4. Ibid.
5. Ibid.
6. Data Governance: An Enabler for ESG (2023).
7. Knowledge Preservation Blog Post (n.d.).
8. Petersen (2023).
9. Ibid.
10. Ibid.
11. Building a Sustainable Path to Cleaner ESG data (n.d.).
12. Apiday Blog (2024).
13. Bergman, Deckelbaum, Karp, Paul, Rifkind, Garrison (2020).
14. Opentext Cybersecurity (n.d.).
15. Ibid.
16. Ibid.
17. Ibid.
18. Ibid.
19. World Economic Forum (2021).
20. ASQ (n.d.).
21. Ibid.
22. Ibid.
23. Global Infrastructure Anti-Corruption Centre (n.d.).
24. Ibid.
25. Ibid.
26. Milone (2023).
27. McKinsey and Co. (2020).
28. Williams and Dolkas (2022).
29. Milone (2023).
30. Ibid.
31. Ibid.
32. Ibid.
33. Ibid.
34. S&P Global Market Intelligence Blog (2023).

35. Ibid.
36. Peterdy (n.d.).
37. KPMG (2020).
38. Jones (2023).
39. Ibid.
40. Ibid.
41. Security and Dolan(2022).
42. Ibid.
43. Ibid.
44. Sanction Scanner Blog (n.d.).
45. Ibid.
46. Ibid.
47. Jones (n.d.).
48. Ibid.
49. Ibid.
50. Knowledge Preservation Blog (n.d.).
51. General Motors (n.d.).
52. Morley (2020).
53. McKevitt (2016).
54. Allianz (2020).
55. Ibid.
56. Littenberg, Dale, Raad, and Rohlfsen (2019).
57. Ibid.
58. Knowledge Preservation Blog (n.d.).
59. Petr Průcha (n.d.).
60. Ibid.
61. Ibid.
62. Panetta (2019).
63. Sustainalytics (2022).
64. Everteam (n.d.).
65. Kaskikallio (2021).
66. Jackson and Hodgkinson (2022).
67. Ibid.
68. Ibid.
69. Ibid.
70. Ibid.

71. Buchholz (2023).
72. Rodriguez (2020).
73. Ibid.
74. Ibid.
75. ETF Trends/Sage Advisory (2021).
76. Ibid.
77. Ibid.
78. Rodriguez (2021).
79. Impakter Index (n.d.).
80. Impakter Index (n.d.).

References

"6 Ways That Information Governance Can Improve AI Compliance." n.d. Knowledge Preservation Blog. www.knowledgepreservation.com/post/6-ways-that-information-governance-can-improve-ai-compliance.

"A Summary of Your Rights Under the Fair Credit Reporting Act." n.d. Federal Trade Commission. www.consumer.ftc.gov/sites/default/files/articles/pdf/pdf-0096-fair-credit-reporting-act.pdf.

"An ESG Lens on Blockchain and Public Equities—Thematic Research Report." March 2022. Sustainalytics. https://connect.sustainalytics.com/inv-an-esg-lens-on-blockchain-and-public-equities.

"Diversity Wins: How Inclusion Matters." May 19, 2020. McKinsey and Co. www.mckinsey.com/featured-insights/diversity-and-inclusion/diversity-wins-how-inclusion-matters.

"Elements of a Best-in-Class Data Privacy Program." Compliance Week. www.complianceweek.com/data-privacy/elements-of-a-best-in-class-data-privacy-program/24745.article.

"ESG Case Study—Boston Properties, Inc.." May 11, 2021. ETF Trends/ Sage Advisory. www.etftrends.com/etf-strategist-channel/esg-case-study-boston-properties-inc/.

Ibid.

Ibid.

"ESG Risk Briefing: Taking Action Against Modern Slavery." October 27, 2020. Allianz. https://commercial.allianz.com/news-and-insights/expert-risk-articles/esg-risk-briefing-4-2020.html.

"ESG: Environmental, Social, Governance: An Introductory Guide for Businesses." July 2020. KPMG. https://assets.kpmg.com/content/dam/kpmg/uk/pdf/2020/08/esg-brochure.pdf.

"Fighting Identity Theft With the Red Flags Rule: A How-to Guide for Business." n.d. Federal Trade Commission. www.ftc.gov/business-guidance/resources/fighting-identity-theft-red-flags-rule-how-guide-business.

"Governance: Taking a Close Look at the 'G' in ESG." May 17, 2023. S&P Global Market Intelligence Blog. www.spglobal.com/marketintelligence/en/news-insights/blog/governance-taking-a-close-look-at-the-g-in-esg.

Ibid.

"Highest Anti-Money Laundering Fines of 2023." n.d. Sanction Scanner Blog. www.sanctionscanner.com/blog/highest-anti-money-laundering-fines-of-2023-829.

Ibid.

Ibid.

"HIPAA Compliance Assistance, Summary of the HIPAA Privacy Rule." n.d. U.S. Department of Health and Human Services. www.hhs.gov/sites/default/files/privacysummary.pdf.

"How Organizations Can Improve Their Ethical Handling of Data." n.d. Knowledge Preservation Blog. www.knowledgepreservation.com/post/how-organizations-can-improve-their-ethical-handeling-of-data.

"Merck & Co Sustainability Report." n.d. Impakter Index. https://impakter.com/index/merck-co-sustainability-report/.

"Overview of International Standard ISO 37001, Anti-Bribery System Management Standard." n.d. Global Infrastructure Anti-Corruption Centre (giaccentre.org).

Ibid.

Ibid.

"PIPEDA Fair Information Principle 10—Challenging Compliance." August 2020. www.priv.gc.ca/en/privacy-topics/privacy-laws-in-canada/the-personal-information-protection-and-electronic-documents-act-pipeda/p_principle/principles/p_compliance/.

"Records and Information Management Guidance: How Do I Know If Records Are Vital?" n.d. United Nations, Archives and Records Management Section. https://archives.un.org/sites/archives.un.org/files/RM-Guidelines/guidance_vital_records.pdf.

Ibid.

Ibid.

Ibid.

"Risk & Compliance Glossary: What Is Anti-Money Laundering (AML)?; "The Role of Blockchain in Information Governance." n.d. Everteam. www.everteam.com/en/role-of-blockchain-in-information-governance/.

Ibid.

Ibid.

"Understanding the LGPD: Basic Elements." n.d. IAPP. https://iapp.org/media/pdf/resource_center/understanding_the_lgpd_basic_elements_ebook.pdf.

"U.S. State Comprehensive Privacy Laws Report: 2024 (2023 Legislative Session)." n.d. IAPP. https://iapp.org/media/pdf/resource_center/us_state_privacy_laws_report_2024_overview.pdf.

"Verizon Sustainability Report." n.d. Impakter Index. https://impakter.com/index/verizon-sustainability-report/.

"What Is 'Dark Data' and How Is It Adding to All of Our Carbon Footprints?" October 5, 2022. World Economic Forum. www.weforum.org/agenda/2022/10/dark-data-is-killing-the-planet-we-need-digital-decarbonisation/.

Ibid.

Ibid.

Ibid.

Ibid.

"What Is ISO 26000? Social Responsibility Guidance Standard." n.d. ASQ. https://asq.org/quality-resources/iso-26000.

Ibid.

Ibid.

"AICPA and Canadian Institute of Chartered Accountants (CICA) Privacy Task Force, Generally Accepted Privacy Principles." August 2009. AICPA and Canadian Institute of Chartered Accountants (CICA) https://op.bna.com/pl.nsf/id/byul-7xhufa/$File/gapp.pdf.

Alder, S. December 1, 2023. "What Is the HITECH Act?" *HIPAA Journal*. www.hipaajournal.com/what-is-the-hitech-act/.

Apiday Blog. January 30, 2024. "How to Collect ESG Data to Improve Reporting?" *Apiday*. www.apiday.com/blog-posts/how-to-collect-esg-data-to-improve-your-reporting.

ARMA International Standards and Best Practices Workgroup: Identifying and Classifying Vital Records." 2017. ARMA Magazine. https://magazine.arma.org/wp-content/uploads/simple-file-list/2017_03_IM_identify_classify_vital_records_ARMA.pdf.

Ibid.

Ibid.

Ibid.

Ibid.

Bergaman, M.S., A.J. Deckelbaum, B.S. Karp, W. Paul, W. Rifkind, Wharton & Garrison LLP. August 1, 2020. "Introduction to ESG." *Harvard Law School Forum on Corporate Governance*. https://corpgov.law.harvard.edu/2020/08/01/introduction-to-esg/.

Ibid.

Bradley, L. August 7, 2023. "Five Things You Need to Know About the SASB Standards." KPMG. https://kpmg.com/xx/en/home/insights/2023/08/ifrs-blog-sasb-standards.html.

Ibid.

Ibid.

Ibid.

Buchholz, L. July 7, 2023. "Top 10: ESG Strategies From the World's Largest Companies." Sustainability Magazine. https://sustainabilitymag.com/top10/top-10.

CDP. n.d. "CDP Scores Explained: CDP Scoring Methodology Guidance."

www.cdp.net/en/scores/cdp-scores-explained.

Ibid.

CDP. n.d. "Why Disclose As a Company." www.cdp.net/en/companies-discloser.

Cheng, L., D.A. Zilberberg and E. Roberts, D. Polk and Wardwell LLP Harvard Law School Forum on Corporate Governance. October 22, 2023. "California Enacts Major Climate-Related Disclosure Laws." https://corpgov.law.harvard .edu/2023/10/22/california-enacts-major-climate-related-disclosure-laws/.

Ibid.

Ibid.

Crowe, UK. March 2020. "Streamlined Energy and Carbon Reporting Summary." www.crowe.com/uk/-/media/crowe/firms/europe/uk/croweuk/pdf-publications/streamlined-energy-and-carbon-reporting-summary-final.pdf

Diamond, M. July 26, 2019. "Association of Corporate Counsel, Quick Overview: Understanding the California Consumer Privacy Act (CCPA)." www.acc.com/resource-library/quick-overview-understanding-california-consumer-privacy-act-ccpa.

Ibid.

Ibid.

Davis, T.E., C.L. Quinn, Seyfarth Shaw, P. Sandhu and S. Estes. June 2022. "Practical Guidance, ESG, Professional Perspective—ESG Data Reliability & Legal Implications of Disclosures: ESG Data Reliability & Legal Implications of Disclosures." Bloomberg Law. www.bloomberglaw.com/external/document/ XECHNMHK000000/esg-professional-perspective-esg-data-reliability-legal-implicat.

Ibid.

Ibid.

Ibid.

Deloitte UK. n.d. "The Task Force on Climate-related Financial Disclosures: Why TCFD Is More Than a Reporting Mechanism." www2.deloitte.com/ uk/en/focus/climate-change/tcfd.html.

Disclosures." https://kpmg.com/kpmg-us/content/dam/kpmg/pdf/2023/streng then-internal-controls-to-navigate-the-soxification-of-esg-reporting.pdf.

Dow Jones. www.dowjones.com/professional/risk/glossary/anti-money-laundering/ compliance-program/.

Elin, P.L. and M. Rapaport. 2023. *A Librarian's Guide to ISO Standards for Information Governance, Privacy, and Security.* Business Expert Press.

Ibid.

Ibid.

European Parliament. January 2021. "Guidance Briefing: Implementation Appraisal, European Parliamentary Research Service: Non-financial Reporting Directive." Nora Hahnkamper-Vandenbulcke, Jan. 2021 Non-financial Reporting Directive (europa.eu).

Hahnkamper-Vandenbulcke, N. n.d. Sustainability-Related Disclosures in the Financial Services Sector.

Hale, J. September 29, 2016. "How Sustainalytics Does Company ESG Research." Yahoo! Finance/Morningstar. https://finance.yahoo.com/news/sustainalytics-does-company-esg-research-100000652.html.

Ibid.

Henisz, W., T. Koller, and R. Nuttall. 2019. "Five Ways That ESG Creates Value: Getting Your Environmental, Social, and Governance (ESG) Proposition Right Links to Higher Value Creation. Here's why." McKinsey & Co. www.mckinsey.com/~/media/McKinsey/Business%20Functions/Strategy%20and%20Corporate%20Finance/Our%20Insights/Five%20ways%20that%20ESG%20creates%20value/Five-ways-that-ESG-creates-value.ashx.

Ibid.

Ibid.

Ibid.

Ibid.

Ibid.

Ibid.

Fasching, D., M. McCarroll, C. Ragan, B. Redgrave, Redgrave LLP, T. Emory, M. Kearney, et al. "Act Now or Pay Later: The Case for Defensible Disposition of Data." Thomson Reuters Law. www.redgravellp.com/act-now-or-pay-later-case-defensible-disposition-data-0.

Fennessy, C. May 12, 2020. "CPRA's Top-10 Impactful Provisions." IAPP. https://iapp.org/news/a/cpra-top-10-impactful-provisions/.

Ibid.

IBM. n.d. "SECR Reporting Explained." www.ibm.com/blog/secr-reporting-explained/.

IBM. n.d. "What Is the Global Reporting Initiative (GRI)?" www.ibm.com/blog/what-is-the-global-reporting-initiative-gri/.

Ibid.

Ibid.

Ibid.

Ibid.

Ibid.

Ibid.

Ibid.

IBM. n.d. "What Is the TCFD?" www.ibm.com/topics/tcfd.

Ibid.

Ibid.

Ibid.

Ibid.

Ibid.

Ibid.

International Integrated Reporting Council. n.d. "Integrated Report Framework." https://integratedreporting.ifrs.org/wp-content/uploads/2013/12/13-12-08-THE-INTERNATIONAL-IR-FRAMEWORK-2-1.pdf.

Invest Europe. n.d. "Invest Europe ESG Reporting Guidelines (Formerly the Carbon Disclosure Project)." www.investeurope.eu/invest-europe-esg-reporting-guidelines/who-is-who/cdp-formerly-the-carbon-disclosure-project/.

Ibid.

Ibid.

ISO. February 7, 2017. "ISO 26000 and OECD Guidelines: Practical overview of the linkages." iso.org/files/live/sites/isoorg/files/store/en/PUB100418.pdf.

KPMG. October 2023. "Fact Sheet: Enhancement and Standardization of Climate-Related .

Ibid.

March 24, 2020. "Principles for Responsible Institutional Investors, Japan's Stewardship Code." www.fsa.go.jp/en/refer/councils/stewardship/20200324/01.pdf.

Jaeger, J. November 26, 2018. "Elements of a best-in-class data privacy program." Compliance Week. www.complianceweek.com/data-privacy/elements-of-a-best-in-class-data-privacy-program/24745.article.

Jones, B. April 25, 2023. "4 Steps to Improving Your ESG Risk Management to Increase Financial Performance." IBM. www.ibm.com/blog/4-steps-to-improving-your-esg-risk-management-to-increase-financial-performance/.

Ibid.

Ibid.

Kaskikallio, K. and EY Nordics Chief Technology Officer. June 23, 2021. "How Blockchain Can Help Achieve Wide-Scope Sustainability Targets." EY Finland. www.ey.com/en_fi/assurance/how-blockchain-can-help-achieve-wide-scope-sustainability-target .

Knowledge Preservation Blog. www.knowledgepreservation.com/post/how-organizations-can-improve-their-ethical-handeling-of-data.

Knowledge Preservation Blog Post. n.d. "Top 10 Ways That Information Governance Supports ESG Compliance." .

Littenberg, M.R., A.J. Dale, A.N. Raad, R. Rohlfsen. April 22, 2019. "Modern Slavery Compliance for U.S.-Based (and Other) Multinationals: A Review of Recent Compliance and Disclosure Developments in the United States and Abroad." Ropes & Gray. www.ropesgray.com/en/insights/alerts/2019/04/modern-slavery-compliance-for-us-based-and-other-multinationals-a-review-of-recent-compliance

Liu, K. n.d. "Guidance: Guide to the Gramm–Leach–Bliley Act." IAPP. https://iapp.org/resources/article/guide-to-the-gramm-leach-bliley-act/

McKevitt, J. October 26, 2016. "Dive Brief: Modern Slavery Allegations Burn

Clothing Supply Chains." Supply Chain Dive. www.supplychaindive.com/news/modern-slavery-clothing-retail-supply-chain/429021/.

Milone, M. February 20, 2023. "Why Mature Data Governance Is Essential for Data-Driven Diversity, Equity, and Inclusion (DEI)" Dataversity. www.dataversity.net/why-mature-data-governance-is-essential-for-data-driven-diversity-equity-and-inclusion-dei/.

Ibid.

Ibid.

Ibid.

Ibid.

Ibid.

Morley, M. January 21, 2020. "Six Steps to an Ethical and Sustainable Supply Chain." Supply Chain Brain Blog www.supplychainbrain.com/blogs/1-think-tank/post/30725-six-steps-to-an-ethical-and-sustainable-supply-chain .

n.d. General Motors. www.gm.com/commitments/sustainability.

Opentext Cybersecurity. n.d. "Data Security and Climate Change How Voltage Supports Carbon-Friendly Strategies." www.opentext.com/assets/documents/en-US/pdf/data-security-and-climate-change-brochure.pdf. www.knowledgepreservation.com/post/top-10-ways-that-information-governance-supports-esg-compliance.

Ibid.

Ibid.

Ibid.

Ibid.

Panetta, K. September 23, 2019. "The CIO's Guide to Blockchain." Gartner. www.gartner.com/smarterwithgartner/the-cios-guide-to-blockchain.

Pearson, A. n.d. "Data Protection Policy: GDPR-Ready Template for Membership Organisations." White Fuse. https://whitefuse.com/blog/data-protection-policy-template/.

Peck, A., J. Feldman, and D. Kiker. January 29, 2021. "Defensible Deletion: The Proof Is in the Planning." *NY Law Journal/DLA Piper*. www.dlapiper.com/en/insights/publications/2021/02/defensible-deletion-the-proof-is-in-the-planning.

Ibid.

Ibid.

Ibid.

Ibid.

Ibid.

Ibid.

Ibid.

Peterdy, K. n.d. "ESG (Environmental, Social, & Governance): A Management and Analysis Framework to Understand and Measure How Sustainably an

Organization Is Operating." https://corporatefinanceinstitute.com/resources/esg/esg-environmental-social-governance/.

Petersen, K. December 12, 2023. "Utilizing Data Analytics to Help Support ESG Reporting." *ESG Data Analytics to Help Support ESG Reporting.* Wolters Kluwer. www.wolterskluwer.com/en/expert-insights/utilizing-data-analytics-to-help-support-esg-reporting.

Ibid.

Ibid.

Petzold, B., M. Roggendorf, K. Rowshankish, C. Sporleder June 26, 2020. *Designing Data Governance That Delivers Value.* McKinsey Digital.Ibid.

Ibid.

Ibid.

Ibid.

Ibid.

Průcha, P. n.d. "Robotic Process Automation as a Driver for Sustainable Innovation And Entrepreneurship." XB-CON Proceedings 2023. Technical University of Liberec, Liberec, Czechia.

Ibid.

Ibid.

PWC. January 2023. "Data Governance: An Enabler for ESG." *Sustainable data.* www.pwc.in/assets/pdfs/consulting/technology/data-and-analytics/govern-your-data/insights/data-governance-an-enabler-for-esg.pdf.

Ibid.

Ibid.

Ibid.

Ibid.

Ibid.

Ibid.

Ibid.

PWC. n.d. "Building a Sustainable Path to Cleaner ESG Data." *ESG Data Collection and Reporting.* PWC. www.pwc.com/us/en/services/esg/library/esg-data-collection-reporting.html.

PWC. n.d. "ESG Reporting and Preparation of a Sustainability Report—Slovakia." www.pwc.com/sk/en/environmental-social-and-corporate-governance-esg/esg-reporting.html.

Rodriguez, S. February 24, 2021. "ESG Case Study—Toyota Motor Corporation." www.etftrends.com/esg-channel/esg-case-study-toyota/.

Rodriguez, S. September 24, 2020. "ESG Case Study—Cisco Systems, Inc.." ETF Trends/Sage Advisory. www.etftrends.com/esg-channel/esg-case-study-cisco-systems-inc/.

Ibid.

Ibid.

Royal, J. n.d. "What Is ESG Investing? A Guide to Socially Responsible Investing." Bankrate.com. www.bankrate.com/investing/esg-investing/.

S&P Global. n.d. "Dow Jones Sustainability Indices (DJSI) Family." www .spglobal.com/esg/performance/indices/djsi-index-family#family.

Sarnek, A., Valence Security and C. Dolan. March 1, 2022. "Cybersecurity Is an Environmental, Social and Governance Issue. Here's Why." www .weforum.org/agenda/2022/03/three-reasons-why-cybersecurity-is-a-critical-component-of-esg/.

Ibid.

Ibid.

SASB Standards. n.d. "SASB Standards Overview." https://sasb.org/standards/.

Ibid.

Ibid.

Ibid.

Social Value International. n.d. "The Principles of Social Value." www .socialvalueint.org/principles

Sustainalytics. n.d. "Overview of Sustainalytics' ESG Risk Ratings." https:// connect.sustainalytics.com/hubfs/SFS/Sustainalytics%20ESG%20Risk%20 Ratings_Issuer%20Backgrounder.pdf

U.S. Federal Trace Commission. n.d. "CAN-SPAM Act: A Compliance Guide for Business." www.ftc.gov/business-guidance/resources/can-spam-act-compliance-guide-business.

Summary of Regulation (EU) 2019/2088 on Sustainability-Related Disclosures in the Financial Services Sector." European Commission. https://eur-lex .europa.eu/legal-content/EN/LSU/?uri=CELEX:32019R2088.

Sustainalytics. n.d. "Overview of Sustainalytics' ESG Risk Ratings." https:// connect.sustainalytics.com/hubfs/SFS/Sustainalytics%20ESG%20Risk%20 Ratings_Issuer%20Backgrounder.pdf

Task Force on Climate-related Financial Disclosure (TCFD)—Aligned Disclosure Application Guidance—Phase 1." www.gov.uk/government/publications/ tcfd-aligned-disclosure-application-guidance/task-force-on-climate-related-financial-disclosure-tcfd-aligned-disclosure-application-guidance.

Ibid.

U.S. Securities and Exchange Commission. March 21, 2022. "SEC Proposes Rules to Enhance and Standardize Climate-Related Disclosures for Investors." www.sec.gov/news/press-release/2022-46.

U.S. Securities and Exchange Commission. n.d. "Fact Sheet: Enhancement and Standardization of Climate-Related Disclosures." www.sec.gov/files/33-11042-fact-sheet.pdf.

UK Government. December 19, 2023. "Guidance: United Nations Global Compact. n.d. "Principles: The Ten Principles of the UN Global Compact.

https://unglobalcompact.org/what-is-gc/mission/principlesWhat Is an AML Compliance Program?" n.d.

World Economic Forum. March 2021. "Bridging Digital and Environmental Goals: A Framework for Business Action." https://www3.weforum.org/docs/WEF_Bridging_Digital_and_Environmental_Goals_2021.pdf.

Williams, J.C. and J. Dolkas. MarchApril 2022. "Diversity and Inclusion: Data-Driven Diversity—To Achieve Your Inclusion Goals, Use a Metrics-Based Approach." https://hbr.org/2022/03/data-driven-diversity

About the Authors

Phyllis L. Elin, PhD, has over three decades of senior information governance (IG) leadership as well as extensive IG consulting experience across a broad range of industries, including higher education, finance, health care, and the public sector. Her unique expertise spans active file management, records retention, technology consulting, and vendor evaluation. In addition, she has authored three recent books on IG published by Business Expert Press, solidifying her reputation as a thought leader in the field. Currently, Phyllis Elin is the CEO of Knowledge Preservation, LLC, an IG consultancy practice based out of New Jersey.

Max Rapaport is an experienced commercial and regulatory attorney with expertise in the areas of IG, data privacy, and commercial intellectual property transactions. Representative experience includes serving as the general counsel for a large outsourcing organization, managing and implementing numerous multijurisdictional IG legal research projects in the United States, the European Union, and Japan, and counseling technology companies on their U.S. and EU data privacy compliance obligations. Max is currently the COO of Knowledge Preservation and, together with Phyllis Elin, has written two books addressing IG challenges.

Index

OTHER TITLES IN THE ENVIRONMENTAL AND SOCIAL SUSTAINABILITY FOR BUSINESS ADVANTAGE COLLECTION

Robert Sroufe, Duquesne University, Editor

- *Making the Connection* by Peter Sammons
- *Sustainable Investing* by Kylelane Purcell and Vivari Ben
- *Confronting the Storm* by David Ross
- *Sustainability for Retail* by Vilma Barr and Ken Nisch
- *People, Planet, Profit* by Kit Oung
- *Bringing Sustainability to the Ground Level* by Susan J. Gilbertz and Damon M. Hall
- *Handbook of Sustainable Development* by Radha R. Sharma
- *Community Engagement and Investment* by Alan S. Gutterman
- *Sustainability Standards and Instruments* by Alan Gutterman
- *Strategic Planning for Sustainability* by Alan S. Gutterman
- *Sustainability Reporting and Communications* by Alan S. Gutterman
- *Sustainability Leader in a Green Business Era* by Amr E. Sukkar
- *Managing Sustainability* by John Friedman
- *Human Resource Management for Organizational Sustainability* by Radha R. Sharma

Concise and Applied Business Books

The Collection listed above is one of 30 business subject collections that Business Expert Press has grown to make BEP a premiere publisher of print and digital books. Our concise and applied books are for...

- Professionals and Practitioners
- Faculty who adopt our books for courses
- Librarians who know that BEP's Digital Libraries are a unique way to offer students ebooks to download, not restricted with any digital rights management
- Executive Training Course Leaders
- Business Seminar Organizers

Business Expert Press books are for anyone who needs to dig deeper on business ideas, goals, and solutions to everyday problems. Whether one print book, one ebook, or buying a digital library of 110 ebooks, we remain the affordable and smart way to be business smart. For more information, please visit www.businessexpertpress.com, or contact sales@businessexpertpress.com.

www.ingramcontent.com/pod-product-compliance
Lightning Source LLC
Chambersburg PA
CBHW061142220326
41599CB00025B/4329